SEEKING EMPLOYMENT IN CRIMINAL JUSTICE AND RELATED FIELDS

Fourth Edition

J. Scott Harr, JD
Attorney at Law
Criminal Justice Chair
School of Human Services
Concordia University, St. Paul

Kären M. Hess, PhD
President
Institute for Professional Development
Instructor
Normandale Community College

THOMSON

WADSWORTH

Australia • Canada • Mexico Singapore • Spain
United Kingdom • United States

THOMSON

WADSWORTH

Dedicated to the pursuit of dreams.

We look forward to hearing from our readers who call with the exciting message, "I got the job!" This book is for you. Good luck! We also wish to provide a special dedication to Henry Wrobleski, former coordinator of the law enforcement department, and Pam Reierson, former media specialist, Normandale Community College, both of whom have contributed a great deal to the advancement of criminal justice and private security as true professions.

Publisher, Criminal Justice: *Sabra Horne*
Acquisitions Editor: *Dawn Mesa*
Development Editor: *Julie Sakaue*
Editorial Assistant: *Lee McCracken*
Technology Project Manager: *Susan DeVanna*
Marketing Manager: *Beverly Dunn*
Marketing Assistant: *Neena Chandra*
Advertising Project Manager: *Bryan Vann*
Project Manager, Editorial Production: *Matt Ballantyne*
Print/Media Buyer: *Judy Inouye*
Copy Editor: *Susan Gall*
Design, graphics, and index: *Christine M. H. Orthmann*
Cover Designer: *Bill Stanton*
Permissions Editor: *Stephanie Keough-Hedges*
Text and Cover Printer: *Von Hoffmann Graphics*

Printed in the United States of America
2 3 4 5 6 7 06 05 04 03

For more information about our products, contact us at:
Thomson Learning Academic Resource Center
1-800-423-0563
For permission to use material from this text, contact us by:
Phone: 1-800-730-2214
Fax: 1-800-730-2215
Web: http://www.thomsonrights.com

Wadsworth/Thomson Learning
10 Davis Drive
Belmont, CA 94002-3098
USA

Asia
Thomson Learning
5 Shenton Way #01-01
UIC Building
Singapore 068808

Australia
Nelson Thomson Learning
102 Dodds Street
South Melbourne, Victoria 3205
Australia

Canada
Nelson Thomson Learning
1120 Birchmount Road
Toronto, Ontario M1K 5G4
Canada

Europe/Middle East/Africa
Thomson Learning
High Holborn House
50/51 Bedford Row
London WC1R 4LR
United Kingdom

ISBN 0-534-57667-2

Library of Congress Control Number: 2002104449

CONTENTS

FIGURES

TABLES

FOREWORD

Abraham Lincoln once said, "Prepare yourself for the day opportunity presents itself, and you will be rewarded." The process of entering a career in criminal justice or private security usually consists of several steps to "prepare yourself."

Philosophical questions regarding your goals must be resolved by practical approaches. As an applicant, you will be seeking to reach one of your most important goals in life. Whatever the situation, you are more likely to realize success if you are prepared to present yourself in the best possible manner to a prospective employer. Different expectations are held by employers and future employees in a situation where there is the beginning of a career.

This book is a genuine contribution to the future of young Americans seeking employment in such careers as law enforcement, juvenile justice, corrections or any of the numerous areas within the private security profession. J. Scott Harr and Kären M. Hess have been heralded by many as being the best in providing information, guidance and direction to those seeking a career in the public or private sectors of the criminal justice system. The authors give applicants a realistic, factual approach in conveying to the reader "this is what it's all about."

The past and present dynamics of seeking employment projected into the future suggest great optimism for applicants who pursue careers and job hunting with a positive attitude. This book goes as far as our knowledge takes it today. It is the best resource for the 21st century and gives the aspirant an enlightened, positive approach to job seeking in these highly competitive fields.

Henry M. Wrobleski
Former Coordinator of Law Enforcement
Normandale Community College

ACKNOWLEDGMENTS

We wish to personally express appreciation to the criminal justice, security and other professionals who have contributed to this book, which is richer because of their personal sharing:

Russell M. Anderson, Field Supervisor and Investigator, Wisconsin Alliance for Fair Contracting;

Richard D. Beckman, Sergeant, Cloverdale (California) Police Department;

Brian Beniek, Officer, Plymouth (Minnesota) Police Department;

Jack R. Cahall, Past Chair, Crime Abatement Committee, New Orleans, Louisiana;

Jim Chaffee, Director of Security, Walt Disney Pictures and Television;

Jim Clark, Chief, Eden Prairie (Minnesota) Police Department;

Dennis L. Conroy, PhD, Sergeant and Director of the Employee Assistance Program, St. Paul (Minnesota) Police Department;

John H. Driggs, Licensed Clinical Social Worker, St. Paul, Minnesota;

Timothy E. Erickson, Assistant Professor, Metropolitan State University;

Lawrence J. Fennelly, Sergeant and Crime Prevention Specialist, Harvard University Police Department;

Bill B. Green, Manager, Security Services, Rosemount, Inc.;

Joe Guy, Officer, Roseville (Minnesota) Police Department;

Marsh J. Halberg, Attorney, Thomsen & Nybeck, P.A.;

Sheldon T. Hess, MD, General Internist, Health Partners;

Robert B. Iannone, CPP, President, Iannone Security Management, Inc.;

Gil Kerlikowske, Police Commissioner, Buffalo (New York) Police Department;

Molly Koivamaki, Emergency Management Coordination, Eden Prairie (Minnesota) Police Department;

John Lombardi, Professor of Criminal Justice and Criminology, Albany State College;

John J. Maas, Deputy Chief, U.S. Probation/Pretrial Services Officer, South Dakota;

Brenda P. Maples, Lieutenant, Memphis (Tennessee) Police Department;

Robert Meyerson, Trooper I, Minnesota State Patrol;

Linda S. Miller, Sergeant, Bloomington Police Department; Executive Director, Upper Midwest Community Policing Institute;

Richard J. Obershaw, Grief Center, Burnsville, Minnesota;

Marie Ohman, Executive Director, Minnesota Board of Private Investigators and Protective Agents;

Penny A. Parrish, Public Information Officer, Minneapolis (Minnesota) Police Department; Parrish Institute of Law Enforcement and Media;

Richard W. Stanek, Sergeant, Minneapolis (Minnesota) Police Department;

Michael P. Stein, Chief, Escondido (California) Police Department;

Albert J. Sweeney, Captain Commanding, Training and Education Division, Boston (Massachusetts) Police Department;

Timothy J. Thompson, Director of Safety and Security, University of St. Thomas;

Kenneth S. Trump, Assistant Director, Tri-City Task Force Comprehensive Gang Initiative; Director of Safety and Security, Parma (Ohio) City School District; National School Safety Consultant;

Luis Velez, Captain, Colorado Springs (Colorado) Police Department;

Henry Wrobleski, Former Coordinator, Law Enforcement Department, Normandale Community College;

Monte D. Zillinger, Special Agent in Charge, Burlington Northern Railroad.

We also wish to thank the reviewers of this text and its various editions for their helpful comments and suggestions:

Frank P. Alberico, Joliet Junior College;
Tim Apolito, University of Dayton;
Jerald C. Burns, Alabama State University;
Robert H. Burrington, Georgia Police Academy;
Dean J. Champion, Minot State College;
Paul V. Clark, Community College of Philadelphia;
Dana C. DeWitt, Chadron State College;
William J. Halliday, Brookdale Community College;
William E. Harver, Widener University;
Robert Ives, Rock Valley College;
Joseph Macy, Palm Beach Community College;
Charles E. Myers; Aims Community College;
James E. Newman, Rio Honda College;
Daniel W. Nolan, Gateway Technical College, Kenosha;
Carroll S. Price, Penn Valley Community College;
Gregory B. Talley, Broome Community College;
Joy Thompson, University of Wyoming;
Rosalie Young, State University of New York at Oswego.

We wish to acknowledge Christine Hess Orthmann for her careful, accurate manuscript preparation, Carol Dunsmore for her friendship and assistance with developing the second edition, Diane Harr for her assistance reviewing the initial manuscript and West/Wadsworth Publishing Company editors Sabra Horne and Dawn Mesa for their encouragement and assistance.

Both authors would like to thank Henry Wrobleski for his influence on both of their careers and professional endeavors. Henry is the kind of friend, colleague and mentor that everyone should experience, and the kind we should strive to be to others.

Kären would like to acknowledge the support of her husband, Sheldon, and children, Christine and Timothy.

Scott would like to acknowledge the support of his wife, Diane, and children, Kelsey and Ricky, with whom he has always shared his dreams. They provide more support than they realize, and their continued interest in these projects and contributions throughout help make them happen. Their smiles, laughter and demands that he put the work down and listen to their piano practice or attend their soccer or baseball games helps keep priorities in check.

Without the patience and encouragement of our families, efforts such as this text could never come to be.

Thank you.

INTRODUCTION

"The longest journey begins with but a single step."

—*Anonymous*

There isn't much about job seeking that is simple. It's difficult to come to grips with just what career you are best suited for, and it's tough to get a job. It can be equally challenging to keep a job, and dealing with job changes or job loss can be particularly difficult. Why? Because work is such an important part of our lives . . . and this is why it is even more important to have a strategy to find meaningful work.

Webster's Dictionary defines *strategy* as "a careful plan or method . . . the art of devising or employing plans. . . toward a goal." Your goal is TO GET A NEW JOB! Whether it is to enter into a profession or to advance within your current profession, it all sounds so simple. Most of us have had no trouble getting work—flipping burgers, washing dishes, baby-sitting. Do not let this lull you into a false sense of security as so many others have. Assuming that getting a job—any job—is easy is a disastrous mistake.

You are interested in a field that has become exceptionally popular; however opportunities abound in the areas of law enforcement and criminal justice as well as the private sector. Not everyone will qualify to work every job. The world of work is constantly changing, and with change comes opportunity. But it still takes significant effort and preparation to get the job you want. No one would expect to walk into an agency or department with little or no preparation and expect to be offered a job. A carefully planned job-search strategy has become more important than ever. Anyone seeking a job must prepare themselves to succeed in this endeavor.

In addition to the vast number of applicants who possess the minimum qualifications, many applicants have excellent experience. Applicants may have worked out of state as law enforcement officers, corrections officers or as private security officers. Military experience has also proven to be very beneficial in the job search, as has advanced college education.

In fact, some agencies and departments require applicants to have a Bachelor's degree. And some applicants have Master's degrees, law degrees, PhDs and a myriad of specialty certifications. In addition, many people have taken advantage of volunteer opportunities related to the field, such as police reserves, volunteer rescue/firefighting and civilian police support jobs. Such work not only provides valuable experience but also demonstrates that the individual can be trusted in a field demanding unqualified ethics. Other vocational and volunteer positions show the applicant is truly well rounded. In short, many applicants begin their job search with exceptional qualifications, making them most attractive candidates.

Do not get discouraged. While all of this may be overwhelming, it should not cause you to give up. You *will* eventually get a job. When and what that job will be depends on your job-hunting strategy. While job hunting sometimes takes longer than anticipated and has occasional discouragements, it is also challenging, exciting and eventually fruitful.

Reflecting on what little was required not too many years ago of those seeking employment in law enforcement, corrections or security work, it is amazing what is expected of job candidates today. Communication skills, computer knowledge, business sense, all are necessities now.

This book addresses both the public and the private sector. It discusses career opportunities throughout the criminal justice system, including law enforcement, the practice of law, courts, corrections and related local, state and federal agencies. It also discusses career opportunities within private security because private security and law enforcement are complementary professions. A private security job can be a stepping stone into a police job. Many students majoring in law enforcement have jobs in private security. Even entry-level security jobs are becoming harder to obtain. Additionally, private security is recognized as an attractive field. Pay, hours and assignments at the management level often are better than in the public sector. Conversely, a police job can lead to a position as a security director or numerous other jobs in criminal justice. Because the fields of criminal justice and private security have so many specific jobs, you can pursue whatever type of position appeals to you, whether it's on the line or in administration. Further, lateral transfers between both professions are occurring more often. You have an opportunity to position yourself for any number of truly rewarding jobs.

This book also addresses promotions and the career ladder. Traditionally, these professions have promoted from within. The ability to advance through the ranks requires many of the same attributes that apply to the entry-level job seeker. But, it also requires an effective strategy. The skills discussed here apply equally to getting a new job in a new field and to getting promoted. Finally, this book examines job loss and change. Many leave a job because they chose to; others leave because they're forced to. To be sure, everyone will eventually leave every job they ever have. Change = Growth. For those dismissed from a job, for reasons deserved or not, this change can be difficult. For those seeking something more than a particular job is providing, this change can be liberating.

Keep in mind that this book was written for individuals throughout the country and is, therefore, general. Each state has different laws you must be aware of, for example, laws regarding licensure requirements, use of polygraph testing and the like. In addition, every employing agency will have its own requirements, for example, what areas in a background investigation will be of particular concern or what types of physical agility testing will be given. Find out what your state and the agency you are interested in require and expect of applicants.

Recognize that searching for a job actually becomes a job in itself. The first step is to develop a personal job-hunting strategy. Always remember, however, your job-hunt strategy should not control you—you should control it. A planned strategy will make the entire process more tolerable, successful and even enjoyable.

Helping you develop such a strategy to get the job you seek is the purpose of this book. The first section gives a general overview of the world of work (Chapter 1). This is followed by a discussion of career opportunities as first responders in law enforcement, public safety and related fields, the most visible components of the criminal justice system (Chapter 2), opportunities in courts and corrections (Chapter 3) and opportunities in private security (Chapter 4). The section concludes with a look at factors to consider when selecting a career (Chapter 5).

The second section focuses on preparing for the job search, including physical fitness and testing (Chapter 6), other tests that might be encountered (Chapter 7), desirable attributes to develop and present (Chapter 8) and the resume (Chapter 9). The section concludes with a critical component of being prepared— facing the risks of failure and building upon them should they occur (Chapter 10).

Section Three presents very specific job-seeking strategies to help you land your "dream job." These strategies are important during the application process (Chapter 11), when presenting yourself (Chapter 12) and during an interview (Chapter 13).

The fourth and final section discusses how you can succeed on the job once you get it, including making it through probation (Chapter 14) and enhancing your chances for promotion (Chapter 15). The final chapter addresses job loss and change and how you move through such set-backs (Chapter 16).

Throughout the book you will be asked to become actively engaged with the topic being discussed, to write down your ideas and plans. Such instances will be indicated like this:

 You are strongly encouraged to keep a journal for this purpose. The more you interact with the content in this book, the more you will get out of it and the more effective your job-search strategy is likely to be.

Each chapter has relevant *Insiders' Views*, written by individuals in the field. These brief, personal essays, found on the Web site, are based on experience and give a variety of perspectives on what is or might be important in seeking a career in law enforcement, corrections, private security or related fields in criminal justice, as well as learning how others have succeeded. The idea for these personal contributions resulted from the enthusiastic reception of speakers sharing similar ideas at our job-seeking seminars. Most job seekers never get a chance to find out what really goes on in the minds of those doing the hiring. The *Insider's Views* fills this void. Repetition occurs within these personal essays. Although the individuals were asked to write about their experience with the topic of the chapter, many felt compelled to add information and advice about other areas as well. As areas are repeated, you will come to realize how critical certain aspects of the job-seeking process are. Every contributor talks about them. You may also find some contradictions with what is said in the text. Use your own judgment as to whose advice you feel suits *you* best. Often no "right" answer exists.

 Each chapter concludes with a series of *Mind Stretches* to get you thinking about the topic as it relates to your particular interests and talents. Again, to get the most out of this book, *do* take time to work through these Mind Stretches, either mentally or in your journal. We have been impressed by our students who have organized job-hunting support groups which discuss issues pertaining to their efforts, including reviewing these Mind Stretch questions together.

Let your first reading be only the beginning. As you get into your job search, use the book as a reference. Also, libraries and bookstores have a tremendous amount of information on the many important aspects of job seeking. Keep practicing your skills such as working up great responses to those "most commonly asked" interview questions. Look at interviews that do not result in a job as opportunities to practice your interviewing skills. Continue to role-play interviews whenever you get the chance.

Experts say that most people will have between *five* and *twenty* careers—not just jobs, *careers*—during a lifetime. The job-hunting process is, indeed, never-ending, so become skilled at it. No one should feel trapped in a job they dislike. Pursue a new one. Or grow in your present job.

We wish you the best of luck in your job search. Here's to developing the skills and strategy that will get you the job you really want!

J. Scott Harr
Kären M. Hess

ABOUT THE AUTHORS

The authors of this book are committed to the advancement of the professionalism of criminal justice and related fields. Both Scott and Kären have been teaching college-level law enforcement classes for many years and have a number of other criminal justice related texts on the national market. Their joint publications with West/Wadsworth include *Criminal Procedure* and *Constitutional Law for the Criminal Justice Professional* (2nd edition).

Scott has been employed in various areas of the law for more than 28 years. He has been a social worker and a youth worker. For over 11 years he served as the chief law enforcement officer and public safety director for a suburb of the Twin Cities and served as a police officer for two other cities before that. In addition, Scott has served as a firefighter and emergency medical technician. He is licensed as a lawyer, police officer and private investigator, and founded Scott Harr Legal Investigations in 1985. Having taught as community faculty at Normandale Community College, and served as resident faculty at Metropolitan State University School of Law Enforcement and Criminal Justice, he is presently the Criminal Justice Chair for the School of Human Services at Concordia University in St. Paul, Minnesota.

Kären is the executive director of Innovative Programming Systems, Inc. and president of the Institute for Professional Development. She holds a PhD in English and a second PhD in criminal justice. Kären conducts in-house workshops on writing effective reports. She has also published extensively. West/Wadsworth publications include *The Police in the Community: Strategies for the 21st Century* (3rd edition), *Criminal Investigation* (6th edition), *Criminal Procedure, Introduction to Law Enforcement and Criminal Justice* (7th edition), *Juvenile Justice* (3rd edition), *Management and Supervision in Law Enforcement* (3rd edition), *Police Operations* (3rd edition) and *Private Security* (4th edition).

September 11, 2001

A day that will never be forgotten . . .

===============

A Note from the Authors.

As this book was being completed, a terrible tragedy fell upon America. We cannot ignore this event. It has affected all of us.

We have long expressed our belief that a person becomes a hero the day he or she pins a badge on that very first time. At some point in their career, they are sure to prove this to be the case. Never did our country expect that so many would prove their heroism under such catastrophic circumstances. If you are reading this book, you are contemplating a career that will, quite literally, have you running towards something that everyone else is running away from. For many of the rescuers, their run to provide aid on September 11, 2001, was to be their last. But they will never be forgotten. Ever.

We wish to acknowledge the thousands of innocent lives lost that day and recognize the countless heroes wearing badges who responded during one of America's darkest hours, many of whom continue their efforts to this day, at Ground Zero, across the United States and around the world. Be they police officers, firefighters, medics and the medical community, emergency managers, military personnel, the clergy, airline passengers and all the other responders, including civilians, each served their fellow Americans in the most noble of ways.

We believe in the work you are considering, and we believe in those choosing these professions. We know you will study hard and train well. From the two of us, please, always remain vigilant and cautious as you are committed to those you serve.

God Bless each of you, and God Bless America.

J. Scott Harr
Kären M. Hess

SECTION ONE

THE CHALLENGE

There are two things to aim at in life;
first, to get what you want; and,
after that, to enjoy it.
Only the wisest . . . achieve the second.

—Langdon Smith

Nothing great was ever achieved without enthusiasm.

—Ralph Waldo Emerson

Before beginning your job search, you should fully understand what you are getting into. Work is so vitally important that choosing a career deserves far more effort than many people give. By taking an educated look at the actual world of work, you begin a *realistic* job search. You've probably read startling statistics about the rate of change facing employees and the job market. These dramatic changes are directly affecting, and will continue to affect, the service sector, including employment in criminal justice and private security services. Chapter 1 addresses how these changes have affected the job market and what the career you're seeking might look like in the 21st century.

Chapter 2 discusses careers in law enforcement, the most visible and familiar component of the criminal justice system. It examines where employment opportunities exist—on the federal, state, county and local levels. Chapter 3 examines careers in the courts and corrections. Corrections is a rapidly expanding field due to the country's increasing intolerance of repeat offenders, the "three strikes and you're out" approach and the mandatory serving of sentences. Included in this chapter is information on careers in probation and parole.

Chapter 4 explores careers in the private sector. Privatization is a current trend, with private security growing much faster than any segment of the criminal justice system. Numerous career opportunities are found in the private security profession, including not only the familiar security officer but alarm services, armed courier services, executive protection services, private corrections and the like. Chapter 5 examines the steps for choosing a career and what factors to consider. It helps you look at the entrance requirements in light of your background, experience and personal likes and dislikes.

If after reading this section you are convinced that a career in criminal justice, private security or a related field is for you, read on. The rest of the book provides strategies and techniques to help you get the job you seek. These fields are demanding, and so is the road to employment.

You have made an important decision by taking this step to develop your job-search strategies. Let's get started!

CHAPTER 1

EMPLOYMENT TRENDS: THE WORLD OF WORK

*Most of our adult lives are spent working. Taking into account commuting time,
overtime, thinking about our jobs, and worrying over work, we spend more of our waking
hours in the office, at the factory, on the road, behind the desk, than we do at home.*
                                                                    —*The Joy of Working, p. ix.*

Do You Know:

➢   What the "hierarchy of needs" is?
➢   What role work has in meeting our needs?
➢   How many job and career changes the average person will make in a lifetime?
➢   How our labor force is changing in terms of gender and race?
➢   Why it is crucial to keep current with technology?
➢   What job areas will expand?
➢   What the projections look like for jobs in criminal justice and security?
➢   What factor education will play in future work?

INTRODUCTION

Work. For most of us, work is a large part of who we are, occupying a vast amount of our time and, to a great degree, shaping how we view ourselves. The fact that you have invested your time, energy and money into working with this book says it is important to you too.

This chapter examines why work is so important to people, what needs it fulfills and how these needs may change. It then presents a brief history of how work has evolved to its present state and some of the massive changes that have occurred, including the impact of technology. This is followed by a look at the changing job market and jobs of the future, including growth trends in the service sector and the need for more education. The chapter concludes with some myths and realities about jobs of the future.

THE IMPORTANCE OF WORK

Working *is* important. It provides you with income, but work is so much more than just a paycheck. Work helps form your identity, and it makes a statement about who you are. Well-known psychologist Abraham H. Maslow developed a hierarchy of needs ranging from the most basic physical needs to the most complex self-actualization needs (Figure 1-1). Once a person's needs are satisfied at the lowest level, he or she is able to move up the hierarchy to the next level. According to this rather simplistic hierarchy, work meets *all* five levels.

According to Maslow's simplified "hierarchy of needs," physical needs are the most basic of human needs and self-actualization needs are the most complex. Security, social and esteem needs fall in between.

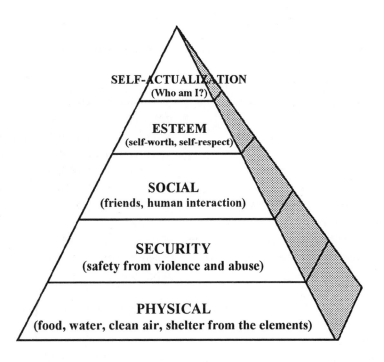

FIGURE 1-1   Maslow's Hierarchy of Human Needs

These needs and their job-related counterparts in a *satisfying* job are often as follows:

➤ Physical: Good working conditions, rest periods, labor-saving equipment, sufficient income, heating/air conditioning

➤ Security: Safe working conditions, good supervision, job security, training in survival

➤ Social: Feeling of belonging to a "job family," agency/department/organization spirit, after-hours get-togethers, picnics and softball games

➤ Esteem: Challenging job, promotions, titles, community recognition, awards

➤ Self-Actualization: Opportunity for growth and development, discretion/decision-making authority, contributing to society/organization

Work has the potential to meet all five levels of human needs; however, only truly *satisfying* jobs will actually fulfill every level.

Think for a few minutes about what's important to **you** in the career you select. Which level(s) of need will influence you the most? Jot down your responses in your journal.

WHAT'S IMPORTANT ON THE JOB

What's important to you as you consider your career? Several factors are listed below. Rank them yourself, using 1 for most important, 17 for least important.

__16__ Amount of feedback given about your job performance.

_____ Amount of freedom you have on your job.

__17__ Amount of fringe benefits.

_____ Amount of job security.

__14__ Amount of pay.

_____ Amount of praise you get for a job well done.

_____ Chance for getting a promotion.

_____ Chance for taking part in making decisions.

__1__ Chance to accomplish something worthwhile.

__15__ Chance to do something that makes you feel good about yourself.

__3__ Chance to do things you do best.

__2__ Chance to learn new things.

_____ Friendliness of people you work with.

_____ How you are treated by your supervisor.

_____ Opportunities to develop your skills and abilities.

__4__ Resources available to do your job.

_____ Respect you receive from people you work with.

Think carefully about your top rankings and how well they would be met in your chosen field. Again, record your thoughts in your journal.

Work satisfies so many human needs that those who find themselves without meaningful employment usually experience a sense of loss. If your work is unfulfilling, your needs must be met elsewhere or anxiety, frustration or even depression may result. If you are suddenly unemployed, as in the case of an unexpected layoff, your lifestyle may become seriously disrupted. Losing a job and being unable to find other work has driven some to such self-destructive behaviors as alcoholism and other substance abuse and even suicide. Truly, work is important as something positive to do to meet your needs—not only your financial needs, but your identity and self-esteem needs.

For these reasons it is important to give careful thought to what work you pursue. This book will help you decide what you want to do with your working life. You will have a chance to look at what is important to you and what you have to offer employers. Many people spend more time planning their next vacation than they do planning what they're going to do for the rest of their lives. To do so is risky.

> Statistics indicate the average person is likely to make more than 10 job changes and 5 career changes in a lifetime.

A brief look at the evolution of work in the United States is revealing.

A BRIEF HISTORY

You may be familiar with Toffler's "three waves" theory, which compares ocean waves to sweeping major changes in society:

➤   The Agricultural Revolution
➤   The Industrial Revolution
➤   The Technological Revolution

The first wave, the Agricultural Revolution, occurred about 8,000 B.C., sweeping aside 45,000 years of cave dwelling. The second wave, the Industrial Revolution, came around 1760, turning our landscape from "amber waves of grain" into smokestacks. This second wave was not without its resistors. A group of workers, called Luddites, systematically destroyed machinery they saw as a threat to manual laborers. But the wave engulfed America, forcing many farmers into factories as blue-collar workers in the new era of industrialization.

Pulley (1997, pp.15–16) notes that the Industrial Revolution had an impact on more than just how and where people worked—it changed the way people identified with each other and how they viewed themselves. Whereas the Agricultural Age saw family members working in the fields together, the Industrial Age separated families, sending its members, young and old, into the factories to labor as nameless "cogs" in the massive machine:

> As people spent more time in the factory than with the family, the importance of work grew. Increasingly it became the principle source of people's identity. For instance, in preindustrial society it was more common to identify yourself in terms of your birthplace or family membership, such as "I'm John of Winchester," or "I'm William's son." In industrialized society people began to tie identity to work . . . . The workplace became the main organizing feature of our life and the source of our identity, status, income, and affiliations. And by the 20th century, identity became specifically tied to *organizations*.

Pulley (p.16) further notes that, over time, these organizations became increasingly "paternalistic," taking care of their employees by providing benefits such as health care insurance, retirement pensions, social functions and activities, as well as rewards for company loyalty, such as bonuses, watches, plaques and dinners. Pulley contends: "Out of this grew the implicit and pervasive understanding between workers and organizations that is now coming apart at the seams—the belief that hard work and loyalty will be exchanged for promotions and job security."

Gradually, the dominance of factories and industrialized business ebbed and a new era was born—"the information age." This third wave, the Technological Revolution, began in the mid-fifties and again changed the face of the American workplace. Brains rather than brawn became important, and white-collar workers began displacing blue-collar workers. Again, resistance occurred. Many people, like the Luddites, have rebelled against computers, fax machines and voice mail. But the third wave *is* here.

OUR CHANGING WORK WORLD

Pulley asserts the third wave has put an end to the assumptions previously mentioned—that hard work and loyalty will be rewarded with job security. The job turnover rate is at an all-time high, leaving many with feelings of collapse and insecurity:

> When our building-block assumptions are pulled out from under us, we often experience a psychological crash that feels as personally damaging as the Kobe earthquake that struck Japan in 1995. . . . What was learned from this disaster, however, is that wood-frame-and-stucco buildings do not survive an earthquake because they do not yield. . . . Likewise both we as individuals and our organizations will need built-in flexibility to weather the future. . . . Our world no longer has the stability and predictability of earlier times (Pulley, pp.16–17).

Others, however, believe this "instability" has a positive impact on contemporary workers as they strive to continuously advance into better and more challenging positions: "As the Great Depression produced a generation of 'organization men,' whose fear of unemployment generated loyalty to their employers, the current period of nearly full employment will create generations of confident and increasingly assertive workers, some experts say" (Tevlin, 1999, p.D5).

Indeed, American workers have reason to feel confident in the current labor "bull market," as our country enjoys the longest economic expansion in history and unemployment remains near record-low levels. Bayer (2000) notes: "More than anything else, our present situation is defined by the high demand for quality labor in contrast to the present limited supply." Nonetheless: "The new economy, in which jobs are plentiful and turnover is high, will not by itself end poverty and want. There are still many people with full-time work who live in poverty. Government has a role in protecting the working poor, as well as in providing a safety net for those hit by this constant churning."

Demographic Trends

As the U.S. population continues to grow, increasing by an estimated 23 million between 1998 and 2008, an important trend impacting employment is the growing proportion of minorities and immigrants. This increasingly diverse population has not only required an expanded range of goods and services, it has also produced corresponding changes in the size and demographic composition of the labor force:

> The U.S. workforce will become more diverse by 2008. White, non-Hispanic persons will make up a decreasing share of the labor force, from 73.9 percent to 70.7 percent. Hispanics, non-Hispanic blacks, and Asians and other racial groups are projected to comprise an increasing share of the labor force by 2008—10.4 to 12.7 percent, 11.6 to 12.4 percent, and 4.6 to 5.7 percent, respectively (*Occupational Outlook Handbook*, 2000, p.2).

The gender composition of the U.S. workforce is also changing: "Between 1998 and 2008, men's share of the labor force is expected to decrease from 53.7 to 52.5 percent while women's share is expected to increase from 46.3 to 47.5 percent (*Occupational Outlook Handbook*, p.2).

> The labor force in America is undergoing many changes, including an increasing percentage of minorities and immigrants, and an increasing percentage of women.

Important demographic changes have also resulted from shifts in some basic societal values, norms and conditions. For example, prior to the technological revolution, American families were generally categorized as warm, secure units with both parents living at home with their children. However, as the 20th century progressed, divorce rates soared and an increasing number of families became categorized as blended or single-parent families. Another trend observed was the declining view of childhood as a carefree time and an increasing rate of children committing violent crimes and being victimized.

Americans have paid tremendous attention to crime and expect it to be contained. And despite the *decrease* in crime in the past few years, Eskridge (1999, p.9) contends: "Concern for criminal activity in our society runs from the suites to the streets. . . . Crime continues to be one of the most significant social-political issues of the day." These trends and demographic changes have produced myriad opportunities for everyone interested in criminal justice and security careers, particularly those who understand and prepare to address these changes.

One of the best ways to prepare for job success in today's rapidly evolving work environment is to build up some critical skills, including communication and technical skills. As Bayer stresses: "Employees are realizing a very critical fact in this rapidly changing labor market: the greatest danger to your career is 'skill obsolescence.' "

As discussed, the U.S. population in general is becoming increasingly diverse, with language barriers presenting a formidable challenge in many professions, particularly those geared toward service to the public. The ability to speak more than one language is a quality many employers now actively seek in job applicants. Many of the other emerging "critical skills" are the direct result of technological advances. This is definitely the case in all areas of criminal justice and security employment.

The Impact of Technology

What remains fascinating is how the working world continues to evolve, being greatly affected by technological advances. Technology is changing so fast it is almost impossible to keep up, much less predict what is ahead. More than ever, successful job seekers will position themselves to showcase their computer knowledge and skills. It is strongly recommended that you bring your computer skill level up as high as possible. You simply must be comfortable at a keyboard.

> Technology is a powerful, rapidly changing force in today's working world. To stay competitive and ensure your value in the work force, keep current with technology.

Technology is not the only driving force behind the changing job market, however. Economic and political forces also have influenced the job market.

A LOOK AT JOBS OF THE FUTURE—WHERE WILL YOU FIT IN?

In the 21st century, interest has heightened in looking ahead at what our world of work might be like. Certain trends, some of which have already been discussed, are pointed out repeatedly:

➢ The total number of jobs will increase rapidly.
➢ The labor force will continue to grow.
➢ Women and minorities will account for a greater share of the work force.
➢ Blue-collar jobs will decline slightly.
➢ The most rapid growth will be in jobs in the *service sector* (which includes criminal justice and security).
➢ More education will be needed for more jobs.

Growth in the Service Industries

The *Occupational Outlook Handbook* estimates a 14.4 percent increase in total number of U.S. jobs between 1998 and 2008. Many of the new jobs will be in the service industries, including social services, legal services and protective services. In fact, a news release by the Bureau of Labor Statistics (BLS) states service-producing industries will account for virtually all of the job growth in industry employment between 1998 and 2008 ("BLS Releases . . . ," 1999).

According to the *Occupational Outlook Handbook*, protective services occupations, which include firefighting occupations, law enforcement occupations and other protective services such as guards, private detectives and investigators, are projected to increase 25.9 percent between 1998 and 2008, adding a total of 717,000 new jobs in this sector. More specifically, firefighting occupations will see an anticipated 6.4 percent increase in the number of jobs (adding 20,000), law enforcement occupations are estimated to increase by 30.8 percent (354,000 new jobs), and other protective service categories will increase by 26.2 percent, including guards (+28.6 % for 294,000 new jobs), and private detectives and investigators (+24.3 % for 15,000 new jobs).

Figure 1-2 illustrates the projected percent change in total employment by major occupational group from 1998 to 2008; Figure 1-3 shows the 20 occupations with fast growth and high pay that have the largest numerical growth, projected 1998–2008.

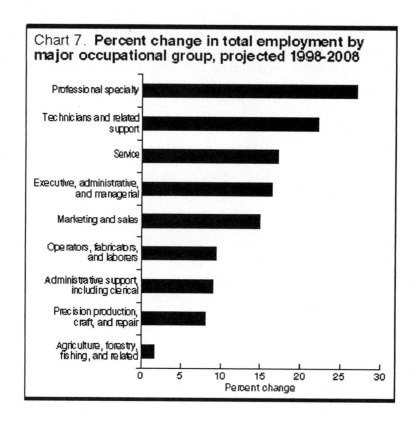

FIGURE 1-2   Percent Change in Total Employment by Major Occupational Group, Projected 1998–2008

SOURCE: *Occupational Outlook Handbook, 2000–2001 Edition.* Washington, DC: Bureau of Labor Statistics, January 2000, Chart 7.

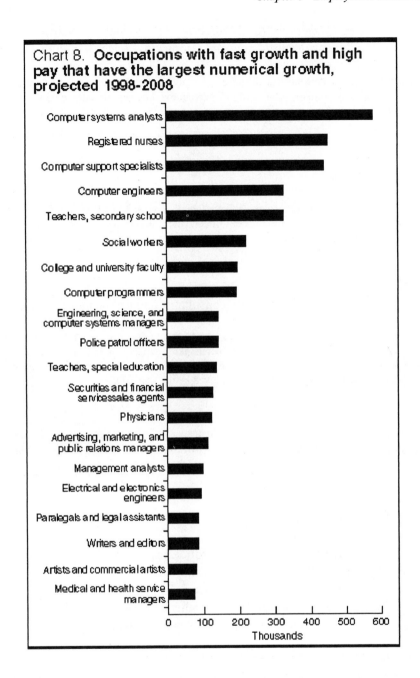

FIGURE 1-3 Occupations with Fast Growth and High Pay that have the Largest Numerical Growth, Projected 1998–2008

SOURCE: *Occupational Outlook Handbook, 2000–2001 Edition.* Washington, DC: Bureau of Labor Statistics, January 2000, Chart 8.

The Top 100: The Fastest Growing Careers for the 21ˢᵗ Century (1998) includes police officers, detectives, corrections officers and security consultants and technicians. According to this document:

> The employment outlook for police detectives is expected to be much faster than the average through the year 2005. High estimates call for an increase of nearly 77 percent over the next decade, to more than 104,000 detectives. Even the lowest estimate calls for an increase of 60 percent over the next decade, to 94,000 detectives.

Regarding corrections officers (p.91):

> Employment in this field is expected to increase much faster than the average for all jobs. It is estimated that another 142,000 jobs will be created within the next fifteen years, an increase in employment of 61 percent. The ongoing war on drugs, new tough-on-crime legislation, and increasing mandatory sentencing policies will add more prison beds and more corrections officers.

The employment outlook is equally positive for security consultants and technicians (p.345):

> Security services is one of the largest employment fields in the United States. About 883,000 persons are employed . . . . The demand for guards and other security personnel is expected to increase much faster than the average through the year 2005, as crime rates rise with the overall population growth. The highest estimates call for more than 1.25 million guards to be employed by the year 2005.

Trends in the changing work force show service-producing industries, including criminal justice and security, will account for most of all job growth. Furthermore, these services will remain the fastest growing major industry during the next decade.

A Need for More Education

New service industry jobs will require enhanced skills and proficiencies, and many will demand successful applicants possess college degrees and other certifications. Data from both the U.S. Labor Department and the U.S. Census Bureau forecast service jobs becoming higher skilled during the next century (Meyers, 1999, p.D5). Ironically, such requirements will lead to both higher and lower unemployment: more joblessness for those who can't read or who don't possess marketable skills and less joblessness among those with higher education.

According to the *Occupational Outlook Handbook*: "Education is essential in getting a high paying job. In fact, all but a few of the 50 highest paying occupations require a college degree. However, a number of occupations—for example . . . police patrol officer—do not require a college degree, yet offer higher than average earnings." Of course, this does not mean that college graduates are unable to fill such positions or that those in service occupations are discouraged from pursuing higher education.

Fleetwood and Shelley (2000, p.4) observe that most jobs in the service field are classified as noncollege level jobs, with the exception of police and detectives: "Training and educational requirements are especially ambiguous and may be changing for a small number of occupations, including police and detective [occupations]." In fact, in 1998, 1.3 million college graduates, or 4 percent, were employed in service occupations, such as police and detective (p.5):

> For some occupations . . . , increases in the proportion of college graduates results from changes in workplace requirements. Some police, for example, are increasingly taking on duties not formerly associated with conventional police work: in addition to patrolling and responding to crime reports, many now perform work that requires familiarity with psychology and social work. These academic subjects are typically learned in college and, over time, the proportion of police officers who need a college degree is expected to increase (p.8).

The reality is that a high-school diploma, while perhaps meeting the bare requirements for some jobs, will seldom be sufficient to assure career advancement opportunities.

> It is projected that more than half of the new jobs created over the next decade will require an educational level beyond high school. Criminal justice and security agencies nationwide are also raising applicants' educational requirements. To stay competitive, you must seek higher education.

The importance of education is discussed more fully in Chapter 8.

KEEPING UP-TO-DATE

One excellent source for finding help in planning careers that require college or technical degrees is the *Professional Careers Sourcebook*, published by Gale Research Publishing, Detroit. It contains job descriptions and the names and addresses of associations able to provide further information on career possibilities.

Another excellent source for keeping current on jobs and employment trends is the *Occupational Outlook Handbook*, produced by the U.S. Department of Labor. Updated every two years, this resource describes about 200 occupations, offering information on the nature of the work involved, salaries, work environments, necessary education and training, and job outlook. It also includes a listing of sources of state and local job information. It can be purchased at any U.S. government bookstore or by calling the office of the Superintendent of Documents in Washington (202-783-3238). You might also want to check with your local library, state agencies and employment offices, as well as your state department of education, state job services agencies and state labor departments.

CONCLUSION

The days of picking one career and sticking with it for 40 years are over. Statistics show the average person is likely to make more than ten job changes and five career changes in a lifetime. Trends in the changing work force show service-producing industries, including criminal justice and security, will account for most of all job growth. Furthermore, these services will remain the fastest growing major industry during the next decade. It is also projected that more than half of the new jobs created over the next decade will require an educational level beyond high school. Criminal justice and security agencies nationwide are raising applicants' educational requirements. Therefore, to stay competitive, you must seek higher education and keep current with technology.

INTRODUCING THE INSIDERS' VIEWS

A supplement to this book is a collection of short articles written by men and women whose careers have intersected with criminal justice and related fields. Each guest writer's contribution, called *An Insider's View*, presents a unique perspective about jobs in criminal justice or related fields and how to obtain them. The backgrounds and credentials of the contributors are quite varied, including police officer, sergeant, captain and chief; railroad police agent; probation/parole officer; private security manager; crime prevention specialist; gang task force member; director of safety for public schools; attorney; professor; medical doctor; and businessman. They also include perspectives from both sides of the interview table—those looking to be hired and those doing the hiring. Whichever angle a particular writer pursues, think about the important insights you are being given from those "on the inside." You will find this supplemental information online under the Student Resources section at http://www.wadsworth.com/criminaljustice_d/.

At the end of each chapter, you will be directed to two or three *Insiders' Views* with relevance to the topic(s) just covered. For this first chapter we've selected articles by Dr. Jack Cahall and Timothy Erickson to introduce you to the "World of Work" as it applies to criminal justice and security professionals.

 MIND STRETCHES

1.   Imagine you have a crystal ball—what changes do you see in the world of work five years from now? Ten years from now? Fifty years from now?

2.   What role do you think education will play in the future?

3.   Do you think work will become more specialized or more generalized in the future? Why? How will your job goals be affected?

4.   What do you think will happen to current age limitations on jobs? Why?

5.   What jobs do you think will become more necessary in the future? Less necessary?

6.   Is your community changing? How? What about neighboring communities?

7.   Why do you think more people don't pursue advanced education or specialized training? Are these reasons legitimate?

8.   Recognizing that our entire society is always changing, what importance will you place on continuing to grow and change yourself?

9.   Is always striving to improve yourself important to you? Is there a danger in not continuing to grow and change?

10. Can you think of jobs that do not now exist but will within the next 10 or 20 years?

REFERENCES

Bayer, Richard. "The U.S. Labor Market: Three Key Issues." *The Five O'Clock Club News*, November 2000.
http://www.fiveoclockclub.com/roundtable/

"BLS Releases New 1998–2008 Employment Projections." Washington, DC: Bureau of Labor Statistics, November 30, 1999 (USDL 99-339). http://stats.bls.gov/news.release/ecopro.nr0.htm

Eskridge, Chris W. *Criminal Justice: Concepts and Issues*, 3rd ed. Los Angeles: Roxbury Publishing Company, 1999.

Fleetwood, Chad and Shelley, Kristina. "The Outlook for College Graduates, 1998–2008: A Balancing Act." *Occupational Outlook Quarterly*, Fall 2000, pp.3–9.

Meyers, Mike. "More Brain, Less Brawn." (Minneapolis/St. Paul) *Star Tribune*, April 11, 1999, p.D5.

Occupational Outlook Handbook, 2000–2001 Edition. Washington, DC: Bureau of Labor Statistics, 2000.
http://stats.bls.gov/oco/oco2003.htm

Pulley, Mary Lynn. *Losing Your Job—Reclaiming Your Soul*. San Francisco: Jossey-Bass Publishers, 1997.

Tevlin, Jon. "Change Will Come Slowly." (Minneapolis/St. Paul) *Star Tribune*, April 11, 1999, p.D5.

The Top 100: The Fastest Growing Careers for the 21st Century. Chicago: Ferguson Publishing Company, 1998.

CHAPTER 2

FIRST RESPONDERS: CAREERS IN LAW ENFORCEMENT, PUBLIC SAFETY AND RELATED FIELDS

The very first step towards success in any occupation is to become interested in it.

—*John Dewey*

Do You Know:

➤ What percentage of time is spent on patrol or doing routine paperwork and how much time is actually taken up with chases and shoot-outs?

➤ What four local agencies you might consider in seeking employment in law enforcement or a related field? Three county agencies? Six state agencies? Fifteen federal agencies?

➤ Where the greatest employment potential is usually found?

➤ At what jurisdictional levels civilian positions in law enforcement are available?

➤ How common promotions in law enforcement are?

➤ Why specialization within the law enforcement profession is important?

➤ How specialized training or expertise may benefit a law enforcement professional?

➤ How job prospects look for those interested in the field of juvenile justice?

➤ What the availability of international jobs in law enforcement is?

➤ What nonsworn civilian career options exist for those interested in law enforcement?

➤ What other careers are available to those interested in public safety and first response?

INTRODUCTION

This chapter discusses the largest and most visible component of the criminal justice system—law enforcement. It begins with a discussion of what law enforcement entails in reality as opposed to what is often seen in movies and on television. Next, employment requirements and the outlook for careers in this field are discussed, followed by an up-close look at the variety of employment available in law enforcement and an explanation of where specific opportunities exist at the local, county, state and federal levels. Salaries for various law enforcement positions, as well as fringe benefits and promotional opportunities, are presented next, followed by a look at advanced jobs and specialization within the field, international job opportunities and a variety of nonsworn civilian jobs that support law enforcement. The chapter concludes with a look at other first responders and a discussion of public safety career opportunities in fire services and emergency response.

IS LAW ENFORCEMENT FOR YOU?

To make informed decisions about your career, you must gather factual data. Some of this information comes from within. Do you possess the personal attributes needed to be a police officer? Can you give orders? Can you take orders? Can you remain calm under stress? Can you treat people professionally and apply the law equally? Can you work the hours under the conditions required by the job?

You also need to consider objective, external data. Much of what happens within law enforcement is not common knowledge. Consequently, many people considering employment in law enforcement may find themselves relying on inaccurate data. Unless you have a personal friend or relative in law enforcement, you are likely to obtain what you know about the field from where most people do: television or the movies.

Because of the popularity of police investigators and detectives, movies and television shows about them abound. But the primary goal of such shows is to entertain, not to educate. Sensationalism is much more likely than realism. A major public misconception about police work is that it is primarily oriented toward catching criminals. *Nash Bridges, NYPD Blue, Homicide* and other television dramas about law enforcement depict police continuously involved in high-speed chases, exciting and dangerous shoot-outs and other dramatic criminal-catching activities.

> The law enforcement profession is grossly misrepresented in television shows and movies. In reality, about 80 percent of duty time is spent on patrol and doing routine paperwork. "Action" such as investigations, high-speed chases, shoot-outs and other dramatic criminal-catching activities consumes only about 20 percent of duty time.

To select a career based on fiction is to set yourself up for disappointment. No one knows better than those in the profession that television shows and movies don't exactly "tell it like it is." The uniforms, the cars, the equipment, the apparent prestige and the legal authority combine to make for a romantic ideal. Don't be fooled. Take a hard look at the law enforcement profession as you make realistic, informed decisions about your future career.

The *Occupational Outlook Handbook, 2000* notes 40-hour workweeks are typical for law enforcement officers, although paid overtime is common. Because most communities require round-the-clock police protection, officers (typically junior officers) are needed to work the night, weekend and holiday shifts. Also, keep in mind that you will not begin your career as a detective—it may be a goal that requires many years to achieve. Other significant points to consider when exploring a career as a police officer, detective or special agent include:

➢ Police work can be dangerous and stressful.
➢ The number of qualified candidates exceeds the number of job openings in federal and state law enforcement agencies but is inadequate to meet growth and replacement needs in many local and special police departments.
➢ The greatest number of job opportunities will be in urban communities with relatively low salaries and high crime rates.

Large, urban departments may offer the widest variety of positions, as well. According to *The Top 100: The Fastest Growing Careers for the 21st Century* (1998, pp.269–270):

> In very large city police departments, officers may fill positions as police chiefs, precinct sergeants and captains, desk officers, booking officers, police inspectors, identification officers, complaint evaluation supervisors and officers, crime prevention police officers, and internal affairs investigators, whose job it is to police the police. Some officers work as plainclothes detectives in criminal investigation divisions. Other specialized police officers include police reserves commanders; police officer commanding officers III, who act as supervisors in missing persons and fugitive investigations; and police officers III, who investigate and pursue nonpayment and fraud fugitives. Many police departments employ police clerks, who perform administrative and community-oriented tasks.

The possibility of officer assaults and fatalities is one aspect of the job many prefer to not think about. Nonetheless, grim statistics attest to the danger law enforcement officers may face on the job. In 2000, 151 local, state and federal law enforcement officers were killed in the line of duty—51 were shot to death, 47 died in automobile accidents, 20 were struck by a vehicle while outside their own vehicle, 8 died in motorcycle accidents, 7 were killed in aircraft accidents, and the rest died from a variety of other causes ("151 Law Enforcement. . . ," 2001, p.7).

Another hazard of police work involves communicable diseases. Officers called to the scene of an accident may come in contact with blood or other bodily fluids. Officers attempting to arrest or contain drunken, high, violent, excited or otherwise "altered" individuals may be bitten, scratched, spit on or worse, increasing their chances of contracting diseases, some of which may be fatal. Many agencies now make hepatitis vaccinations available and have regular HIV testing for officers involved in needle pricks and other high-risk incidents. Furthermore, police work often takes an emotional and psychological toll on officers, who routinely witness death and suffering resulting from accidents and criminal behavior. Officers' private lives may also suffer under such stress.

This information is presented not to discourage you from considering a career in law enforcement but to raise your awareness about some potential hazards of a very worthwhile profession. Caution, alertness and good judgment are critical, possibly lifesaving, qualities every good officer should possess. Other personal characteristics such as honesty, integrity and a sense of responsibility are especially important in law enforcement. You must also consider the level of education, training and other qualifications necessary to apply for a law enforcement position.

EMPLOYMENT REQUIREMENTS

According to the *Occupational Outlook Handbook*:

> Candidates must be U.S. citizens, usually at least 20 years of age, and must meet rigorous physical and personal qualifications. Physical examinations for entrance into law enforcement often include tests of vision, hearing, strength, and agility. Eligibility for appointment usually depends on performance in competitive written examinations and previous education and experience. In larger police departments, . . . applicants usually must have at least a high school education. Federal and State agencies typically require a college degree.

Law enforcement agencies are encouraging applicants to complete college-level courses in criminal-justice related subjects: "Many entry-level applicants for police jobs have completed some formal postsecondary education and a significant number are college graduates. Many junior colleges, colleges, and universities offer programs in law enforcement or administration of justice. Other courses helpful in preparing for a career in law enforcement include accounting, finance, electrical engineering, computer science, and foreign languages" (*Occupational Outlook Handbook*).

EMPLOYMENT OUTLOOK

The outlook for jobs in law enforcement is positive, although continuing budgetary constraints may keep the field from growing as much as is needed. Nonetheless: "The opportunity for public service through law enforcement work is attractive to many because the job is challenging and involves much personal responsibility" (*Occupational Outlook Handbook*). Furthermore:

Law enforcement officers in many agencies may retire with a pension after 20 or 25 years of service, allowing them to pursue a second career while still in their 40s. Because of relatively attractive salaries and benefits, the number of qualified candidates exceeds the number of job openings in Federal law enforcement agencies and in most State, local, and special police departments—resulting in increased hiring standards and selectivity by employers. Competition is expected to remain keen for the higher paying jobs with State and Federal agencies and police departments in more affluent areas.

The *Occupational Outlook Handbook* states: "Employment of police officers and detectives is expected to increase faster than average for all occupations through 2008," meaning employment in these fields is projected to increase 21 to 35 percent. The Bureau of Labor Statistics (BLS) projects a 31.6 percent increase in employment for police patrol officers between 1998 and 2008, raising their numbers from approximately 446,000 to 586,000.

Some aspects of law enforcement require careful, realistic consideration. But these fields continue to draw people to them. Ask a hundred officers why they're in it, and you'll hear a hundred different responses. And, yes, police officers complain a lot—about the hours, the pay and the administration. But there is something about law enforcement that gets in your blood.

LAW ENFORCEMENT—UP CLOSE

The public generally believes that being a police officer means wearing a uniform and pushing a squad car around town. Few people outside the field have any idea of the variety of employment available. Consider the vocational spectrum shown by the following partial listing of positions, many obtained by reviewing the 1999 *International Association of Chiefs of Police Membership Directory*:

Arson Investigator	Document Specialist	Police Surgeon
Attaché	Emergency Management Coordinator	Polygraph Operator
Ballistics Expert	Evidence Technician	Professor
Booking Officer	FBI Special Agent	Psychiatric Advisor
Border Patrol Officer	Fingerprint Expert	Public Relations Officer
Chaplain	Firearms Instructor	Public Safety Director
Chief of Police	Forensic Scientist	Radio Communications
Chief of Staff	Gaming Enforcement Agent	Record Management
Director		
Commander of Field Operations	Gang Investigator	Scientist
Commissioner	Inspector	Security Specialist
Communications Officer	Instructor	Secret Service Agent
Community Safety Coordinator	Intelligence Officer	Serology Specialist
Community Service Officer	Investigator	Sheriff
Conservation Officer	Jailer	Street Crimes Specialist
Crime Lab Technician	Juvenile Specialist	Superintendent of Police
Crime Prevention Specialist	K-9 Handler	S.W.A.T.
Customs Officer	Narcotics Agent	Traffic Officer
Data Processing Specialist	Operations Specialist	Training Director
Deputy	Patrol Officer	Treasury Agent
Deputy Chief	Personnel Specialist	Trooper
Detective	Photographer	Undercover Operative
Detention Officer	Pilot	Undersheriff
Director of Research and Development	Police Attorney/Legal Advisor	U.S. Marshal
Director of Scientific Services	Police Psychologist	Water Patrol
Director of Standards and Training	Police/School Liaison Officer	Witness Protection Agent

WHERE OPPORTUNITIES EXIST

To begin your look at law enforcement, consider the basic jurisdictions in which you might work. Jurisdiction in this sense basically addresses both *where* particular agencies work and *what* their enforcement emphasis is. The primary jurisdictional levels are local, county, state and federal.

Different levels of law enforcement agencies have different areas of responsibility. For example, while Secret Service agents are law enforcement officers, they do not do traffic enforcement. Similarly, local law enforcement officers are seldom called on for diplomatic protective service. The following descriptions of local, county, state and federal agencies are adapted from *Introduction to Law Enforcement and Criminal Justice,* 6th edition (Wrobleski and Hess, 2000, pp.16–19. Reprinted by permission).

Local Agencies

Local agencies and offices with law enforcement responsibilities include (1) township and special district police, (2) the constable, (3) the marshal and (4) municipal police.

Township and Special District Police. The United States has approximately 19,000 townships, which vary widely in scope of governmental powers and operations. Most townships provide a limited range of services for predominantly rural areas. Some townships, often those in well-developed fringe areas surrounding a metropolitan complex, perform functions similar to municipal police.

The Constable. Several states have established the office of constable, especially in New England, the South and the West. The constable is usually an elected official who serves a township, preserving the peace and serving processes for the local justice court. The constable may also be the tax collector or be in charge of the pound, execute arrest warrants and transport prisoners.

The Marshal. In some parts of the United States, a marshal serves as a court officer, serving writs, subpoenas and other papers issued by the court and escorting prisoners from jail or holding cells in the courthouse to and from trials and hearings. The marshal also serves as the bailiff and protects the municipal judge and people in the court. In some jurisdictions, the marshal is elected; in other jurisdictions, the marshal is appointed.

Municipal Police. The United States has more than 40,000 police jurisdictions and approximately 450,000 police officers, all with similar responsibilities but with limited geographical jurisdictions. The least uniformity and greatest organizational complexity are found at the municipal level due to local autonomy. The majority of these police forces consist of fewer than 10 officers, yet this is what most people think of when they think of law enforcement.

County Agencies

County agencies with law enforcement responsibilities include (1) the county sheriff, (2) the county police and (3) the county coroner or medical examiner.

The County Sheriff. Many state constitutions designate the sheriff as the chief county law enforcement officer. The sheriff is usually elected locally for a two- or four-year term and may appoint deputies to help provide police protection as well as to (1) keep the public peace,   (2) execute civil and criminal process throughout the county, (3) maintain and staff the county jail, (4) preserve the court's dignity and (5) enforce court orders.

The hundreds of sheriff's departments vary greatly in organization and function. In some states, the sheriff is primarily a court officer; criminal investigation and traffic enforcement are delegated to state or local agencies. In other states, notably in the South and West, the sheriff and deputies perform both traffic and criminal duties. The sheriff's staff ranges from one (the sheriff only) to several hundred, including sworn deputies and civilian personnel. A major difference between sheriffs' and municipal police departments is that sheriffs often place greater emphasis on civil functions and operating corrections facilities.

The County Police. The county police are often found in areas where city and county governments have merged and are headed by a chief law enforcement officer.

The County Coroner or Medical Examiner. The coroner's principal task is to determine the cause of death and to take care of the remains and personal effects of deceased persons. The coroner need not be a medical doctor or have any legal background to be elected. In some jurisdictions, however, the coroner has been replaced by the medical examiner, a physician, usually a pathologist who has studied forensic science. Still other jurisdictions are using medicolegal death investigators or deputy coroners, discussed shortly.

State Agencies

State agencies with law enforcement responsibilities include (1) state investigative agencies, (2) state fire marshal divisions, (3) departments of natural resources, (4) driver and vehicle services divisions, (5) departments of human rights and (6) state police and highway patrol agencies.

State Investigative Agencies. State Investigative Agencies place investigators throughout the state to help investigate major crimes, organized criminal activity, and the illegal sale or possession of narcotics and prohibited drugs; conduct police science training courses for peace officers; provide scientific examination of crime scenes and laboratory analysis of evidence; and maintain a criminal justice information and telecommunications system.

State Fire Marshal Divisions. Designated state fire marshals investigate suspicious and incendiary fire origins, fire fatalities and large-loss fires; tabulate fire statistics; and provide education, inspection and training programs for fire prevention.

State Department of Natural Resources (Fish, Game and Watercraft). Conservation officers investigate complaints about nuisance wildlife, misuse of public lands and waters, violations of state park rules and unlawful appropriation of state-owned timber. They also dispose of big game animals struck by motor vehicles, assist state game managers on wildlife census projects and assist in identifying needed sites for public access to lakes and streams. The department also issues resident and nonresident boat licenses and licenses for hunting, fishing and trapping.

Driver and Vehicle Services Division. The *Motor Vehicle Section* registers motor vehicles, issues ownership certificates, answers inquiries, licenses motor vehicle dealers, supplies record information to the public and in some states, registers bicycles. The *Driver's License Section* tests, evaluates and licenses all drivers throughout the state; maintains accurate records of each individual driver including all violations and accidents occurring anywhere in the United States and Canada; interviews drivers whose record warrants possible revocation, suspension or cancellation; records the location of every reported accident; assists in driver education efforts and administers written and road tests to applicants.

Department of Human Rights. The Department of Human Rights enforces the Human Rights Act, which prohibits discrimination on the basis of race, color, creed, religion, national origin, sex, marital status, status with regard to public assistance or disability in employment, housing, public accommodations, public service and education.

State Law Enforcement—State Police and Highway Patrol Agencies. Some state police enforce all state laws; others enforce primarily traffic laws on highways and freeways and are usually designated as state highway patrol. A major difference between the two officers is that state police generally have more investigative duties than do the highway patrol.

Usually, *state police* work within jurisdictions on request or following up on their own cases. State police typically have specialized units of special agents or criminal investigators, plainclothes detectives who investigate various violations of state law such as drug trafficking.

Most *state patrol* agencies enforce state traffic laws and all laws governing operation of vehicles on the state's public highways. Officers usually work in uniform and drive marked cars and motorcycles. Duties include (1) maintaining preventive patrol on the highways, (2) regulating traffic movements and relieving congestion, (3) investigating traffic accidents and (4) making surveys and studies of accidents and enforcement practices to improve traffic safety. (NOTE: *Highway patrol*, while still used, is becoming less common, with many states replacing the term with *state patrol*. While their training emphasizes traffic-related matters, state patrol officers are trained in all areas of professional law enforcement.)

State officers seeking additional specialization should research their state's specialized units, such as canine units, aircraft units, special response and tactical teams, investigation units and executive protection teams. Sources of further information regarding state law enforcement careers are provided at the end of this chapter.

Federal Agencies

Reaves and Hart (2001, p.1) report: "As of June 2000, Federal agencies employed more than 88,000 full-time personnel authorized to make arrests and carry firearms." In 2000, women and minorities accounted for 14.4 and 30.5 percent of Federal officers, respectively.

Federal agencies to consider when looking for a job in law enforcement or a related field include (1) Federal Bureau of Investigation; (2) Federal Drug Enforcement Administration; (3) U.S. Marshals; (4) Immigration and Naturalization Service; (5) Bureau of Prisons; (6) Bureau of Customs; (7) Federal Aviation Administration; (8) Bureau of Diplomatic Security; (9) Internal Revenue Service; (10) U.S. Secret Service; (11) Bureau of Alcohol, Tobacco and Firearms Tax; (12) U.S. Mint; (13) Postal Inspectors; (14) Coast Guard and (15) military services.

The Federal Bureau of Investigation (FBI). The FBI is the primary investigative agency of the federal government. Its special agents have jurisdiction over more than 200 federal crimes and are responsible for investigating espionage; interstate transportation of stolen property and kidnapping; unlawful flight to avoid prosecution, confinement or giving testimony; sabotage; piracy of aircraft and other crimes aboard aircraft; bank robbery and embezzlement; and enforcement of the Civil Rights Act.

The FBI also provides valuable services to law enforcement agencies throughout the country. The *Identification Division* is a central repository for fingerprint information, including the automated fingerprint identification system (AFIS), which greatly streamlines the matching of fingerprints with suspects. The *National Crime Information Center* (NCIC-2000) is a computerized, electronic data exchange network developed to complement computerized systems already in existence and those planned by local and state law enforcement agencies. The *FBI Laboratory*, the world's largest criminal laboratory, is available without cost to any city, county, state or federal law enforcement agency in the country. The *Uniform Crime Reports* (UCR) is a national clearinghouse for U.S. crime statistics.

The Federal Drug Enforcement Administration (FDEA). FDEA agents seek to stop the flow of drugs at their source, both domestic and foreign, and to assist state and local police in preventing illegal drugs from reaching local communities. They are involved in surveillance, raids, interviewing witnesses and suspects, searching for evidence and seizing contraband.

The U.S. Marshals. In 1789 Congress created the office of U.S. Marshal. Marshals are appointed by the president and are responsible for (1) seizing property in both criminal and civil matters to satisfy judgments issued by a federal court, (2) providing physical security for U.S. courtrooms, (3) transporting federal prisoners and (4) protecting government witnesses whose testimony might jeopardize their safety.

The Immigration and Naturalization Service (INS). The Immigration and Naturalization Service has border patrol agents who serve throughout the United States, Canada, Mexico, Bermuda, Nassau, Puerto Rico, the Philippines and Europe. They investigate violations of immigrant and nationality laws and determine whether aliens may enter or remain in the United States. The INS is the largest employer of Federal officers with arrest and firearm authority.

The Bureau of Prisons (BOP). The BOP is responsible for the care and custody of persons convicted of federal crimes and sentenced to federal penal institutions. The Bureau operates a nationwide system of maximum-, medium- and minimum-security prisons, halfway houses and community program offices. The BOP is the second largest employer of Federal officers.

The Bureau of Customs. The Bureau of Customs has agents stationed primarily at ports of entry to the United States, where people and/or goods enter and leave. Customs agents investigate frauds on customs revenue and the smuggling of merchandise and contraband into or out of the United States.

The Federal Aviation Administration (FAA). In 1970, President Nixon began a sky marshal program as part of the Customs Service. Following the 1985 hijacking of TWA Flight 847, this elite team of sharpshooters re-formed under the FAA. Dressed in civilian clothes, air marshals board flights at random or in response to specific threats, carrying guns and special ammunition designed to kill without penetrating the skin of the airplane.

Bureau of Diplomatic Security. Part of the U.S. Department of State, these special agents investigate passport and visa fraud, conduct personnel security investigations, issue security clearances and protect the Secretary of State and foreign dignitaries. They also train foreign civilian police and administer counter-terrorism and counter-narcotics rewards programs. Their numbers are expected to grow rapidly as the threat of terrorism increases and the battle against it intensifies.

The Internal Revenue Service (IRS). The Internal Revenue Service, established in 1862, is the largest bureau of the Department of the Treasury. Its mission is to encourage the highest degree of voluntary compliance with the tax laws and regulations. Internal Revenue Service agents investigate willful tax evasion, tax fraud and the activities of gamblers and drug peddlers.

The U.S. Secret Service. The Secret Service was established in 1865 to fight currency counterfeiters. In 1901 it was given the responsibility for protecting the president of the United States, the president's family members, the president-elect and the vice president.

The Bureau of Alcohol, Tobacco and Firearms Tax (BATF). The Bureau of Alcohol, Tobacco and Firearms Tax is primarily a licensing and investigative agency involved in federal tax violations. The Firearms Division enforces the Gun Control Act of 1968.

The U.S. Mint. Officers are responsible for protecting $100 billion of the United States' gold, silver and coins at the nation's six Mint facilities, 24 hours a day, seven days a week. They also safeguard Mint employees, visitors and tourists, and guard the Declaration of Independence, the U.S. Constitution, the Articles of Confederation and Lincoln's Gettysburg Address.

Postal Inspectors. Postal inspectors enforce federal laws pertaining to mailing prohibited items such as explosives, obscene matter and articles likely to injure or cause damage, including biological and chemical agents sent with intent to kill and terrorize, such as anthrax and cyanide. Any mail that may prove to be libelous, defamatory or threatening can be excluded from being transported by the postal service. Postal inspectors protect the mails and recipients of mail. They also investigate any frauds perpetrated through the mails such as chain letters, gift enterprises and similar schemes.

The Coast Guard. The Coast Guard helps local and state agencies that border oceans, lakes and national waterways. They have been actively involved in preventing the smuggling of narcotics into this country.

The Military Services. The armed forces also have law enforcement responsibilities. The uniformed divisions are known as the Military Police (Army), the Shore Patrol (Navy) and the Security Police (Marine Corps and Air Force). The military police are primarily concerned with the physical security of the various bases under their control. Within each operation, the security forces control criminal activity, court-martials, discipline, desertions and the confinement of prisoners. Military law enforcement assignments such as the military police provide exceptional experience. Other non-law enforcement assignments, however, also provide proof that the individual can take orders, assume responsibility and successfully accept challenges.

Even if you are not interested in the military as a career, it is a great background when job seeking. The military is particularly well suited for those who are younger and less certain as to what career direction to take. Any military experience is better than just throwing those years away aimlessly wandering from job to job. Military experience is usually directly applicable to successful employment in law enforcement.

New recruits with most federal law enforcement agencies throughout the country receive their initial training at the Federal Law Enforcement Training Center (FLETC) in Glynco, Georgia. Many receive further training at Quantico, Virginia. Again, sources of further information regarding federal law enforcement careers are provided at the end of this chapter.

JURISDICTIONS COMPARED

Each agency level has its own particular benefits. Federal work may be considered prestigious, dynamic and usually has the best pay and benefits. However, it also usually has high standards and often requires relocating, which can substantially interfere with today's common two-profession families. Because of the large number of people employed by the federal system, the bureaucracy can be frustrating, with a possibility of feeling lost or engulfed in the numbers. Age may also be a drawback; you cannot be older than 35 at the time you are hired due to laws governing retirement in the federal law enforcement system.

Employment with local law enforcement has its own benefits, frequently associated with being part of a more concentrated law enforcement effort. One community benefit to a local police department is local identity and control. Many officers enjoy being a recognized part of a smaller community. Smaller agencies may have fewer transfer or promotional opportunities, but may also permit officers to assume more responsibilities on the job.

Usually, the larger the geographic jurisdiction, the greater the number of employment opportunities. According to the Bureau of Justice Statistics, or BJS (*Law Enforcement Management* . . . , 1999, p.1): "In 1997, the Nation's larger municipal police departments employed an average of 23 full-time officers per 10,000 city residents. Larger county police and sheriffs' departments employed 13 and 12 officers per 10,000 county residents, respectively." In considering where you might find your best employment potential, consider which governmental agencies have the greatest number of employees because with numbers go advancement potential.

Some departments are also more aggressive in their hiring of women and minorities, although generally the employment outlook has improved tremendously for both groups over the last quarter century. For example, according to a survey by the National Center for Women in Policing (NCWP) of the nation's 100 largest law enforcement agencies, the number of women police officers grew from 2 percent to 12 percent between 1972 and 1997 ("The Future of Women in Policing: Mandates for Action," 1999, p.53).

Local police departments offer more than half the jobs available, including many civilian opportunities. BJS data shows: "As of June 1997, local police departments had an estimated 531,496 full-time employees, including 420,000 sworn personnel" (*Local Police Departments, 1999*, p.1). These figures indicate more than 20 percent of full-time employees at local police departments were non-sworn civilians. Similarly: "As of June 1997, sheriffs' departments had an estimated 263,427 full-time employees, including about 175,000 sworn personnel," meaning nearly 33 percent of the full-time positions were filled by civilians (*Sheriffs' Departments, 1999*, p.1).

> To find the greatest employment potential, consider agencies that have the greatest number of employees. Remember, more than half of all law enforcement positions are found in local police departments, and civilian opportunities exist at all three levels—local, state and federal.

Since the number of employees at various jurisdictional levels changes from year to year, the most current available data can be found at www.ojp.usdoj.gov/bjs. We encourage you to reference this site for valuable and timely information regarding careers in law enforcement.

SALARIES

Simply put, government work will never share the nearly limitless compensation potential of private employment. This is not to say that law enforcement personnel are destined to be destitute. On the contrary, pay at the local, county, state and federal levels is certainly comfortable. Considering the benefits associated with government work—pensions, medical coverage, vacation and sick time and greater job security than that found in the private sector—a career in law enforcement is well compensated. Deferred compensation and generous retirement plans may allow for excellent early retirement. The advice here: Start early and contribute the most you possibly can.

In many agencies, additional opportunities may make law enforcement employment more attractive. For example, most jurisdictions allow for some part-time work. This may include overtime work (usually paying more than the 40-hour-per-week pay scale), or moonlighting for local businesses doing security work, traffic control for special events, etc. While it is usually something other than money that motivates the law enforcement officer, salary is an important consideration. Different jurisdictions pay differently, and advancement offers pay incentives.

Local, County and State Salaries

According to *The Top 100*, salaries for detectives and police officers vary greatly, depending on location and the size of the population served. An online survey by *Police* magazine of law enforcement personnel nationwide revealed a general trend of slightly higher salary ranges on the East and West coasts when compared to the Midwest/Central regions ("2001 Salary Survey," 2001, p.12). Table 2-1 contains salary information for sworn local and county law enforcement personnel in 1998. For the most current figures, check the Bureau of Labor Statistics (BLS) Web site: www.stats.bls.gov.

TABLE 2-1   1998 Salaries for Sworn Local and County Law Enforcement Personnel

Jurisdiction/Rank	1998 Median Annual Salary	Lowest 10% Earned . . .	Middle 50% Earned . . .	Highest 10% Earned . . .
Local				
Police Patrol Officers	$37,710	< $22,270	$28,840–$47,890	$63,530+
Detectives & Criminal Investigators	$46,180	< $27,950	$35,540–$62,520	$80,120+
Police & Detective Supervisors	$48,700	< $28,780	$37,130–$69,440	$84,710+
County				
Sheriffs/Deputy Sheriffs	$28,270	< $19,070	$23,310–$36,090	$44,420+

SOURCE: *Occupational Outlook Handbook, 2000–2001 Edition*. Bureau of Labor Statistics, 2001. Online: www.stats.bls.gov/oco

Federal Salaries

Federal jobs in law enforcement fall under the *General Schedule,* or *GS,* system. This salary scale has 15 grades (GS-1 to GS-15), defined according to level of responsibility, type of work and required qualifications. Salary increases as the grade increases. Each grade has 10 steps, also with increasing salary. Table 2-2 presents the 2001 special salary rates for law enforcement officers. The 2001 General Schedule and other special salary schedules for federal employees can be found online at the U.S. Office of Personnel Management (OPM) Web site: www.opm.gov/oca/01tables. For those interested in salaries in a particular geographic area, a complete set of locality pay tables is also available at this Web site.

TABLE 2-2   2001 Special Salary Rate Table for Law Enforcement Officers

	1	2	3	4	5	6	7	8	9	10
GS-3	$20,966	$21,548	$22,130	$22,712	$23,294	$23,876	$24,458	$25,040	$25,622	$26,204
4	23,540	24,194	24,848	25,502	26,156	26,810	27,464	28,118	28,772	29,426
5	27,071	27,803	28,535	29,267	29,999	30,731	31,463	32,195	32,927	33,659
6	28,538	29,353	30,168	30,983	31,798	32,613	33,428	34,243	35,058	35,873
7	30,809	31,715	32,621	33,527	34,433	35,339	36,245	37,151	38,057	38,963
8	32,115	33,119	34,123	35,127	36,131	37,135	38,139	39,143	40,147	41,151
9	34,362	35,470	36,578	37,686	38,794	39,902	41,010	42,118	43,226	44,334
10	37,842	39,063	40,284	41,505	42,726	43,947	45,168	46,389	47,610	48,831

NOTE: These special salary rates for law enforcement officers (as defined in 5 U.S.C. 5541(3) and 5 CFR 550.103) are authorized by section 403 of the Federal Employees Pay Comparability Act of 1990. By law, these rates are the basis for computing locality and other geographic adjusted rates of pay. (See section 404 of FEPCA and 5 CFR part 531, subparts C and F.)
SOURCE: U.S. Office of Personnel Management Web site: www.opm.gov/oca/01tables/LEOann/leoanpdf/01tb491.pdf

The *Occupational Outlook Handbook* adds:

> Federal special agents and inspectors receive law enforcement availability pay (LEAP) or administratively uncontrolled overtime (AUO)—equal to 25 percent of the agent's grade and step—awarded because of the large amount of overtime that these agents are expected to work. For example, in 1999 FBI agents enter service as GS-10 employees on the government pay scale at a base salary of $34,400, yet earned about $43,000 a year with availability pay. They can advance to the GS-13 grade level in field non-supervisory assignments at a base salary of $53,800 which is worth almost $67,300 with availability pay.

Fringe Benefits

As civil service employees, police officers typically receive generous benefits, including health insurance, paid sick leave and paid vacation. *The Top 100* (p.272) adds: "In addition, most police departments offer retirement plans and retirement after twenty or twenty-five years of service, usually at half pay."

Promotions and Transfers

Law enforcement has definite upward salary limitations, but the main frustration for most is that promotions are limited, corresponding to the number of officers in the particular department.

> Advancement in [law enforcement] occupations is determined by several factors. An officer's eligibility for promotion may depend on a specified length of service, job performance, formal education and training courses, and results of written examinations. Those who become eligible for promotion are listed on the promotional list along with other qualified candidates. Promotions generally become available from six months to three years after starting, depending on the department (*The Top 100*, p.271).

Larger city departments usually offer greater numbers of advancement opportunities, whereas police forces in smaller communities are typically more limited by the rank and number of law enforcement personnel needed (*The Top 100*, pp.271–272). The fact is, most police officers will retire at the employment level at which they were hired. While intermediate supervisory positions between patrol officer and chief exist, there are far fewer of these than there are officers. A major contributing factor to police "burnout" is that many officers consider lack of promotion as a lack of recognition.

Promotions in law enforcement are limited. Most police officers retire at the employment level at which they were hired.

Promotions and transfers generally come from within a department. Not only does the administration know the individual, but the promotion bolsters morale by serving as recognition for that officer's work. There are, however, benefits to bringing in an outsider, particularly if no one from within the department is qualified or if internal problems require someone without prior ties to the department. Lateral and promotional opportunities outside one's department are occurring more often. The career ladder is the focus of Chapter 15.

Like other professions, getting ahead in law enforcement requires time and commitment—sometimes combined with luck. People do make sergeant, lieutenant, captain and chief. But you can't rise to the top without landing that first entry-level position. From there, your job-seeking skills become job-advancing skills.

Many other employment opportunities exist in specialty positions within a department. Becoming a specialist in such areas as traffic enforcement, accident investigation, juvenile, narcotics enforcement, K-9 handling or internal affairs may prevent officers from falling into a rut.

ADVANCED JOBS AND SPECIALIZATION

While a majority of officers do, and possibly should, begin their careers as generalists, most upwardly mobile, successful police professionals will specialize at some point in their careers: juvenile specialists, crime prevention specialists, polygraph specialists, and the list goes on. As technology continues to develop, specialists in these areas will be sought. As our society changes, becoming older and more diverse in demographic and cultural makeup, other needed specialties will emerge as well. As Stone (2000, p.18) asserts: "Police work is much more than fast cars and top guns. When it comes to many 'non-traditional' policing jobs, highly specialized training is key."

> A need exists for specialization within the law enforcement field. While a majority of officers begin as generalists, those who wish to progress up the ladder of responsibility and salary will usually need to specialize.

This does not mean that the day of the "generalist" police officer on patrol is nearing an end. It is highly likely that patrol officers will continue as the backbone of any law enforcement agency. However, the reality is that every aspect of our world is becoming more complex and specialized, and the people putting themselves in a good position for future advancement will be those who anticipate and prepare for change by learning and honing specific skills.

Criminal justice involves many areas requiring special expertise in such diverse fields as training and firearms instruction, handwriting and fingerprint identification, or forensic sciences such as chemical and microscopic analysis. Others work as part of special units such as mounted, motorcycle, bicycle or harbor patrol, K-9, or special weapons and tactics (SWAT) or other emergency response teams.

Other specialists needed in the criminal justice system include psychologists, physicians, scientists and accountants. The FBI, for example, specifically seeks people with very specialized training. Police officers with degrees in law, psychology or medicine are of great value to their departments. In addition, the many skills that can be taken into the private sector not only fill important department needs, but also create attractive and lucrative specialty positions. A law degree, for instance, is an excellent education for any area of law enforcement, whether the person wants to use it in a courtroom or "in the trenches." This topic is discussed further in Chapter 3. Expertise in such areas as drawing, photography, computers, firearms, flying or even public relations can help any police professional on the move. Almost *any* specific area of interest you have can be successfully woven into a satisfying and advancing career.

> Specialized training or expertise, whether in the form of a law degree, a talent for drawing or the ability to pilot an aircraft, can benefit any law enforcement professional seeking advancement.

Preparing for advancement may be as basic as obtaining a generalized advanced education to effectively interact with those of similar educational levels in other professions. It may be acknowledging the increasing cultural diversity of the United States and learning a foreign language or two. It may be acquiring a degree in management, computer science or public relations. It's your call. *Anything* you can do to set yourself positively apart from others is important. If you have the chance to acquire specialized skills, take that chance. Don't merely keep up with the others. Take advantage of the myriad opportunities available to meet the challenge and forge ahead.

Working in law enforcement with specialized degrees can provide attractive pay and benefits. The downside, however, is that your work may not vary and travel may be a requirement. In particular, federal agencies may require a number of relocations throughout a career, which can be seen as exciting opportunities or extreme inconveniences. To illustrate the wide variety of career options within law enforcement, the following is a brief look at five specialty areas: juvenile justice officer, deputy coroner/ medical examiner/medicolegal death investigator, profiler, U.S. Mint police and armed sky marshal.

The Juvenile Justice Officer

For those who enjoy working with youths and families, the juvenile system provides very satisfying employment. With the growing amount of juvenile delinquency and serious, violent offenses committed by youth, the juvenile justice system is expanding at a phenomenal rate and should be a major employer of personnel in the years ahead.

> Work in the juvenile justice system is very challenging, and the need for juvenile officers is growing.

The juvenile officer faces a particular challenge in that the system "lumps" youths who are violent criminals together with youths who commit relatively minor offenses (such as smoking) and youths who are victims of neglect or abuse. According to Drowns and Hess (2000, p.2):

> Our juvenile justice system is a complex, changing network that is apart from, yet a part of, the broader criminal justice system. It is apart *from* that system in that it is charged with protecting youths from harm, neglect and abuse, both emotional and physical. This protection frequently involves the criminal justice system as well as numerous public agencies and organizations. The juvenile justice system is a part *of* the criminal justice system in that it is charged with dealing with youths who break the law, and some juveniles may end up in the adult system.

In most departments, juvenile work is considered a promotion after three to five years as a patrol officer. In addition, many departments have school resource officers (SROs) who work within local schools and whose roles include the multiple duties of law enforcement officer, teacher and counselor. According to Burke (2001, p.73): "The tragedies that have occurred in schools in the recent years combined with the Department of Justice dedicating millions of dollars to hiring SROs for schools have made SROs the fastest growing field in law enforcement."

Deputy Coroner/Medical Examiner/Medicolegal Death Investigator

Two systems exist in the United States to deal with death investigations, particularly sudden deaths. Some jurisdictions use the elected sheriff-coroner system while others use the appointed medical examiner (M.E.) system:

> In jurisdictions using the sheriff-coroner system, sworn, armed deputy coroners carry out investigative duties. Said [one assistant deputy chief coroner], a former paramedic, "A lot of cases we deal with involve crime—just by the nature of the position." He said that deputies sometimes do apply arrest powers, though that's not their primary duty.

> In jurisdictions using the M.E. system, the investigators are often called death investigators or medicolegal death investigators. In some areas, civilians carry out these roles, in others it is patrol officers or detectives who perform these functions (Stone, p.19).

More than 3,100 death investigation jurisdictions are scattered throughout the country. The American Board of Medicolegal Death Investigators stresses those interested in this field must have a combination of education and skills encompassing the areas of medicine and law. In addition to studying basic death and homicide investigation, medicolegal training academies teach investigators how to deliver death notification and deal with the grief process. Stone (pp.19–20) adds:

> Whatever training investigators can tuck under their belts goes toward supporting responsibilities that range from collecting evidence to testifying in court. . . . Investigator responsibilities [include] the assumption of responsibility for the deceased or anything on the deceased; determining cause of death, particularly sudden deaths outside the medical system; determining manner of death; identifying the deceased; safeguarding property of the deceased until next of kin can be located; and taking reports.

Other responsibilities include collecting evidence and taking photographs, which are sent to the state police forensic science lab for examination. The lab, in turn, issues a report back to the investigator who then tries to recreate the scene: "When, where did it happen? We determine motive. Was it passion, politics, a love triangle, etc.? Then we try to determine who's responsible and present our findings in court" (Stone, p.20).

Criminal Profiler

Only 40 full time in FBI

The FBI refers to criminal profilers as criminal investigative analysts, "highly trained and experienced law enforcement officers who study every behavioral aspect and detail of an unsolved violent crime scene in which a certain amount of psychopathology has been left at the scene" (O'Toole, 1999, p.44). Psychopathology is the study of an offender's behavioral and psychological indicators left at a violent crime scene that result from his physical, sexual and, in some cases verbal, interaction with his victim(s). According to O'Toole (p.45):

> An experienced, well-trainer profiler is intuitive, has a great deal of common sense, and is able to think and evaluate information in a concise, logical manner. A successful profiler is also able to suppress their personal feelings about the crime by viewing the scene and the offender-victim interaction from an analytical point of view. Most important, a successful profiler is able to view the crime from the offender's perspective rather than from his or her own. The successful profiler possesses an in-depth understanding of human behavior, human sexuality, crime scene investigation and forensics, and has extensive training and experience in studying violent crimes and providing interpretations of his or her insights and observations to investigators.

Mint Police

Created at the end of the 1690s, the U.S. Mint Police is one of the nation's oldest police forces. Mint Police possess expertise in high-level security, and officers' primary responsibility is protecting the country's gold, silver and coins located at Mint facilities in Fort Knox, Denver, San Francisco, West Point, Philadelphia and Washington, DC. The agency is currently expanding its mission to include offering consulting services to foreign governments on how best to protect their gold and precious metals, and offering assistance to other federal agencies in protecting and transporting valuable assets:

> Currently, each mint is staffed with firearm instructors, field training officers, an emergency response team, a hostage negotiator and a detective specializing in areas such as cyber-fraud. These officers have backgrounds in the Secret Service, FBI, Defense Department and local police departments. Maintaining a full roster, however, has been difficult due to a 20 percent turnover rate and the fact that the Mint Police have maintained a low profile in the past, making applications somewhat sparse (Hanson, 2001, p.66).

Current Mint Police Chief William Daddio, however, has recently begun a campaign to raise his police force's profile, teaming Mint officials with Capitol Hill colleagues to increase capital investments and reward his officers with bigger pay raises. His efforts have produced positive results: "Word has spread about the Mint Police and they recently received 800 applications for 60 job openings—with nearly 50 percent of these from women. The need for qualified officers is going to continue to grow as expansion takes place and new challenges arise" (Hanson, p.67).

Armed Sky Marshals

Until the deadly September 11, 2001, airborne terrorist attacks on the World Trade Center and the Pentagon, most Americans had never heard of the Federal Air Marshals. Hawley (2001) notes: "The FAA has always been secretive about the air marshals, refusing to divulge their number, how they work or what they look like. The assault teams wear masks when giving rare public demonstrations." In the wake of the attacks, however, several Congressional leaders and members of the Air Transportation Association, the trade organization for the U.S. airlines, have strongly urged expansion of the air marshal program, and it is likely this "shadowy force" will be strengthened in the coming years.

Among other skills, sky marshals must be very comfortable with firearms. FAA spokesperson Rebecca Trexler states: "They have some of the highest, if not the highest, firearms qualifications in the federal government. They don't miss" (Hawley). Each agent spends at least three hours a week in shooting practice at their training base near Atlantic City, NJ, which includes a five-story simulated control tower, three outdoor shooting ranges with moving targets and two retired airliners.

Other Venues Requiring Law Enforcement

In addition to the more traditional police agencies, you might consider working in a more specialized environment. Many institutions, facilities and industries operate their own police forces. Examples include college and university campus police and transportation police for railroads and airports.

INTERNATIONAL JOBS

The vast majority of career areas have a new emphasis on international employment. Law enforcement is no exception. Many people are eager to travel, and if it can be part of their job, all the better.

International jobs are available in law enforcement, but obtaining them is not easy. Most overseas positions are classified jobs with special requirements such as security clearances and confidentiality. Because of such factors as jurisdiction, these jobs tend to be covert. Federal agencies such as the FBI, Drug Enforcement Administration and Secret Service have agents around the world. Although it is not part of the criminal justice or law enforcement field, the Central Intelligence Agency (CIA) also offers opportunities for excitement and travel. Again, travel can be a perk as well as a potential difficulty.

As the field of law enforcement expands, so does the geographic availability of jobs. International job opportunities in law enforcement are slowly increasing, but obtaining them is still difficult.

In addition to the multitude of sworn positions, both domestic and abroad, you may also find a nonsworn position in a career field related to law enforcement.

NONSWORN CAREER OPTIONS RELATED TO LAW ENFORCEMENT

Positions traditionally filled by sworn personnel are now often being filled by nonsworn personnel. The simple reason for this trend is economic—nonsworn personnel may be every bit as qualified and yet not need to be paid at the salary level of sworn, often unionized, personnel. More regular hours, the varied and interesting assignments and the relative lack of danger are just a few factors that might motivate you to consider some exciting careers that *support* law enforcement. These positions may also serve as a "stepping stone" to a sworn job. You can work out of a police station or sheriff's office without being subjected to some of the less desirable aspects of police work.

> Civilians are becoming more common in various careers that support traditional law enforcement, including crime prevention specialists, juvenile specialists, animal control officers and dispatchers.

Community Crime Prevention Specialists

The last decade has seen an increasing interest in and reliance on community crime prevention. While some law enforcement agencies have sworn officers conduct such work, others assign civilians. Crime prevention specialists have the luxury of working with the community in a positive effort *before* crisis occurs, with the hope of *preventing* crime. Or, they may be the contact that lends valuable assistance after a crisis.

Crime prevention specialists educate the community about such issues as locks, lighting, alarms and personal safety. It is an excellent opportunity to be creative because much of crime prevention involves developing programs, designing brochures, presenting speeches and even directing videos and slide presentations. Salaries vary, but the more regular schedule and the opportunity to step into the private sector make this an area worth considering.

Juvenile Specialists

As previously discussed, the juvenile justice system is expanding at a phenomenal rate and is projected to be a major employer of personnel in the future. In addition to working in police agencies, careers in juvenile justice include such areas as group home childcare workers and counselors, intake officers and childcare workers in juvenile detention facilities or correctional facilities, including boot camps, juvenile probation, etc.

If you enjoy working with youths, a career in the juvenile justice system may be right for you. If you think you might be interested in this area of law enforcement, start volunteering with some youth groups to gain experience in working with youths and to confirm that this is, indeed, an area of special interest to you. Some suggest this area offers the greatest opportunity to impact the community.

Animal Control, Humane Officers and Cruelty Investigators

Animal control is one area within the realm of community service that can effectively serve as both an entry-level stepping stone to a job in law enforcement or as a specialty area that many find rewarding in itself. If you have a special interest in animal welfare, this is an area where you can get paid for doing what you love.

In recent years, there has been a strong push to professionalize animal control and humane investigations. While some jurisdictions have police officers or sheriff's deputies handle these tasks, others are turning to civilians to fulfill this role:

> Kathy Gilstrap, Animal Control Manager of the Lakewood (Colo.) Police Department, . . . and her officers are non-sworn, unarmed state class III peace officers and only have authority to make arrests for animal control-related issues. But, they are uniformed, badged, wear vests, carry a bite stick and OC spray and work under the police department as part of the patrol division. They have authority to take an animal from its owner, depending on the situation. . . .

> One agency, whose humane officers, known as special agents, are, in fact, armed and sworn peace officers is New York's American Society for Prevention of Cruelty to Animals (ASPCA) Humane Law Enforcement. They wear vests, uniforms the same color as NYPD's officers and drive marked Crown Vic units complete with lights, siren and decals (Stone, p.22).

Animal control officers' responsibilities are multifaceted: "New York ASPCA investigators are charged, among other things, with checking on the wellbeing of animals and investigating blood sports, felony offenses involving mainly dog fighting and cock fighting. In these 'sports,' abused dogs are forced to fight to the death and birds are fitted with razor-sharp spurs to achieve the same end" (Stone, p.23).

In addition to investigating abuse and other animal-related issues, many humane officers perform community education services, taking their expertise into schools, talking with students about pet care and answering their questions. Humane officers also train police officers in the skills needed to handle situations in the field where animals are involved, such as guard dogs at drug "labs." Animal control officers may accompany police officers on raids when an informant has warned of a guard dog in the house. Animal control may tranquilize or otherwise contain a threatening animal until police are able to complete their duties, making sure no one gets bitten in the process.

Dispatchers

Police, fire and ambulance dispatchers, also called public safety dispatchers, monitor the location of emergency service personnel within their jurisdiction. The *Occupational Outlook Handbook* states:

> They dispatch the appropriate type and number of units in response to calls for assistance. Dispatchers, or call takers, often are the first people the public contacts when they call for emergency assistance. If certified for emergency medical services, the dispatchers may provide medical instruction to those on the scene until the medical staff arrives.

> Police, fire and ambulance dispatchers work in a variety of settings: they may work in a police station, a fire station, a hospital, or a centralized city communications center. In many cities, the police department serves as the communications center. In these situations, all 911 emergency calls go to the police department, where a dispatcher handles the police calls and screens the others before transferring them to the appropriate service.

Dispatchers held 248,000 jobs in 1998, about one-third of which were for police, fire and ambulance services. However, employment of public safety dispatchers is expected to grow more slowly than average for all occupations over the next decade. The *Occupational Outlook Handbook* states: "To balance the increased demand for emergency services, many districts are seeking to consolidate their communications centers into a shared, area-wide facility. . . . Individuals with computer skills and experience will have a greater opportunity for employment as public safety dispatchers."

FIRE SERVICE

Because many communities have a public safety department, encompassing both law enforcement and firefighting responsibilities, a look at careers in the fire service seems appropriate for this chapter.

> As with police work, a career in the fire service attracts many applicants seeking a position that combines challenging, action-oriented work and excitement with the chance to perform an essential public service.

Some communities have full-time, paid firefighters while others maintain a staff of volunteers, also referred to as *paid-on-call*, because almost all "volunteer" departments provide some, albeit minimal, pay. Some communities have experimented with private fire companies. Their responsibilities are generally the same: to protect the public against the dangers of fire and other emergencies:

> Firefighters work in a variety of settings, including urban and suburban areas, airports, chemical plants, other industrial sites, and rural areas like grasslands and forests. In addition, some firefighters work in hazardous materials units that are trained for the control, prevention, and cleanup of oil spills and other hazardous materials incidents. . . .
>
> Firefighters have assumed a range of responsibilities, including emergency medical services. In fact, most calls to which firefighters respond involve medical emergencies, and about half of all fire departments provide ambulance service for victims. Firefighters receive training in emergency medical procedures, and many fire departments require them to be certified as emergency medical technicians (*Occupational Outlook Handbook*).

Between extinguishing fires and responding to medical emergencies, firefighters clean and maintain equipment, conduct practice drills and fire inspections, and participate in physical fitness activities. They also prepare written reports on fire incidents. Fire service officers are often involved in prevention efforts including community education aimed at public assemblies, school groups and civic organizations.

Some firefighters become certified fire inspectors, checking existing structures for fire code compliance and working with developers and planners to ensure new buildings meet those codes. Other firefighters specialize in fire investigation, becoming involved when the cause of a fire is suspicious, perhaps criminal negligence or arson. These investigators collect evidence, interview witnesses, write fire reports and, if necessary, testify in court.

Working conditions are often strenuous, dangerous and complex. Firefighting involves risk of injury or death from structural collapse, exposure to flames and smoke, and the increased potential for traffic accidents when responding to alarms. As witnessed during the tragic unfolding of events on September 11, 2001, when terrorists attacked the World Trade Center, firefighters (and other first responders) are expected to run *into* a situation that all others are running *away from*. Firefighters may also be exposed to poisonous, flammable or explosive gases or chemicals, and radioactive or other hazardous materials, presenting immediate and/or long-term negative health impacts.

Shift hours are longer and vary more widely than hours of most other workers. Many full-time firefighters work shifts that last several days in a row, requiring them to eat and sleep at the fire station. In 1998, the median annual salary of firefighters was $31,170, with yearly earnings ranging from less than $14,310 to more than $50,930. Benefits typically include medical and liability insurance, pension plans, vacation time, sick leave and some paid holidays. Nearly all fire departments provide necessary uniforms and equipment.

The job outlook for firefighters is projected to remain keenly competitive, with employment increasing more slowly than average for all occupations through 2008. Total employment of firefighters in 1998 was 239,000 and is projected to increase only 4.7 percent by 2008, for a total of 251,000 positions. Turnover in this field is unusually low and layoffs are uncommon. According to the *Occupational Outlook Handbook*:

> Most applicants for firefighting jobs must have a high school education or its equivalent and pass a civil service examination. In addition, they need to pass a medical examination and tests of strength, physical stamina, coordination, and agility. Experience as a volunteer firefighter or as a firefighter in the Armed Forces is helpful.

> As a rule, entry-level workers in large fire departments are trained for several weeks at the department's training center or academy. Through classroom instruction and practical training, the recruits study fire fighting techniques, fire prevention, hazardous materials control, local building codes, and emergency medical procedures, including first aid and cardiopulmonary resuscitation. They also learn how to use axes, chain saws, fire extinguishers, ladders, and other fire fighting and rescue equipment.

Personal qualities necessary for firefighting include mental alertness, self-discipline, courage, mechanical aptitude, endurance, strength and a sense of public service. Continuing education is also part of the job, as firefighters must stay current with new technology and equipment and must continuously practice their skills and coordination with others on their team. The *Occupational Outlook Handbook* adds:

> Most experienced firefighters continue studying to improve their job performance and prepare for promotional examinations . . . Opportunities for promotion depend upon written examination results, job performance, interviews, and seniority. . . . Many fire departments now require a bachelor's degree, preferably in fire science, public administration, or a related field, for a promotion to positions higher than battalion chief.

EMERGENCY MEDICAL TECHNICIANS AND PARAMEDICS

As discussed, many jurisdictions have a public safety department combining law enforcement, fire service and emergency medical response activities. The medical response component may be assigned to the police, to the fire department or to an entirely separate entity.

> Emergency medical technicians (EMTs) and paramedics respond to a variety of incidents where people are in need of immediate medical attention, including automobile accidents, heart attacks, drownings, childbirths and gunshot wounds.

EMTs and paramedics provide stabilizing medical care on site and transport the sick or injured to a medical facility. Formal training and certification is required of all EMTs and paramedics. All 50 states possess a certification procedure.

Working conditions of these professionals varies but is usually physically strenuous and fast-paced. EMTs and paramedics work both indoors and outdoors, in all types of weather. Their jobs involve considerable kneeling, bending and heavy lifting. They come in regular contact with bodily fluids and face increased exposure to diseases, some of which may be fatal. They may also be attacked or assaulted when responding to persons high on drugs or who are psychologically disturbed.

Earnings of EMTs vary based on employment setting, geographical location, training and experience. The median annual salary of EMTs was $20,290 in 1998, with the lowest paid EMTs earning less than $12,700 annually and the highest paid earning more than $34,480. EMTs who are part of fire or police departments receive the same benefits as firefighters or police officers:

> EMTs and paramedics employed by fire departments work about 50 hours a week. Those employed by hospitals frequently work between 45 and 60 hours a week, and those in private ambulance services, between 45 and 50 hours. Some of these workers, especially those in police and fire departments, are on call for extended periods. Because emergency services function 24 hours a day, EMTs and paramedics have irregular working hours that add to job stress (*Occupational Outlook Handbook*).

EMTs and paramedics held approximately 150,000 jobs in 1998, not including the thousands of volunteers who supplement these services. Employment of EMTs is projected to grow faster than average for all occupations through 2008. In a related field, employment of ambulance drivers and attendants is also projected to increase faster than average through 2008.

CONCLUSION

A multitude of agencies exist for those considering a career in law enforcement or related fields, including federal agencies, state agencies, county agencies and local agencies. To find the greatest employment potential, consider agencies that have the greatest number of employees. Remember, more than half of all law enforcement positions are found in local police departments, and civilian opportunities exist at all three levels—local, state and federal.

Keep in mind a need exists for specialization within the law enforcement field. While a majority of officers begin as generalists, those who wish to progress up the ladder of responsibility and salary will usually need to specialize. Specialized training or expertise, whether in the form of a law degree, a talent for drawing or the ability to pilot an aircraft, can benefit any law enforcement professional seeking advancement. Also consider that as the field of law enforcement expands, so does the geographic availability of jobs. International job opportunities in law enforcement are slowly increasing, but obtaining them remains difficult.

Civilians are becoming more common in the various careers that support traditional law enforcement, including crime prevention specialists, juvenile specialists, animal control officers and dispatchers.

Other public safety careers that routinely interface with law enforcement include firefighting and emergency medical response. As with police work, a career in the fire service attracts many applicants seeking a position that combines challenging, action-oriented work and excitement with the chance to perform an essential public service. Emergency medical technicians (EMTs) and paramedics respond to incidents where people need immediate medical attention, including automobile accidents, heart attacks, drownings, childbirths and gunshot wounds.

ADDITIONAL CONTACTS AND SOURCES OF INFORMATION

Law Enforcement

AFOSI, Public Affairs Office
1535 Command Drive, Suite B-304
Andrews AFB, MD 20762-7000
(301) 981-6860

American Federation of Police
3801 Biscayne Boulevard
Miami, FL 33137
(305) 573-9819

American Police Academy
1000 Connecticut Avenue NW, Suite 9
Washington, DC 20036
(202) 293-9088

American Society for the Prevention of Cruelty to
    Animals (ASPCA): (212) 876-7700
http://www.aspca.org

Bureau of Indian Affairs
(202) 208-3711

Drug Enforcement Administration (DEA)
Washington, DC 20537
(202) 401-7834
(800) DEA-4288
http://www.usdoj.gov/dea

FBI Special Agent: http://www.fbi.gov

FCF Jobs
P.O. Box 2176
Brunswick, GA 31521-2176
http://www.gate.net/~fcfjobs
    * *Federal Law Enforcement Careers* ($9.95)
    * *State Trooper Careers* ($9.95)
    * *Federal Law Enforcement Testing Guide* ($6.95)
    * *State Handgun Laws* ($4.95)

Federal Air Marshals Program: http://www.faa.gov/fam

Humane Officers (Animal Control and Cruelty Investigation)
    The Law Enforcement Training Institute, University of
    Missouri, Columbia: http://www.missouri.edu/~letiwww/

International Association of Chiefs of Police (IACP)
515 North Washington Street, 4th Floor
Alexandria, VA 22314
(703) 836-6767
http://www.theiacp.org

International Security and Detective Alliance (ISDA)
P.O. Box 6303
Corpus Christi, TX 78466-6303
(512) 888-6164

International Union of Police Associations
1421 Prince Street, Suite 330
Alexandria, VA 22314
(703) 549-7473

Medicolegal Death Investigators
http://www.slu.edu/organizations/abmdi/

National Association of Investigative Specialists (NAIS)
P.O. Box 33244
Austin, TX 78764
(512) 719-3595
Fax: (512) 719-3594
http://www.pimall.com/nais/home/html

National Law Enforcement Officers Memorial Fund
    (NLEOMF): http://www.nleomf.com

National Park Service
1849 C Street NW
Washington, DC 20240
(202) 208-6843
http://www.nps.gov

National Police Officers Association of America
P.O. Box 22129
Louisville, KY 40252-0129
(800) 467-6762

National United Law Enforcement Association
256 East McLemore Avenue
Memphis, TN 38106
(901) 774-1118

U.S. Border Patrol
Chester A. Arthur Building
425 I Street NW
Washington, DC 20536
Hiring: (912) 757-3001, extension 9916
        http://www.usborderpatrol.gov

U.S. Bureau of Alcohol, Tobacco and Firearms (ATF)
Personnel Division
650 Massachusetts Avenue NW
Room 4170
Washington, DC 20226
http://www.atf.treas.gov

U.S. Coast Guard Law Enforcement
http://www.uscg.mil/welcome/html

U.S. Customs
Job hotline: (800) 944-7725
http://www.customs.ustreas.gov

U.S. Marshals Service
Employment and Compensation Division
Field Staffing Branch
600 Army Navy Drive
Arlington, VA 20220
http://www.usdoj.gov/marshals/

U.S. Mint Police
Recruitment Information: (202) 354-7300

U.S. Secret Service
Personnel Division
Room 912
1800 G Street NW
Washington, DC 20223
http://www.ustreas.gov/usss

Dispatchers

Association of Public Safety Communications Officials
2040 S Ridgewood
South Daytona, FL 32119-2257
http://www.apcointl.org

Fire Services

International Association of Firefighters
1750 New York Avenue NW
Washington, DC 20006
http://www.iaff.org/iaff/index.html

National Fire Academy
U.S. Fire Administration
16825 South Seton Avenue
Emmitsburg, MD 21727
http://www.usfa.fema.gov/nfa/index.htm

Emergency Medical Services

National Association of Emergency Medical Technicians
408 Monroe Street
Clinton, MS 39056
http://www.naemt.org

National Registry of Emergency Medical Technicians
P.O. Box 29233
Columbus, OH 43229
http://www.nremt.org

National Highway Transportation Safety Administration
EMS Division
400 7th Street SW, NTS-14
Washington, DC
http://www.nhtsa.dot.gov/people/injury/ems

General

   Applying for Federal Jobs—A Guide to Writing Successful Applications and Resumes for the Job You Want in Government
      by Patricia B. Wood. May be ordered from: Workbooks, Inc., 9039 Sligo Creek Parkway, #316,
         Silver Springs, MD 20901
         Phone/FAX (301) 565-9467
         Also available: *The 171 Reference Book*
                  The 171 Writing Portfolio
                     Promote Yourself! How to Use Your Knowledge, Skills and Abilities . . . and Advance in the
                     Federal Government

Occupational Outlook Handbook
Browse contents online: http://stats.bls.gov

Bureau of Justice Statistics (BJS)
http://www.ojp.usdoj.gov/bjs

The Top 100: The Fastest Growing Careers for the 21st Century
Published and distributed by:
      Ferguson Publishing Company
      200 West Madison Street, Suite 300
      Chicago, IL 60606
      (312) 580-5480

Bureau of Labor Statistics (BLS)
http://stats.bls.gov

U.S. Office of Personnel Management (OPM)
http://www.opm.gov

 MIND STRETCHES

1.   What do most people think of when they think of a "police job"? Where did you acquire the information on which you base your answer?

2.   Do you see law enforcement changing to respond to new challenges?

3.   Why might you *not* want to consider a job as a police officer "on the street"?

4.   Do "nonsworn" law enforcement positions, such as civilian crime prevention specialists, have career benefits not available to police officers? What negatives would you want to be aware of in considering a career such as a community service officer?

5.   What other vocational or avocational skills could blend well with a police career? Can you think of unique skills that could make a candidate for a job more attractive to a hiring agency?

6.   Why might someone interested in a career in policing fail to consider other jobs in the security or criminal justice fields?

7.   Can law enforcement continue as it has been in serving communities, or is some change inevitable? What change do you foresee, if any? What can you begin doing right now to meet the challenge?

8.   Why do you think the entertainment field is so obsessed with law enforcement? Do you think this obsession helps or hurts the profession? Why?

9.   What is your favorite television police show? Why? Do you think television and the movies have influenced your career choice?

10.   Are police salaries more or less than you had anticipated? Does salary affect your decision as to what field of employment you will eventually pursue? Why or why not?

INSIDERS' VIEWS

For this chapter, read the *Insiders' Views* by Dennis L. Conroy, Ph.D. ("It's Not Like on TV"), and Molly Koivamaki ("A Wealth of Opportunities"), found on the Web site: http://www.wadsworth.com/criminaljustice_d/.

REFERENCES

Burke, Sean. "The Advantages of a School Resource Officer." *Law and Order*, September 2001, pp.73–75.

Drowns, Robert W. and Hess, Kären M. *Juvenile Justice*, 3rd ed. Belmont, CA: West/Wadsworth Publishing Company, 2000.

"The Future of Women in Policing: Mandates for Action." *The Police Chief*, March 1999, pp.53–56.

Hanson, Marce. "U.S. Mint Police." *Police*, August 2001, pp.66–67.

Hawley, Chris. "Armed Sky Marshals May Increase." *Associated Press*, as reported on LATimes.com (*Los Angeles Times*), September 15, 2001.

Law Enforcement Management and Administrative Statistics, 1997. Washington, DC: Bureau of Justice Statistics Executive Summary, April 1999. (NCJ-175712)

Local Police Departments, 1997. Washington, DC: Bureau of Justice Statistics Executive Summary, October 1999. (NCJ-178934)

Occupational Outlook Handbook. 2000–2001 Edition. U.S. Department of Labor. Bureau of Labor Statistics. Washington, DC: U.S. Government Printing Office, 2000. http://stats.bls.gov/oco

"151 Law Enforcement Officers Killed in Line of Duty in 2000." *Criminal Justice Newsletter*, January 10, 2001, p.7.

O'Toole, Mary Ellen. "Criminal Profiling: The FBI Uses Criminal Investigative Analysis to Solve Crimes." *Corrections Today*, February 1999, pp.44–46.

Reaves, Brian A. and Hart, Timothy C. *Federal Law Enforcement Officers, 2000.* Washington, DC: Bureau of Justice Statistics Bulletin, July 2001. (NCJ-187231)

Sheriffs' Departments, 1997. Washington, DC: Bureau of Justice Statistics Executive Summary, October 1999. (NCJ-179011)

Stone, Rebecca. "Adventures in Law Enforcement 2000." *Police*, March 2000, pp.18–28.

The Top 100: The Fastest Growing Careers for the 21st Century. Chicago: Ferguson Publishing Company, 1998.

"2001 Salary Survey." *Police*, August 2001, p.12.

Wrobleski, Henry M. and Hess, Kären M. *Introduction to Law Enforcement and Criminal Justice*, 6th ed. Belmont, CA: West/Wadsworth Publishing Company, 2000.

CHAPTER 3

CAREERS IN THE COURTS, CORRECTIONS AND RELATED FIELDS

The pessimist complains about the wind; the optimist expects it to change; the realist adjusts the sails.

—*Anonymous*

Do You Know:

➤ How a law degree may be useful to someone not seeking to become a lawyer?
➤ Besides lawyers, what other professionals work in our nation's courts?
➤ What the purpose of corrections is in our criminal justice system?
➤ What the primary difference between adult corrections and juvenile corrections has traditionally been and whether this is still the case?
➤ Who the majority of corrections employees are?
➤ What corrections officers do and how the future looks for those seeking this job?
➤ What the primary difference is between probation and parole?
➤ How the job outlook is for probation and parole officers?
➤ What impact home detention and electronic monitoring have on jobs in corrections?

INTRODUCTION

As you learned in Chapter 2, an incredible variety of jobs are available within the law enforcement profession—everything from patrol officer to police surgeon—assuring a niche for almost every interest. Beyond that, the criminal justice field offers even more than you may have ever considered. You may be destined for a job you have never thought of or even knew existed—until now.

Directing your career toward one of these other areas could open a whole new world of employment satisfaction. The criminal justice system is so complex it needs a tremendous number of participants. While many of these jobs may not appear as glamorous as those frequently depicted on television, they are extremely important and provide exceptional opportunities.

This chapter presents the numerous job opportunities within the other two components of the criminal justice system—the courts and corrections. It begins with a discussion of the judicial system in the United States and the critical role played by lawyers. It also discusses numerous other careers within this system that might interest those wishing to become part of criminal justice. The chapter then discusses corrections in the United States, including the adult and juvenile systems as well as careers at the local, state and federal levels.

OPPORTUNITIES IN OUR JUDICIAL SYSTEM—THE COURTS

Before exploring the various jobs within the judicial system, briefly review the nature of our legal system. It is highly complex and, by design, adversarial—accuser versus the accused. The entire affair is presumed to involve a challenge of the individuals as well as a challenge to the system. While this process has been criticized for being too complicated, full of loopholes and technicalities, one thing is certain: the system requires a lot of employees.

Lawyers

When you think of job opportunities within the legal system, you usually begin by thinking of attorneys. And if you are like a lot of other people, you may not think too highly of lawyers. However, lawyers are essential in our courts, acting both as advocates and advisers.

The judicial process generally requires at least two lawyers, one representing each side. In criminal cases, one lawyer (or a team of lawyers) represents the state, or "the people" (the prosecutor), and another lawyer (or legal team) represents the defendant (the defense attorney). Civil cases also involve prosecutors and defense lawyers, but the clients are generally private individuals. Each lawyer must represent his or her client aggressively within the boundaries of the law.

Many people who don't understand the system look down on defense lawyers because of what their clients have been accused of doing when, in actuality, these lawyers are simply doing their job—providing the constitutionally guaranteed right to legal representation. In addition, some people may feel the system is unfair because it seems to favor the wrongdoer with such rules as prohibiting certain evidence from being admitted. Although some attorneys find this side of the system unappealing and may prefer to be a prosecutor, many attorneys find working for the defense a great challenge.

The practice of law requires a law degree, otherwise known as a doctor of law or a juris doctorate (J.D.). To obtain this degree you must complete three to four years of intense study beyond your bachelor's degree. The competition for getting into law school is intense, requiring a strong academic background and experience. The demands of obtaining a law degree are both difficult and expensive. Law school is very competitive, and the level of student ability is extremely high. Kasanof (2000, p.48), a police lieutenant who also holds a law degree, offers this advice:

> Know that a law degree is *not* an automatic ticket to big money and status. While partners at big law firms, and lawyers who sue tobacco companies or do big personal injury cases, may make a lot of money, many lawyers do not. Some lawyers who work for non-profit organizations, or for some government agencies, may make less than police officers. A lot of legal work is not very glamorous: it's reading, writing, talking on the phone, etc. Even trial lawyers don't spend most of their time actually *in* court.

He (p.49) further suggests:

> If you plan to work primarily in law enforcement, in certain other government agencies, as a solo practitioner or in many smaller law firms, you may be able to get by with a solid record from a typical state law school, or from a less prestigious private law school. . . . If you want to work at a large law firm, you will need top grades, usually from a prestigious law school. While big law firms may pay a lot of money, they can be very unpleasant places to work. And you *will* work long and hard.

Other realities of law school are that it takes a significant amount of time (three years if you go full time and take summers off for internships/clerkships; four years for part-time/night school) and a significant amount of money (tuition alone runs anywhere from $6,000/year to $24,000/year). Such sacrifices require you to consider this avenue carefully and discuss it with those important to you—spouse, significant other, family—because you will need their support (Kasanof, p.49).

Attorneys can practice in many areas besides criminal law, such as corporate, insurance and personal injury law. Some lawyers specialize in bankruptcy, divorce or environmental law, while others are committed to working with the poor and disadvantaged. Others use their law degrees in their current jobs as their employers discover it helpful to have people knowledgeable about the law on staff. Others simply enjoy the academic challenge of attaining this level of degree and continue in their present line of work.

A trend developing in criminal justice is for employees to obtain law degrees to help them achieve professional goals, which may or may not include the traditional practice of law. This trend has generated so many lawyers that the salaries are not what they once were.

> A career option for those seeking active employment in our nation's courts is that of law. In fact, many already employed in the field of criminal justice are pursuing law degrees to help them achieve their professional goals, even if they do not include the traditional practice of law.

Lawyers held about 681,000 jobs in 1998. Employment for lawyers is expected to increase 17.2 percent through 2008, for a total of 798,000 law positions. Nearly 70 percent of lawyers are in private practice; most of the remaining 30 percent held positions in government, the greatest number at the local level. According to the *Occupational Outlook Handbook* (2000, p.42), the median annual earnings of all lawyers was $78,170 in 1998. That same year, the median salaries of lawyers six months after graduating from law school varied significantly by the type of work obtained:

All law school graduates–$45,000 (median)

Private practice–$60,000	Academe–$38,000	Government–$36,000
Business/industry–$50,000	Judicial Clerkship–$37,500	Public interest–$31,000

Many lawyers advance to become judges or other judicial workers.

Judges, Magistrates and Other Judicial Workers

The *Occupational Outlook Handbook* (p.141) states:

> Judges apply the law and oversee the legal process in courts according to local, State, and Federal statutes. They preside over cases concerning every aspect of society, from traffic offenses to disputes over management of professional sports, or from the rights of huge corporations to questions of disconnecting life support equipment for terminally ill persons. They must ensure that trials and hearings are conducted fairly and that the court administers justice in a manner which safeguards the legal rights of all parties involved.

Judges' duties and powers are dictated by the jurisdictional levels over which they preside—general trial court, municipal court, county court, appellate court, federal district court, circuit court, state supreme court and U.S. Supreme Court are some of the jurisdictional levels. Federal and state judges are generally required to have first been lawyers, although nearly 40 states allow non-lawyers to hold limited jurisdiction judgeships.

Judges, magistrates and other judicial workers held about 71,000 jobs in 1998. That number is projected to increase only 2.9 percent through 2008, for an estimated total of 73,000 positions. All judicial positions are government positions—local, state or federal—with about 40 percent employed by the federal government. Earnings of judicial workers vary greatly by jurisdiction, with the Chief Justice of the U.S. Supreme Court earning $175,400 in 1998 to state judges of general jurisdiction trial courts earning between $72,000 and $115,000.

Many fascinating, lucrative and very satisfying non-lawyer job opportunities also exist within our judicial system. In fact, most people are not aware of the multitude of other careers within the courts.

Legal Assistants and Paralegals

Whether they are called legal assistants or paralegals, these occupations have generated a great deal of interest recently. They require considerably less schooling than a law degree and often pay very well. Many in this field feel they get the opportunity to do almost as much as the lawyers—they investigate the facts of the case; research precedent case law; and help lawyers prepare for closings, hearings, trials and corporate meetings. Because they often interact with the clients and witnesses and are actively involved in working up the cases, there can be a great deal of job satisfaction. All states require a license to actually practice law; thus, legal assistants and paralegals must work under a supervising lawyer. The *Occupational Outlook Handbook* states:

> There are several ways to become a paralegal. Employers usually require formal paralegal training obtained through associate or bachelor's degree programs or through a certification program. Increasingly, employers prefer graduates of 4-year paralegal programs or college graduates who have completed paralegal certificate programs. Some employers prefer to train paralegals on the job, hiring college graduates with no legal experience or promoting experienced legal secretaries.

Paralegals held about 136,000 jobs in 1998, the vast majority with private law firms (p.146). These jobs are projected to be among the fastest growing occupations through 2008 because, in part, of the cost-effectiveness of their services. Paralegals generate much of the information and documentation needed by lawyers but at a fraction of the cost. In 1998, the median annual earnings of paralegals were $32,760 (p.147).

Court Reporters

You've seen them on TV or in the movies. As testimony and questioning swirls about the courtroom, the court reporter sits before a tiny typewriter, nearly motionless, except for her fingers, which seem to be moving considerably slower than the words being spoken by others in the room. Yet the entire proceeding is captured verbatim. Using a stenotype machine, the reporter presses multiple keys at a time to record combinations of letters representing sounds, words or phrases, which are recorded electronically onto computer disks or CD-ROM and subsequently translated into text through a process called computer-aided transcription. Accuracy is crucial because there is only one person creating this official transcript:

Although many court reporters record official proceedings in the courtroom, the majority of court reporters work outside the courtroom. Freelance reporters, for example, take depositions for attorneys in offices and document proceedings of meetings, conventions, and other private activities. Others capture the proceedings in government agencies of all levels, from the U.S. Congress to State and local governing bodies. . . .

Court reporters usually complete a 2- or 4-year training program, offered by about 300 postsecondary vocational and technical schools and colleges. Currently, the National Court Reporters Association (NCRA) has approved about 110 programs, all of which offer courses in computer-aided transcription and real-time reporting. NCRA-approved programs require students to capture 225 words per minute. Court reporters in the Federal Government usually must capture at least 205 words a minute (*Occupational Outlook Handbook*).

This important skill is currently in high demand. What may appear to be a rather mundane job is, in fact, a very rewarding one. Not only are court reporters right in the middle of very interesting events, but the pay is excellent. A National Court Reporters Association survey of its members found average annual earnings for court reporters were about $54,000 in 1999.

Many court reporters work a standard 40-hour week, although part-time work is also common. While some court reporters work for judges, a substantial number of court reporters are self-employed and have very lucrative businesses, which may result in irregular working hours. The *Occupational Outlook Handbook* projects overall employment of court reporters to grow about as fast as average for all occupations through 2008.

Bailiffs

Bailiffs are officers, usually deputy sheriffs, who are assigned to facilitate the court process. While some are sworn, armed law enforcement officers, others are not. Duties of the bailiff include maintaining order in the court and helping to move those involved with the court process, including defendants and the jury. If a particular assignment requires a sworn officer, all the regular requirements for any police officer apply. Nonsworn bailiffs may require less education or experience.

Clerks

Court clerks play many roles that assist the administration of justice. The role of the clerk includes maintaining accurate records and ensuring that court schedules are made and kept. The system, whether criminal or civil, revolves around records and paperwork, and it is the duty of the clerks to see that all records are properly maintained. While many of these positions are clerical, those who work their way up to be *the* Clerk of Court attain a position that is both prestigious and well paying.

Other "Helping" Professions Necessary to the Justice System

One of the wonders of the criminal justice field is the number and types of jobs available. Psychologists, social workers and case managers are involved with both the adult and juvenile systems. Chemical dependency and domestic abuse counselors work hand in hand with financial, marriage and vocational counselors. If you are interested in criminal justice as a career path, you should be able to find a niche that suits you.

Because our legal system seeks to help people who become involved with the system, including those who are being punished, almost every job that people have in the helping professions outside the legal system can be found within the system. It is the opportunity to positively affect the lives of those who find themselves in the legal system that appeals to those who enjoy being a part of it. The *Occupational Outlook Handbook* (p.157) states:

> Human service workers and assistants is a generic term for people with various job titles, including social service assistant, case management aide, social work assistant, community support worker, alcohol or drug abuse counselor, life skill counselor, and gerontology aide. . . . Human service workers and assistants . . . assess clients' needs, establish their eligibility for benefits and services, and help clients obtain them.

In addition: "Opportunities for human service workers and assistants are expected to be excellent, particularly for applicants with appropriate postsecondary education. The number of human service workers and assistants is projected to grow much faster than the average for all occupations between 1998 and 2008" (p.158). Total employment of social workers is expected to rise 36.1 percent between 1998 and 2008. In 1998, the median annual earnings of human service workers and assistants were $21,360.

Counseling is another occupation projected to grow faster than average through 2008. Counselors help people with a variety of issues, ranging from personal and family matters to educational problems, mental health concerns, addictions, substance abuse, stress and anger management. Counselors are employed by various social agencies, correctional institutions and residential care facilities, such as halfway houses for criminal offenders. The *Occupational Outlook Handbook* suggests: "Counselors must possess high physical and emotional energy to handle the array of problems they address. Dealing daily with these problems can cause stress."

In addition to becoming a lawyer, a multitude of other career alternatives exists for those wishing to work in a courtroom setting. Possibilities to consider include jobs as a legal assistant or paralegal, court reporter, bailiff, clerk, psychologist, social worker, case manager or a variety of counseling positions.

The judicial system provides work for people of all levels of education, experience and background. In fact, some people who were "on the wrong side" of the law earlier in their lives are now playing valuable roles in the criminal justice field. Some believe that those who have been in trouble themselves, and possibly even served jail or prison time, can address the issues and concerns of those presently involved better than those who have merely read about it. Similarly, some exceptional chemical dependency and domestic abuse counselors have police records dating back to before they received treatment. Such experiences give them valuable insight for helping those currently needing treatment. So, whether you like to work with the young or the old, those accused of committing a crime or those victimized by it, or even if you enjoy administrative work, the legal system has a place for you.

OPPORTUNITIES IN OUR JUDICIAL SYSTEM—CORRECTIONS

The corrections portion of our criminal justice system serves several purposes:

➤ To punish offenders.
➤ To rehabilitate wrongdoers.
➤ To make society safer for the public.

> The purpose of corrections is to punish and rehabilitate offenders while protecting the public and making our society safer.

Like law enforcement and the courts, corrections is divided into an adult and a juvenile system. Traditionally, the adult system has tended to be more punitive and punishment-oriented while the juvenile system has emphasized treatment and rehabilitation. Typical of state statutes regarding *adult offenders* is Chapter 609 of the Minnesota Statutes, which states that the purpose of the adult criminal code is:

> To protect the public safety and welfare by preventing the commission of crime through the deterring effect of the sentences authorized, the rehabilitation of those convicted, and their confinement when the public safety and interest requires.

In contrast, typical of state statutes regarding *juveniles* is Chapter 260 of the Minnesota Statutes:

> The purpose of the laws relating to juvenile courts is to secure for each child alleged or adjudicated to be delinquent is to promote the public safety and reduce juvenile delinquency by maintaining the integrity of the substantive law prohibiting certain behavior and by developing individual responsibility for lawful behavior. This purpose should be pursued through means that are fair and just, that recognize the unique characteristics and needs of children, and that give children access to opportunities for personal and social growth.

The trend of punishing adults and "treating" juveniles seems to be reversing itself to some extent. More emphasis is being placed on the *treatment* of adult offenders while, at the same time, more traditional penalties, such as incarceration and even manual labor, are being used more frequently as "treatment" for juvenile offenders. Nonetheless, some people prefer working with juveniles because the system remains more treatment oriented, and our society holds the belief that youths are generally as capable as, if not more than, adults in redirecting their lives. It is particularly satisfying to see young people get their lives straightened out.

> The primary difference between adult corrections and juvenile corrections has traditionally been the *punishment* of adults and the *treatment* of juveniles, although this difference seems to be reversing itself to some extent.

Is corrections as exciting as being in on the action-packed arrest? (Remember, that's only 20 percent of police work.) Maybe not. But then, police work doesn't offer the long-range benefits of really helping people to change. Many police officers are frustrated by seeing only the misery caused by crime and not having a positive influence on people, as those who work in corrections often do, particularly those in probation and parole, as will be discussed shortly. But first, look at the most prevalent professional in corrections—the corrections officer, or C.O.

Corrections Officers

Corrections begins after the arrest and involves everything from the initial "booking" to long-term "guarding." Some positions involve counseling inmates, while others are limited to an armed position in a watchtower. For some, work in corrections is a step towards getting somewhere else, a legitimate "stepping stone" to other jobs in law enforcement. It is also, however, an opportunity to be part of a whole other world of the criminal justice system, which many find appealing and very satisfying.

As noted by the *Occupational Outlook Handbook* (p.359):

> Correctional officers are responsible for overseeing individuals who have been arrested and are awaiting trial, or who have been convicted of a crime and sentenced to serve time in a jail, reformatory, or penitentiary. They maintain security and inmate accountability in order to prevent disturbances, assaults, or escapes.

It is worth making the distinction here between corrections officers and detention officers. Though they both perform their functions behind bars, and their jobs are similar in some ways, their jobs are also different in several critical ways. One major distinction is the different constitutional justifications for doing what they do. Individuals held in detention have not yet appeared before the court and, therefore, retain the presumption of innocence. Consequently, any punitive aspect of the correctional environment is not justified with such "inmates." The officer's duty regarding such individuals is to keep them safe and secure until they can be brought before a judge.

Working conditions in correctional institutions may be stressful and occasionally dangerous. Correction officers may be assaulted, injured or even killed by inmates. As with police work, officers in correctional facilities must provide security 24 hours a day. Most corrections officers work 8 hours a day, 5 days a week, but the hours may occur during the night shift, and the days may fall on weekends or holidays. Paid overtime is also common. The *Occupational Outlook Handbook* (p.359) notes:

> Most institutions require that correctional officers be at least 18 to 21 years of age, have a high school education or its equivalent, have no felony convictions, and be a United States citizen. Promotion prospects may be enhanced through obtaining a postsecondary education.

> Correctional officers must be in good health. Candidates for employment are generally required to meet formal standards of physical fitness, eyesight, and hearing. . . . Good judgment and the ability to think and act quickly are indispensable. Applicants are typically screened for drug abuse, subject to background checks, and required to pass a written examination.

Shaffer (1999, p.85) adds: "Some of the characteristics of successful corrections professionals . . . include a sense of fairness, professionalism, integrity, common sense, intelligence, communications skills, patience, honesty, flexibility and self-confidence."

Hill (1997, p.2) has compiled a competency profile of correctional officers, offering a glimpse at some of the duties, roles and responsibilities of this career:

> A correctional officer ensures the public safety by providing for the care, custody, control and maintenance of inmates; and to carry out this mission, must manage and communicate with inmates; intervene in crises and manage conflicts; maintain health, safety and sanitation; communicate with staff; participate in training; and distribute authorized items to inmates.

Desirable correctional officer traits and attitudes include: adaptable/change-oriented, analytical, assertive, compassionate, consistent, cooperative, credible, dependable, emotionally stable, empathetic, ethical, fair, flexible, leader, neat, optimistic, perceptive, positive role model, professional, punctual, self-motivated, sensible and sincere (Hill, p.2). Skill in stress management, CPR/first aid, self-defense, interpersonal communication, public relations and the use of prison tools and equipment are also advantageous to those seeking employment as a correctional officer.

A career in corrections, while demanding and challenging, can be extremely rewarding. Consequently, as noted by Stephens (1999, p.29): "The field has become much more competitive in recent years. . . . This means that people today choosing correctional careers are, increasingly, those who are preparing for it. Vanishing from the landscape are those people simply experimenting with corrections as one among several career options." Furthermore, the trend toward new generation prisons and direct supervision gives corrections officers more involvement with inmates and more control over the populations they supervise, which translates into enhanced professionalism and greater job satisfaction.

Corrections is considered a growth industry. The outlook for jobs for corrections officers at all levels—local, state and federal—is very favorable over the next decade, given the projected increases in the number of individuals incarcerated across the country. Beck and Karberg (2001, p.4) report the national prison incarceration rate has risen sharply since 1990: "Since 1990 the number of sentenced inmates per 100,000 residents has risen an average of 5.4% annually, increasing from 292 to 481." They further note from yearend 1990 to midyear 2000, local, state and federal governments had to accommodate an additional 82,438 inmates per year, or the equivalent of 1,585 new inmates per week (p.1).

As noted in *The Top 100: The Fastest Growing Careers for the 21st Century* (1998, p.91): "Employment in this field is expected to increase much faster than the average for all jobs. . . . The ongoing war on drugs, new tough-on-crime legislation, and increasing mandatory sentencing policies will add more prison beds and more corrections officers." Kiekbusch (2001, p.1) warns: "Corrections in America soon will be confronted by a serious manpower problem: the severe shortage of properly trained and highly motivated correctional officers to staff the nation's correctional facilities. During the next 10 years, there will be an estimated 25,300 openings per year for correctional officers." The *Occupational Outlook Handbook* (p.360) projects a 38.7 percent increase in total employment for correctional officers between 1998 and 2008, rising from 383,000 positions to 532,000.

In 1998, the median annual earnings of correctional officers were $28,540 (*Occupational Outlook Handbook*, p.361). Salaries vary greatly across the country for all positions and personnel of all experience levels: "Beginning salaries for State correctional officers ranged from $14,600 in California to $34,100 in New Jersey. . . . At the Federal level, the starting salary was about $20,600 to $23,000 a year in 1999" (p.361). Benefits commonly available to corrections officers include uniforms or a clothing allowance to buy their own work clothes, medical and dental insurance, disability and life insurance, vacation, sick leave and retirement pensions.

While a majority of this discussion on corrections officers has focused on prison staff, jail officers are another group whose employment outlook appears bright: "Significantly, one of the fastest-growing sectors of today's jail population consists of sentenced offenders serving time in local jails because overcrowded prisons cannot accept them" (Schmalleger, 1999).

A career option for those seeking work in corrections is that of a corrections officer. Corrections officers make up over half of all employees in corrections today. Duties include maintaining the security and safety of persons being held within the correctional facility, enforcing rules and regulations and possibly providing a degree of counseling to inmates. Present and predicted increases in inmate populations mean more corrections officers will be needed in the future.

For prospective criminal justice applicants interested in long-term personal interaction, the fields of probation and parole are worth considering.

Probation and Parole Officers

Careers in probation and parole are other options for those seeking employment in corrections. Like corrections officers, probation and parole officers counsel offenders, but they also evaluate their progress in becoming productive members of society. Unlike corrections officers, probation and parole officers work outside the steel bars and high brick walls, in the community corrections environment.

The primary difference between probation and parole is that probation is an alternative to incarceration, while parole is supervised release from incarceration before the expiration of the sentence. Each involves considerable interaction with offenders.

The probation officer oversees a correctional plan outside detention. The parole agent helps offenders prepare for eventual discharge from the system. It is becoming increasingly common to have one officer handle both probationers and parolees.

Most states require at least a bachelor's degree for probation and parole officers. Careers in the correctional field are quite different from those in law enforcement, but probation officers can take defendants from the crisis point at which they enter the criminal justice system and work with them to help them alter their lives. This long-term payoff makes probation and parole work rewarding.

Probation and parole officers are professionals with vital roles in our corrections system. The job outlook for those interested in becoming probation and/or parole officers is positive, as the entire area of corrections is expanding rapidly.

Community Corrections – Alternatives to Incarceration

Because of increasing jail populations, both the adult and juvenile systems are being forced to examine community alternatives to incarceration. Some of these options are residential facilities such as halfway houses, prerelease centers, transition centers, work furlough and community work centers, community treatment centers and restitution centers. These facilities employ a wide range of staff, including probation/parole officers, counselors, caseworkers, educators, health care workers and numerous administrative, management and support/clerical personnel.

Nonresidential correctional alternatives, such as day reporting centers, require similar personnel. Carlson et al. (1999, p.168) explain: "Day reporting centers are nonresidential locations at which offenders must appear daily to participate in programmed activities and to work out a schedule detailing their activities outside the center. Offenders are also required to maintain frequent phone communications with center staff and to submit to random drug testing."

Another option that eases overcrowded jails and prisons is to allow offenders to remain in their own homes under house arrest.

Electronic Monitoring and House Arrest. Used in conjunction with *electronic monitoring* (EM), house arrest or home detention offers an effective, inexpensive method of supervising probationers. A typical electronic monitoring system (EMS) consists of a bracelet worn on the offender's wrist or ankle. The bracelet contains a transmitter that emits a signal that is continuously monitored, enabling authorities to know the whereabouts of the offender at all times. The increasing use of home detention and electronic monitoring is creating new work opportunities for those who implement and manage these programs.

As house arrest and electronic monitoring gain popularity and grow in use, new job opportunities are created for those who implement and manage such programs.

Juvenile Corrections

If you're interested in working with youths, the same positions needed in adult corrections can generally be found in the juvenile justice system. In fact, considering the historical focus of juvenile justice has been treatment and rehabilitation, this area of corrections is heavily dependent on probation officers, counselors, case workers, social workers, educators and those interested in providing "surrogate" families for troubled youth. Carlson et al. (p.344) state:

> Community-based corrections for juveniles includes both nonresidential (community supervision, family crisis counseling, proctor programs, service-oriented programs and day treatment programs) and residential (shelters, group homes, foster homes, foster group homes and other nonsecure facilities such as correctional farms, ranches and camps) alternatives.

Other Careers in Corrections

Although corrections officers make up the largest number of those with careers in corrections, numerous other careers are available, including administrative, clerical, educational, professional/technical and maintenance/food service positions. Many departments of corrections now employ public information officers (PIOs) to interface with the media and perform other functions. In California, for example, the PIOs also serve as administrative assistants to the warden: "He or she has other duties in addition to working with the media. PIOs often schedule certain days of the week for media tours and visits" (Harry, 2001, p.114). According to Scott (2001, p.102): "PIOs should educate the public, particularly about treatment and conditions of inmates, to positively promote the department. Through news articles, broadcasts or letters to the editor, one can tout the benefits of inmate rehabilitation programs and taxpayer costs involved." Furthermore (p.103): "In today's information age, PIOs also have to concern themselves with the Internet and its abundance of Web sites that foster inmate propaganda."

According to Carlson et al. (p.450): "Treatment professionals [in corrections] include medical staff, psychologists and mental health staff, caseworkers and counselors, correctional educators, chaplains and other religious personnel, recreational specialists and other program coordinators." Furthermore, those facilities involved in prison labor must also staff personnel knowledgeable in the specific industry and products being produced. Finally, bear in mind that as more correctional facilities are built, an increasing number of staff in *all* these categories must be hired to keep the institution operating effectively and constitutionally.

Kelly (1996, pp.135–136) provides the following summary of jobs in corrections (Reprinted by permission):

While correctional job titles and descriptions vary according to the structure and needs of each institution and agency, a few titles are commonly accepted. Occupations within corrections are as varied as those outside the field. Some positions require a high degree of formal education and training, yet there are opportunities for those with more modest education and experience. The education, training, and experience required for the following occupations differ from one place to another. Check with the Federal Bureau of Prisons, as well as your state or local correctional agency for specific job descriptions and requirements. Remember that advancement within the system is possible with continued education and training. The following is a sample of the types of opportunities available in the corrections field.

MANAGERIAL/ADMINISTRATIVE SUPPORT

Warden/Jail Manager: Oversees all operations and programs within the superintendent facility.

Personnel/Human Resources Manager: Responsible for recruiting, advising, hiring, and firing staff; implements the institution's policies and procedures; provides leadership and supervision; advises and assists staff with benefits.

Employee Development Specialist: Plans, supervises or leads programs designed to train and develop employees; consults with or guides management on employee training and development issues.

Budget Administrator: Plans and coordinates the use of resources for a facility.

Financial Manager: Maintains financial services such as auditing and credit analysis; coordinates financial policies and procedures.

Facility Manager: Manages and maintains buildings, grounds and other facilities. Requires managerial skills and a broad technical knowledge of operating capabilities and maintenance requirements of various kinds of physical plants and equipment.

Safety Manager: Offers technical advice on or manages occupational safety programs, regulations, and standards. Requires knowledge of the techniques of safety and pertinent aspects of engineering, psychology and other factors affecting safety.

Ombudsman: Acts as an unbiased liaison between inmates and facility administration; investigates inmate complaints, reports findings, and helps achieve equitable settlements of disputes between inmates and the correctional administration.

Librarian/brarian: Manages and che facility's collection of books, recordings, films, and other materials.

Computer Specialist: Manages or designs use and maintenance of computer systems. This is an area of great need in the corrections field.

Researcher: Analyzes data for budgets and for projected needs and assists in the evaluation of programs.

Food Service Manager: Manages and supervises the operation of the institution's or department's food services, including the storeroom, kitchen, dining rooms, and procurement. Often requires certification as a registered dietician and familiarity with federal, state, and local health codes and sanitary standards.

Correctional Officer: Supervises the treatment and custody of offenders in correctional institutions.

Probation/Parole Officer: Advises and counsels individuals who are on probation or parole; enforces and monitors compliance with the rules imposed on the offender by either the court or parole board.

Juvenile Services Officer: Advises and counsels juveniles in aftercare; evaluates and initiates treatment plans for juveniles in aftercare and makes referrals to appropriate support agencies.

COUNSELING/TRAINING

Psychologist/Counselor: Works with inmates and corrections professionals. Provides counseling and testing. Generally requires professional training. Closely allied specialists may include art therapists and drama therapists. Certified drug and alcohol abuse counselors are in great demand.

Chaplain: Offers religious guidance and spiritual counseling to inmates. Requires ordination by a recognized ecclesiastical body; chaplains may be called upon to minister to inmates not of their faith.

Recreation Specialist: Plans, organizes, and administers programs that promote inmates' physical, creative, artistic and social development.

Vocational Counselor: Provides educational programs or career training for inmates; determines learning needs, abilities, and other facts about inmates. May participate in discussions with other staff professionals to aid in inmates' rehabilitation.

Vocational Instructor: Provides both classroom and hands-on training in a variety of trades.

Industrial Specialist: Assists or manages a prison industry, such as printing, carpentry, agriculture, and sign-making programs.

Juvenile Caseworker: Supervises the treatment and custody of juvenile offenders in correctional or rehabilitation facilities. Often provides support and counseling to juvenile offenders and participates in the development and implementation of treatment plans.

Teacher: Leads classes on subjects for both juveniles and adult offenders. Requires a bachelor's degree plus certification by the state education authority in specific subject area. Teachers certified in special education are in great demand.

MEDICAL

Health System Administrator: Responsible for the administrative management of the health care delivery system and
use of outside resources to provide patient care.

Medical Officer: Performs professional and scientific work in one or more fields of medicine. Requires, at a minimum,
the degree of Doctor of Medicine and, in most states, a current license to practice medicine. Medical support staff may include physicians' assistants, nurses, nurses' assistants, and pharmacists.

CONCLUSION

Many career options exist for those seeking work in our nation's courts and corrections. One of the most popular career choices is that of law. A multitude of other alternatives exists for those wishing to work in a courtroom setting, including jobs as a legal assistant or paralegal, court reporter, bailiff, clerk, psychologist, social worker, case manager or a variety of counseling positions. The field of corrections is experiencing phenomenal growth. Possible career options for those seeking work in corrections include corrections officers in both adult and juvenile facilities, probation officers and parole officers. The job outlook for those interested in becoming corrections officers and probation/parole officers is positive, as the entire area of corrections is expanding rapidly.

While government agencies find their challenge "doing more with less" to appease the very vocal "no new taxes" constituency, the less traditional fields of employment will expand. Even if it's in the areas providing alternatives to more expensive imprisonment, including probation and parole work, the areas that can lessen the burden on taxpayers will flourish. Beyond government employment, all areas of the system will continue to take advantage of private responses. No doubt a "partnership" will develop, allowing people to move from one area to another, with new possibilities always on the horizon.

ADDITIONAL CONTACTS AND SOURCES OF INFORMATION

American Bar Association (ABA)
750 North Lake Shore Drive
Chicago, IL 60611
http://www.abanet.org

American Correctional Association (ACA)
4380 Forbes Boulevard
Lanham, MD 20706
(301) 918-1800
http://www.corrections.com/aca

American Jail Association (AJA)
2053 Day Road, Suite 100
Hagerstown, MD 21740
http://www.corrections.com/aja/index.html

American Probation and Parole Association
c/o Council of State Governments
Iron Works Pike
P.O. Box 11910
Lexington, KY 40578
(606) 244-8203
E-mail: appa@csg.org

Federal Bureau of Prisons (BOP)
320 First Street NW, Room 460
Washington, DC 20534
(800) 347-7744
http://www.bop.gov

International Association of Correctional Officers (IACO)
P.O. Box 81826
Lincoln, NE 68501
http://www.acsp.uic.edu/iaco

Law School Admission Council
P.O. Box 40
Newtown, PA 18940
http://www.lsac.org

National Court Reporters Association
8224 Old Courthouse Road
Vienna, VA 22182
http://www.verbatimreporters.com

Standing Committee on Legal Assistants
http://www.abanet.org/legalassts

United States Court Reporters Association
1904 Marvel Lane
Liberty, MO 64068
http://www.uscra.org

American Correctional Association Publications – Call (800) 222-5646, extension 1860
   Correctional Officer Resource Guide, 3rd ed.; Item #631-CC01, $29.95
   Correctional Law for the Correctional Officer, 3rd ed., by William C. Collins, J.D.; Item #630-CC01; $19.95
   Mental Health in Corrections: An Overview for Correctional Staff, by Wesley Sowers, M.D., Kenneth Thompson,
      M.D. and Stephen Mullins, M.D.; Item #210-CC01; $15.00
   Staff Supervision Made Easy, by Scott D. Hutton, Ph.D.; Item #194-CC01; $19.95

 MIND STRETCHES

1. How do you feel about lawyers?

2. If you were to become a criminal lawyer, would you rather be a prosecutor or a defense attorney?

3. Do you think judges should be elected public officials or appointed by members of local and state
    government?

4. What do most people think of when they think of a "correctional officer job"? Where did you acquire
    the information on which you base your answer?

5. What benefits would you find in a job in corrections that may not exist in a street police job?

6. What negatives would you want to be aware of in considering a job as a correctional officer?

7. Can you think of unique skills that could make a job candidate more attractive to a hiring agency?

8. Is there a danger in pursuing a specific job that "really excites" you, to the point you do not believe any
    other job would be worthwhile?

9. What corrections jobs do you think will become more necessary in the future? Less necessary?

10. How do you predict corrections will change? Why?

INSIDERS' VIEWS

For this chapter, read the *Insiders' Views* by Marsh J. Halberg, J.D. ("Lawyers Wear Many Hats: Which One Is Right for You?") and John J. Maas ("The Path to a Career in Corrections"), found on the Web site: http://www.wadsworth.com/criminaljustice_d/.

REFERENCES

Beck, Allen J. and Karberg, Jennifer C. *Prison and Jail Inmates at Midyear 2000.* Washington, DC: Bureau of Justice Statistics Bulletin, March 2001. (NCJ-185989)

Carlson, Norman A.; Hess, Kären M.; and Orthmann, Christine M. H. *Corrections in the 21ˢᵗ Century: A Practical Approach.* Belmont, CA: Wadsworth Publishing Company, 1999.

Harry, Jennifer L. "An Interview with Margot Bach: Information Officer II for the California Department of Corrections." *Corrections Today*, June 2001, pp.114–119.

Hill, Gary. "Correctional Officer Traits and Skills." *Corrections Compendium*, August 1997, pp.1–12.

Kasanof, Adam. "Is Law School Right for You?" *Police*, July 2000, pp.48–49.

Kelly, Michael. "Is a Career in Corrections for You?" *Corrections Today*, July 1996, pp.134–136.

Kiekbusch, Richard G. "The Looming Correctional Work Force Shortage: A Problem of Supply and Demand." *Corrections Compendium*, April 2001, pp.1–3, 24–25.

Occupational Outlook Handbook. 2000–2001 Edition. U.S. Department of Labor, Bureau of Labor Statistics, Washington, DC: U.S. Government Printing Office, 2000.

Schmalleger, Frank. *Criminal Justice Today: An Introductory Text for the Twenty-First Century*, 5ᵗʰ ed. Upper Saddle River, NJ: Prentice Hall, 1999.

Scott, Gerges. "So, You Want to Be a Public Information Officer for a Corrections Department." *Corrections Today*, June 2001, pp.102–104.

Shaffer, John S. "Life on the Installment Plan: Careers in Corrections." *Corrections Today*, December 1999, pp.84–88, 147.

Stephens, W. Richard, Jr. *Careers in Criminal Justice.* Boston: Allyn and Bacon, 1999.

The Top 100: The Fastest Growing Careers for the 21ˢᵗ Century. Chicago: Ferguson Publishing Company, 1998.

CHAPTER 4

CAREERS IN PRIVATE SECURITY

Private security is the invisible empire of criminal justice.

—Christopher A. Hertig

Do You Know:

➢ The difference between proprietary, contractual and hybrid security?
➢ The difference between public and private policing?
➢ Why cooperation between public law enforcement and private security is necessary and what some examples of such cooperation are?
➢ What areas of public justice are being affected by privatization?
➢ What trend is occurring in corrections and who the largest provider of such services currently is?
➢ Why many law enforcement officers desire jobs as private security directors?
➢ What typical entry-level positions exist in private security and what the duties are for these individuals?
➢ What mid-level and top-level positions exist in private security?
➢ Where job opportunities in private security are most likely? Least likely?
➢ How common licensing and registration requirements are for private security professionals? Where to obtain information about such requirements?
➢ What qualities employers seek in private security applicants?
➢ How private security and public law enforcement compare in terms of employment and spending?
➢ What the outlook is for jobs in private security?
➢ What kind of salary you might expect from a job in private security?
➢ How available promotions are in private security?

INTRODUCTION

No area in the criminal justice system is growing as rapidly as careers in private security. Why? *People want lower taxes!* This unquestionably means that the private sector will pick up where the government leaves off. Lower taxes mean fewer police; fewer police mean fewer programs; fewer programs mean the burden of paying for whatever additional protection people desire will fall on the specific populations requesting it. Here is where opportunities abound for private entrepreneurs.

Private security *is* big business and a protective presence that continues to get bigger every year: "The world market for private contractual security services will grow 8.4 percent annually through 2004, approaching $100 billion" ("Worldwide Security Services . . . ," 2001, p.8). The American Society for Industrial Security (ASIS) (n.d., p.2) notes that all businesses, regardless of size, have numerous security concerns relating to fraud, theft, computer hacking, industrial espionage and workplace violence:

Security is one of the fastest growing professional careers worldwide. A career in the security field provides a multitude of opportunities. These opportunities range from entry level security officer positions to investigators specializing in specific areas and managers and directors of security at major corporations and organizations around the world. The demand for heightened security is being increased by theft of information, workplace violence, terrorism and white-collar crime.

Matison and Hess (1997, p.4) add:

Crime, violence and workplace safety are major concerns of businesses and organizations. They want to prevent crime, violence and accidents and when prevention fails, they want to be able to find out who is responsible and how to avoid future incidents. Industrial espionage and corporate theft are areas which plague some larger companies. Store security, shoplifting, vandalism and even arson are significant problems for other businesses. This is a very major market.

This chapter begins with a comparison of the private security officer and the public law enforcement officer. It then examines the relationship between these two fields and discusses the criticality of cooperation between them. This is followed by an up-close look at career opportunities within the security profession, including salaries and the potential for growth in this field.

PUBLIC VS. PRIVATE OFFICERS

Because public policing and private security are closely related, and because people employed in one field often become involved at some time in the other, start by looking at how the two fields basically differ.

A primary difference between public policing and private security, as the names imply, is who you work for. Who pays your salary? Individuals in public policing are paid with tax dollars and, consequently, are accountable to the tax-paying citizens, whether on a local, county, state or federal level. They are under constant scrutiny by both the public and the politicians charged with overseeing expenditures of public funds, and their incomes are heavily influenced by the tax dollars allocated to policing. Private security positions, in contrast, are funded by business, industry or any entity in the private sector wanting protection beyond what public law enforcement provides.

Another basic difference between public policing and private security is the essential goals of each. Public law enforcement is quite reactive, operating as a service to the jurisdiction that pays for it. Ideally, it serves everyone within its jurisdiction equally, without a profit motive. People call, and the police are expected to respond. Private security is proactive, seeking to prevent problems and limit losses for a particular private employer. Whether a private security operation is *proprietary* (the security officers are actual employees of the company) or *contractual* (the security officers are hired from an independent security company), the private security profession is profit oriented and serves the employer paying for such service. The current trend is *hybrid security*, which combines contractual and proprietary security.

Proprietary security officers are actual employees of the company they guard. Contractual security officers work for an independent security company and are assigned to guard a company without its own internal security staff. The trend is toward using hybrid security, combining both proprietary and contractual security services.

A third basic difference between public and private policing is in the statutory power involved. Public police officers are an arm of the government and act with its full authority, including the authority of arrest. Although police powers of arrest are awesome, police may be denied access to private facilities that are accessible to those facilities' security officers. Without a warrant, public police could well be denied access to an industrial facility that relies on its own security department to deal with such concerns as industrial espionage.

Private security officers have no more power than that of private citizens. However, as citizens, they can carry weapons, conduct investigations, defend property and make arrests. And they may, in fact, *appear* to have more authority than regular citizens as a result of wearing a uniform, carrying a weapon and having the approval and support of the organization to defend the property.

Differences between public police and private security officers include:
1. Where the paycheck comes from (public tax dollars vs. private sector budgets)
2. Whether the response is reactive or proactive
3. The statutory power involved

Frequently public policing and private security are viewed as being competitors. Additionally, some people in public law enforcement may look down on security officers, calling them "wanna-bes," that is, individuals who really want to be police officers but didn't make it. But this is simply no longer true—private security as a profession has come of age.

PUBLIC/PRIVATE COOPERATION

Private security has become a major player in safeguarding Americans and their property. As our increasing elderly and business populations are likely to continue their inhabitation of high-rise condos and office buildings, their reliance on private security will also increase. The traditional police officer patrolling public roads or a beat officer on foot cannot practically be expected to patrol such structures. Unlike public police officers, private security officers can and do patrol specific buildings, even specific floors or rooms within buildings. It can be anticipated that the fields of public law enforcement and private security may tend to blend together as society recognizes the need for each and as these professions themselves learn how they can best work together—to the benefit of all.

An obvious reason for cooperation is that individuals often move from one field to the other. Some individuals use private security as a stepping stone into public policing. Likewise, some individuals in public policing enter private security, sometimes as a consultant, sometimes after retiring from public policing, sometimes as a part-time job while working as a public police officer, and sometimes as a highly paid corporate security director.

Cooperation between public law enforcement and private security can benefit both sides and is an important step toward enhanced safety for all. Examples of cooperation between the public and private sector include combined efforts at the sites of natural disasters, common initiatives in controlling and securing large public events and cooperation in preventing and handling neighborhood crime.

PRIVATIZATION OF PUBLIC JUSTICE

The privatization trend has extended to more than just police officers. It is working its way into other areas of the justice system as well.

The trend toward private justice can also be found in the areas of corrections and juvenile justice.

Private Corrections

The privatization of corrections is highly controversial. Critics fear the quality of inmate care will be compromised as private facilities focus on generating a profit and raise concerns about the degree of control the government will have over the nation's criminals if they are housed in privately operated facilities. Nonetheless, the privatization of corrections has been slowly gaining ground since the 1980s: "In the United States, there are a total of 158 private correctional facilities operating in 30 states, Puerto Rico, and the District of Columbia. Texas has the most facilities, with 42, followed by California, Florida, and Colorado" ("Privatization Can Save . . . ," 2001, p.3)

Numerous companies are capitalizing on the expanding niche for private corrections, some of the largest companies being the Corrections Corporation of America; Concept, Inc.; U.S. Corrections Corporation; Mid-Tex Detention, Inc.; Esmor Correctional Services, Inc., and Wackenhut Corrections Corporation.

The privatization of corrections has been increasing since the 1980s. In 1995 Wackenhut Corrections Corporation became the largest company in the national private corrections industry.

Factors to consider in the private sector, however, concern staffing levels and the resultant impact on staff security. Private prisons, concerned about the bottom line, often can reduce expenditures by having smaller staffs or paying employees less: "The survey of private prisons showed that they have 'significantly lower staffing levels' than comparable public prisons . . .—28 staff members per 100 inmates in private facilities, as opposed to 32 staff members per 100 inmates in public prisons" ("Privatization Can Save . . . ," p.4). Furthermore: "Major incidents of violence were more common in private prisons. . . . The rate of inmate assaults on staff members was 12.2 per 1,000 inmates in private prisons, and 8.2 per 1,000 in public prisons" (p.4).

Private Sector Involvement in Juvenile Justice

Some juvenile justice agencies, finding their jurisdictions lack adequate services and expertise, are contracting with private sector vendors to meet their clients' needs. A survey by Levinson and Chase (2000, p.158) found the most common private sector services and programs provided to juvenile justice agencies involved health/mental health programs, programs for special needs juveniles, services for females, residential (secure) programs, community-based programs and inpatient substance abuse programs. The survey (p.159) also showed the private sector to be a growth area for juvenile correctional programs and services: "There has been an increase in the use of for-profit contractors—from 60 percent in 1991 to 80 percent in 1999. Further, it appears that this trend will continue into the future."

PRIVATE SECURITY—UP CLOSE

Because private security is profit oriented, opportunities exist that are not available in the public sector. With corporate America recognizing that security and loss prevention are as critical to a successful business as management and marketing, an increasing number of very appealing job opportunities are developing.

The stereotype of the retiree sitting at a guard desk overnight is no longer an accurate portrayal of what has become a profession in every sense of the word. Like law enforcement, much of what happens in this profession is not common knowledge. Consequently, many people considering employment in private security may find themselves relying on inaccurate data. Unless you know someone in the field, you probably obtained what you know about security work where most people do: television or the newspaper. Television may lead you to believe *security work* consists primarily of solving crimes the police cannot or will not deal with. Television shows about private detectives frequently do two injustices to the profession. First, they unrealistically glamorize it. Second, they fail to explain what a lucrative and necessary area of business it is.

Law enforcement officers are able to do only so much, and their work may not cover all aspects necessary to other participants in the criminal justice system, such as lawyers. Remember, the role of the police is to investigate *crimes*. Once they have done this, their job is over. But what about facts surrounding a civil, noncriminal negligence case such as a car accident which falls short of criminal activity but which might spawn significant litigation? Even if it *is* a police matter, police don't always put as much emphasis on obtaining evidence as a defense attorney might like—evidence that could help exonerate the accused. Furthermore, the police have little interest in personal matters such as infidelity investigations or even workers' compensation violations. Here are excellent opportunities for the private investigator.

When you consider that the private sector may provide more advancement potential and more overall control of one's professional and personal life, it is easy to see why many law enforcement officers set eventual goals to become private security directors.

Employment in the private sector usually provides more advancement potential and greater control over one's professional and personal life, explaining why many law enforcement officers desire jobs as private security directors.

While many individuals who have enjoyed a successful career in law enforcement will enjoy a "second career" in private security, many people successfully use work in the private sector as a "stepping stone" into the public sector. Law enforcement is a popular career, and jobs as police officers are difficult to come by. Having worked as a security officer at any level says a number of things about an applicant for a police job:

➤ The applicant has been successfully employed.
➤ The applicant has worked in a position of trust.
➤ Unusual hours do not present a problem.
➤ The uniform does not create a power-hungry person.
➤ The applicant can keep cool under stressful circumstances.

Types of Jobs Available

The continuously evolving complexity of our society is necessitating specially trained private security officers in all phases of life. Businesses need individuals who can effectively use highly technical surveillance equipment. They rely on private suppliers of search dogs and strike/civil disobedience response teams. Some businesses need 24-hour surveillance. Services commonly identified as candidates for privatization include animal control, court security, funeral escorts, parking enforcement, patrolling of public parks, prisoner transport, public building security, public housing development patrol and special event security.

An ASIS survey of security professionals found them handling a variety of specific responsibilities, including physical security; loss and crime prevention; general management and administrative functions; fraud and economic crime investigation; business continuity, contingency planning and disaster management; fire and life safety; background investigations; executive protection; human resources related functions; information security; and computer/Internet/network security ("Comp and Circumstance...," 2001, p.x).

With the enhanced function of private security has come the opportunity for specialization. As the private security profession expands, so have the kinds of jobs available. ASIS lists the following (p.18) as security specialties with career opportunities:

Construction Security	Hi-Tech Security	Security Design and Engineering
Contingency Planning	Insurance Security	Security Education and Training
Corporate Security	Nuclear Security	Security Investigations
Crisis Management	Pharmaceutical Security	Special Event Security
Entertainment Security	Proprietary/Information Security	Terrorism Counteraction
Executive Protection	Real Estate Management Security	Wholesaling and Warehousing
Government Operations Security	Residential Security	Security
High-Rise/Office Building Security	Security Consulting	

Regardless of the specific security discipline or specialty, opportunities in the private sector are typically categorized as entry-level, mid-level and top-level positions.

Entry-Level Positions. Typical entry-level jobs include private security guards and private patrol officers. Private security guards control access to private property; protect against loss through theft, vandalism or fire; enforce rules; maintain order and lower risks of all kinds. The *Occupational Outlook Handbook* (2000) states:

> In department stores, guards protect people, records, merchandise, money, and equipment. They often work with undercover store detectives to prevent theft by customers or store employees and help in the apprehension of shoplifting suspects prior to arrival by police. In office buildings, banks, and hospitals, guards maintain order and protect the institutions' property, staff, and customers. At air, sea, and rail terminals and other transportation facilities, guards protect people, freight, property, and equipment. They may screen passengers and visitors for weapons and explosives using metal detectors and high-tech equipment, ensure nothing is stolen while being loaded or unloaded, and watch for fires and criminals.
>
> Guards who work in public buildings such as museums or art galleries protect paintings and exhibits by inspecting people and packages entering and leaving the building. . . . Armored car guards protect money and valuables during transit. In addition, they protect individuals responsible for making commercial bank deposits from theft or bodily injury.

Most guards wear a uniform and some carry a baton or other weapons, such as a gun. Security guards may work inside and/or outside, patrolling the interior of buildings or the exterior grounds. They may be stationed at a desk to monitor security cameras and to check the identification of persons coming and going. As with many other jobs, a typical guard shift lasts eight hours, although many guards work at night, and many work alone. Because of the flexible hours and limited formal training requirements, this occupation is attractive to those seeking a second or part-time job.

Private patrol officers are similar to patrol units of the public police force. They move from one location to another, on foot or in a vehicle, protecting property and preventing losses. Some patrol officers work for a single employer; others have several employers.

Typical entry-level jobs include private security guards and private patrol officers. Private security guards control access to private property; protect against loss through theft, vandalism or fire; enforce rules; maintain order and lower risks of all kinds. Private patrol officers, similar to patrol units of the public police force, move from one location to another, on foot or in a vehicle, protecting property and preventing losses.

In 1998, more than 1 million guard jobs were held, with 60 percent of all wage and salary guards employed by industrial security firms and guard agencies. Guard jobs exist throughout the country but are most common in metropolitan areas. More than 25 percent of guards worked part time: "A significant number of law enforcement officers work as security guards when off-duty to supplement their incomes. Often working in uniform and with the official cars assigned to them, they add a high profile security presence to the establishment with which they have contracted" (*Occupational Outlook Handbook*).

Mid-Level Positions. Mid-level jobs in private security include private investigators, detectives, armed couriers, central alarm respondents and consultants. Private investigators and detectives may "freelance" or may work for a specific employer. Often the work involves background checks for employment, insurance and credit applications, civil litigation and investigation of insurance or workers' compensation claims. Sometimes investigators are brought in to work undercover to detect employee dishonesty, shoplifting or illegal drug use:

> Private detectives and investigators offer many services, including executive, corporate, and celebrity protection; pre-employment verification; and individual background profiles. They also provide assistance in civil liability and personal injury cases, insurance claims and fraud, child custody and protection cases, and pre-marital screening. Increasingly, they are hired to investigate individuals to prove or disprove infidelity. . . .

> Private detectives and investigators often specialize. Those who focus on intellectual property theft, for example, investigate and document acts of piracy, help clients stop the illegal activity, and provide intelligence for prosecution and civil action. Other investigators specialize in financial profiles and asset searches. Their reports reflect information gathered through interviews, investigation and surveillance, and research, including review of public documents (*Occupational Outlook Handbook*, p.369).

Regarding the employment of such professionals, the *Occupational Outlook Handbook* (p.370) states:

> Private detectives and investigators held about 61,000 jobs in 1998. About 1 out of 4 was self-employed. Approximately a third of salaried private detectives and investigators worked for detective agencies, while another third were employed as store detectives in department or clothing and accessories stores. The remainder worked for hotels and other lodging places, legal services firms, and in other industries.

> Mid-level jobs in private security include private investigators, detectives, armed couriers, central alarm respondents and consultants. Top jobs in security include loss prevention specialists, security directors and risk managers.

Top-Level Positions. Top jobs in security include managing a private security company or heading up security for a private concern. Common titles include loss prevention specialist, security director and risk manager.

As with guard positions, higher-level security positions are most likely to exist in urban regions with higher populations. International jobs are also available in security, but obtaining them is not easy. Many businesses and establishments, such as hotels, are opening facilities in foreign countries. Often the security director of such businesses and establishments are sent to set up the security system.

> Job opportunities in private security are greater in metropolitan areas. Security jobs are more difficult to obtain in foreign countries and in less populated areas of the United States.

Those seeking careers in private security may also wish to consider public security positions as well as those of special deputies, code enforcement officers and others with limited law enforcement authority. Many government agencies hire "special deputies" who possess law enforcement authority while on duty. These special deputies perform many of the same functions carried out by private security forces but do so for the government. At the local level, special deputies may be under the direct authority of the sheriff, or they may constitute a security department within a government organization. In New York, for example, security officers working for local governments are called *peace officers* to distinguish them from their public police officer counterparts.

Special deputies are also found in the federal government. For example, the U.S. Marshals assign special deputy marshals to courthouses. Such deputies are often contract employees who possess law enforcement authority only while on duty and only at their assigned venue. The Department of Energy (DOE), through its contractors, employs hundreds of individuals to perform security and safeguard responsibilities related to classified documents and materials. While such individuals are not DOE inspectors and lack law enforcement authority, they do work closely with local police departments and the FBI to investigate all levels of security breaches, thefts of government property and other crimes impacting government property and issues. Furthermore, compensation in this area can be quite lucrative.

As technology advances, the types of security jobs available also expand. One of the newest arenas of security involves cyber-crime, as Weinstein (1999, p.J1) explains:

> A few years ago, cyber-crime served only as the subject of sci-fi novels. Today, it is a serious problem affecting everyone. . . . According to the annual CSI/FBI Computer Crime and Security Survey conducted by the Computer Security Institute and the San Francisco FBI Computer Intrusion Squad, system penetration by outsiders increased for the third year in a row, along with unauthorized access by insiders and financial losses because of computer security breaches (amounting to losses of more than $100 million).
>
> That's not the half of it. Many cyber-thieves are becoming instant millionaires by bilking brokerages and, especially, the insurance industry, according to Jay Valentine, CEO of Austin, Texas-based InfoGlide, a company that makes fraud-busting software. . . .

In the past 18 to 24 months, tracking down cyber-thieves has ascended to high priority. More companies are creating computer security departments manned by cyber-sleuths or computer security investigators. "They used to be former police officers with technical skills. Now they're mainly young techies, many of whom are recent college grads, with a knowledge of C++, Java and Internet applications," Valentine said.

About 300 of the Fortune 500 companies are hiring cyber-sleuths, according to Valentine. It all adds up to yet another emerging field with undefined job titles and job tracks. Valentine estimated that six to 10 computer security jobs exist at any midsize to large company, and the pay scale ranges from $60,000 to $100,000-plus at the senior levels.

Whether entry-level or management, it's anything but a dull career. "A security person, for example, may be investigating multiple attempts to log on, monitoring log-on procedures, passwords, tracing attempts to break into a network or trying to discover what type of computer it originated from," Valentine said.

Obviously, this type of security work requires a specialized skill and degree of technical knowledge. While such technical knowledge is not a prerequisite for most security positions, employment requirements in the growing field of private security are becoming increasingly higher.

Employment Requirements

Private security is joining the trend of other fields that stress the importance of achieving certain basic professional requirements. Employers with proprietary forces usually set their own standards for security officers. Contractual security companies often are regulated by state law. Individuals who wish to provide security services on their own may need to be licensed by their state. Requirements vary, so it is important to check on your local situation.

While some states require few, if any, qualifications be met by those wishing to work in private security, other states are very strict as to who may practice in this field, either as an individual or a company supplying security services. Of the three professional licenses author Harr holds, his private detective license required more comprehensive administrative requirements and was more expensive to initially obtain than his licenses as a police officer or a lawyer. Minnesota statutes stipulate who needs to be licensed as a private investigator in the state, what the application consists of and what must accompany the application, including:

➤ A surety bond for $5,000.
➤ Verified certificates of at least five citizens not related to the signer who have known the signer for more than five years, certifying that the signer is of "good moral character."
➤ Two photographs and a full set of fingerprints for each signer of the application.

A majority of states now recognize that some controls have to be in place to ensure responsible involvement by those operating in this field: "Most States require that guards be licensed. To be licensed as a guard, individuals must be at least 18 years old, pass a background check, and complete classroom training in such subjects as property rights, emergency procedures, and detention of suspected criminals. Drug testing is often required, and may be random and ongoing (*Occupation Outlook Handbook*). Additionally (p.370): "There are no formal education requirements for most private detective and investigator jobs, although many private detectives have college degrees. . . . The majority of the States and the District of Columbia require private detectives and investigators to be licensed by the State or local authorities. Licensing requirements vary widely. Some States have few requirements, . . . while others have stringent regulations."

Be sure to investigate the requirements of the state(s) in which you want to work. Some county and city governments also require certification or licensure of those working in private security positions within their jurisdiction. Because many duties of private security officers can have consequences as critical as those of the law enforcement officer—for example, using firearms, K-9s and other weapons, arresting people, rendering emergency medical assistance and the like—it makes sense to have basic requirements in place. Most common are regulations regarding background checks, certain minimal knowledge and posting some sort of bond. Some states have a residency requirement. Many states have policies on autos and uniforms.

> Nearly every state now has licensing or registration requirements for guards who work for contract security agencies. Some states have a residency requirement, and many states have regulations concerning autos and uniforms. Be sure to investigate these employment requirements by contacting the appropriate regulatory agency.

Training requirements and other qualifications vary among different agencies; however, some applicant qualities are fairly common. Most employers prefer guards who are high school graduates. Some jobs require a driver's license. Some employers seek individuals who have had experience in the military police or in state and local police agencies. Furthermore: "Applicants are expected to have good character references, no serious police record, and good health. They should be mentally alert, emotionally stable, and physically fit in order to cope with emergencies. Guards who have frequent contact with the public should communicate well." The *Occupational Outlook Handbook* (p.370) notes:

> For private detective and investigator jobs, most employers look for individuals with ingenuity who are persistent and assertive. A candidate must not be afraid of confrontation, should communicate well, and should be able to think on his or her feet. Good interviewing and interrogation skills are also important and are usually acquired in earlier careers in law enforcement or other fields.

Because competition for prime security positions is increasing, applicants should strive to increase their marketability by gaining knowledge of the field through education and other types of experiences. According to ASIS (p.2): "Students seeking careers in security should pursue course work in security, computer science, electronics, business management, law, police science, personnel and information management."

In addition, some individuals may want to be certified by the ASIS through their *Certified Protection Professional (CPP) program*. This program, organized in 1977, is designed to recognize individuals meeting specific criteria of professional protection knowledge and conduct. To be eligible to take the examination, candidates must either have 10 years of experience with no degree, eight years of experience and an associate's degree, five years of experience and a bachelor's degree, four years of experience and a master's degree or three years of experience and a doctoral degree. At least half the experience must be in "responsible charge" of a security function. The examination takes a full day, with the morning devoted to general security knowledge and the afternoon devoted to a choice of four specialty tests selected from a wide variety of areas.

> Most employers seek security applicants with high school diplomas and some experience in the military police or in state or local level police work. Other important qualities include good character references, good health, good personal habits and no police record. A valid driver's license may also be required. Eligible individuals may benefit by becoming a Certified Protection Professional, or CPP.

Job Outlook

According to one security expert: "Private security is now clearly the nation's primary protective resource, outspending public law enforcement by 73 percent . . . and employing nearly three times the people . . . . The annual growth rate will be 8 percent for private security, double that of public law enforcement" (Hess and Wrobleski, 1996, p.716).

> Private security is the nation's primary protective resource today, outspending public law enforcement by more than 73 percent and employing nearly three times the workforce.

According to *The Top 100: The Fastest Growing Careers for the 21st Century* (1998, p.345):

> Security services is one of the largest employment fields in the United States. . . . The demand for guards and other security personnel is expected to increase much faster than the average through the year 2005, as crime rates rise with the overall population growth. The highest estimates call for more than 1.25 million guards to be employed by the year 2005.

The *Occupational Outlook Handbook* adds: "Opportunities for most jobs as guards should be very favorable through the year 2008," with the employment of guards, private detectives and investigators expected to grow faster than the average for all occupations (p.371). Employment projections indicate the addition of 15,000 private detective and investigative positions between 1998 and 2008, a 24.3 percent increase in employment. Given the enhanced state of alert within the United States following recent terrorist attacks, it seems safe to say the demand for security forces will most certainly remain high in the foreseeable future.

> The private security field is expected to grow more rapidly through the year 2005 than the average for all occupations, requiring the hiring of many employees to meet the increasing security needs.

Certain areas within the security industry are also projected to grow more rapidly than others. Bias (1999, p.1) reports on the results of an ASIS survey: "The fields where the most security management job growth is expected are computer security and information technology. Contract security and investigations also appear to be gaining job positions due to the swell in outsourcing, and companies looking for cost-effective technology that allows a reduction in officer staffing are creating jobs in electronics security and alarm system design and installation."

Salaries

It is difficult to provide an accurate listing of "average" pay in private security because the range is extreme. Entry-level jobs may start at the minimum wage, but the upper wage is virtually unlimited. Owners of successful private security or investigation firms and upper-level security directors can expect lucrative salaries, with perks like bonus plans and company cars.

The *Occupational Outlook Handbook* reports median annual earnings of guards were $16,240 in 1998, while median annual earnings of private detectives and investigators were $21,020 that same year (p.371). The *Handbook* also notes:

> Earnings of private detectives and investigators vary greatly depending on their employer, specialty, and the geographic area in which they work. According to a study by Abbott, Langer & Associates, security/loss prevention directors and vice presidents averaged $65,500 a year in 1998; investigators, $49,300; and store detectives, $17,700.

The Top 100 (p.345) adds:

> Earning for security consultants vary greatly depending on the consultant's training and experience. Entry-level consultants with a bachelor's degree commonly start at $26,000 to $32,000 per year. Consultants with graduate degrees begin at $34,000 to $41,000 per year, and experienced consultants may earn $50,000 to $100,000 per year or more. Many consultants work on a per-project basis, with rates of up to $75 per hour.

In an interesting twist, while the earning potential of private security professionals generally exceeds that of public police officers, private security managers working in publicly held companies typically earn more than security managers in privately owned enterprises: "Those who worked for publicly owned companies earn on average 16 percent more than those employed by privately owned ventures" (Anderson, 2001, p.69). However: "Company revenue appears to be a less significant determinant of salary than the size of the security budget and the breadth of the territory covered" (p.66). Furthermore (p.70): "With regard to the business sector, the highest average salaries were earned by security managers working in energy, financial services, and IT." Tables 4-1 and 4-2 show salary data for security officers, console operators, investigators and managers.

Table 4-1   2000 Annual Salary Ranges for Security Officers, Console Operators and Investigators

ANNUAL SALARY RANGES		
	Low End	*High End*
Security Officers		
Contract – Unarmed	$17,000	$23,600
Proprietary – Unarmed	$21,500	$30,700
Contract – Armed	$22,600	$43,000
Proprietary – Armed	$27,000	$33,700
Console Operators		
Contract	$20,000	$20,800
Proprietary	$22,000	$30,000
Investigators		
Contract	$41,000	$56,500
Proprietary	$42,000	$43,300

SOURCE: Adapted from "Comp and Circumstance: ASIS International 2000 Employment Survey." *2001 Security Industry Buyers Guide*, 2001, p.xii.

Table 4-2   2000 Annual Average Salary of Security Managers, as Related to Several Factors

NUMBER OF EMPLOYEES		NUMBER OF LOCATIONS		SIZE OF SECURITY BUDGET MANAGED	
Under 100	$57,931	One location (building or facility)	$60,941	$250,000 and under	$55,965
100–1,000	$59,249	Two or more locations within one state	$65,404	$250,001 to $500,000	$61,839
1,001–10,000	$71,392	Two or more locations in more than one state	$82,156	$500,001 to $1,000,000	$76,378
More than 10,000	$85,852	Two or more locations in more than one country	$103,473	$1,000,001 to $2,500,000	$80,120
				More than $2,500,000	$127,913

SOURCE: Adapted from Teresa Anderson. "Putting Payday in Perspective." *Security Management*, Vol.45, No.9, September 2001, pp.67–68.

Anderson (p.71) adds: "Personal development factors such as certification and education affect salaries. Those holding a Certified Protection Professional (CPP) designation have higher salaries, as do those with advanced degrees. Most notably, . . . security professionals who are also CPPs earn about 21 percent more than those with no certification of any kind. The average salary for a CPP is $83,765, while those with no certification earn $69,100." Furthermore, security managers who work for publicly held companies and who handle security budgets greater than $2.5 million earned an average $163,480 (p.70).

Salaries in the field of private security vary greatly, ranging from around $17,000 a year for unarmed contract security officers to $150,000 or more a year for corporate security managers working for large public companies.

Fringe Benefits

Most security professionals receive benefits from their employers, although various surveys indicate different percentages of employees are receiving certain benefits (Anderson; "Comp and Circumstance;" "2001 Salary Survey"). Nonetheless, most security employees receive vacation (97%), holidays (93%), health care coverage (92–97%), life insurance (90–93%), sick leave (87%), dental insurance (84–93%), 401(k) plan (74–91%), and long-term disability plan (73–89%). Other benefits frequently provided include tuition reimbursement (68%), pension plan (65–71%), personal time (65%), vision insurance (61–75%), short-term disability (60%), cellular/airtime usage (53%), trade show/convention expenses (52%) and association memberships (50%).

In addition to these benefits, nearly half of security employees receive performance bonuses (45–48%), stock options or stock purchase plans (16–34%) and participation in a profit sharing plan (14–25%). Furthermore, 18–21% of employers offer child-care support (Anderson, p.71). The "2001 Salary Survey" (2001, p.S7) reports security professionals employed by transportation/utility firms receive the greatest number of benefits of any industry surveyed, while government workers received the fewest.

Promotions

Like law enforcement, security careers can meet a stumbling block not as prevalent in other careers. Promotions can come few and far between—if at all. The problem is that jobs in the security field tend to be at one end of the spectrum or the other. At the entry level, security jobs can be minimum wage jobs, with minimal raises. "Middle management" positions are usually few in number. The money is in top management jobs, either for a corporation or for one's own business. At these levels there is literally no upward limit.

> As in law enforcement, promotions in private security may be scarcer than in other professions, particularly into middle management where positions are limited.

Those aspiring to become security managers must also possess critical technical and computer skills, as asserted by Wilson (2001, p.37):

> Security managers are no longer able to concern themselves solely with the physical access or perimeter security of a facility or campus. Today's security managers also must deal with securing a company's computer network, preventing e-mail viruses, restricting employee access to computer databases, and protecting and facilitating the flow of corporate information from facility to facility. Successful security professionals need to be able to incorporate traditional security skills with the IT skills now required.

CONCLUSION

Private security is the nation's primary protective resource today, outspending public law enforcement by more than 73 percent and employing nearly three times the workforce. The private security field is expected to grow rapidly through the year 2008, requiring the hiring of a large number of employees to meet the increasing security needs. A security job can serve as a stepping stone to other employment or a chance to obtain supplemental income as a second job or while attending school. Whether you seek employment in private security as a chance to acquire valuable training to help gain future employment in law enforcement or because the security field has exceptional future potential, private security can provide satisfying work.

ADDITIONAL CONTACTS AND SOURCES OF INFORMATION

ASIS International Customer Service
1625 Prince Street
Alexandria, VA 22314
(703) 519-6200
http://www.asisonline.org

National Association of Legal Investigators (NALI)
P.O. Box 905
Grand Blanc, MI 48439
http://www.nalionline.org

Professional Training Resources
P.O. Box 439
Shaftsbury, VT 05262
(802) 447-7832 or (800) 998-9400
 Publishes: *Cashing In on Consulting for the Private
    Security Professional*, by Jim R. Matison and
    Kären M. Hess, 1997.

 MIND STRETCHES

1.   Why do you think the entertainment field is obsessed with depicting private security? Do you think this obsession helps or hurts the profession? Why?

2.   Do you personally know any security officers? Are they like the private investigators depicted on television?

3.   What is your favorite private detective show? Why?

4.   Do you think television and the movies have influenced your career choice?

5.   Do you think security work will become more specialized or more generalized in the future? Why? How will your job goals be affected?

6.   What stereotype do you think private security officers have? Why? Is it justified?

7.   Why do you think the trend to license all professions exists? Do you think it is helpful?

8.   Are security salaries more or less than you had anticipated? Does salary affect your decision as to what field of employment you will eventually pursue? Why or why not?

9.   How do you predict the field of private security will change? Why?

INSIDERS' VIEWS

For this chapter, read the *Insiders' Views* by Robert B. Iannone, CPP ("Career Opportunities in Private Security"), and Marie Ohman ("The Changing Face of Private Security"), found on the Web site: http://www.wadsworth.com/criminaljustice_d/.

REFERENCES

Anderson, Teresa. "Putting Payday in Perspective." *Security Management*, Vol.45, No.9, September 2001, pp.66–71.

ASIS International. *Career Opportunities in Security*. Alexandria, VA: ASIS International, no date.

Bias, Bronson S. "Bright Employment Future." *ASIS Dynamics*, January/February 1999, pp.1, 9.

 "Comp and Circumstance: ASIS International 2000 Employment Survey." *2001 Security Industry Buyers Guide*, 2001, pp.ix–xii.

Hess, Kären M. and Wrobleski, Henry M. *Introduction to Private Security*, 4th ed. St. Paul, MN: West Publishing Company, 1996.

Levinson, Robert B. and Chase, Raymond. "Private Sector Involvement in Juvenile Justice." *Corrections Today*, April 2000, pp.156–159.

Matison, Jim R. and Hess, Kären M. *Cashing In on Consulting for the Private Security Professional*. Shaftsbury, VT: Professional Training Resources, 1997.

Occupational Outlook Handbook. 2000–2001 Edition. U.S. Department of Labor, Bureau of Labor Statistics, Washington, DC: U.S. Government Printing Office, 2000.

"Privatization Can Save Money in Prison Construction, Study Says." *Criminal Justice Newsletter*, May 25, 2001, pp.3–4.

The Top 100: The Fastest Growing Careers for the 21st Century. Chicago: Ferguson Publishing Company, 1998.

"2001 Salary Survey." Supplement to *Access Control and Security Systems Integration*, 2001, pp. S1–S7.

Weinstein, Bob. "Investigate the Job Prospects in Cyber-Crimefighting." (Minneapolis/St. Paul) *Star Tribune*, May 9, 1999, p. J1.

Wilson, Jeff M. "Money Matters." *Security Products*, May 2001, pp.36–40.

"Worldwide Security Services Demand Expected to Grow Through 2004." *Access Control and Security Systems Integration*, January 2001, p.8.

CHAPTER 5

ON CHOOSING A CAREER:
KNOWING THE JOB AND YOURSELF

People are always blaming their circumstances for what they are. I don't believe in circumstances. The people who get on in this world are the people who get up and look for the circumstances they want, and if they can't find them—make them.

—*George Bernard Shaw*

Do You Know:

➤   Why job satisfaction is so important?
➤   The best way to avoid job dissatisfaction?
➤   What the four steps of the career development process are?
➤   What specific requirements and limitations you should consider when choosing a career?
➤   How your background could prevent employment in the criminal justice or security fields?
➤   What an *inventurer* is? If you are one?
➤   What five essential parts of a dream job must be considered before it can become a reality?
➤   The importance of taking risks?

INTRODUCTION

Previous chapters discussed some realities of careers in criminal justice and security. As you consider these professions, understand what they are—and what they are *not*. Also, take a serious inventory of your abilities and interests to determine if your career goals are realistic.

In this chapter you'll combine knowledge about your chosen field with an honest look at yourself, to make certain you are, indeed, on a road that will take you where you want to be. How often would you get into your car and just drive with no thought of where you want to go? Yet many people launch themselves toward a career with very limited forethought—or with unrealistic dreams. Many job seekers have dreams—dreams of a successful career and a carefree, pleasurable lifestyle. However, as Leider and Shapiro (1996, p.94) state:

> The "perfect job" isn't really about enjoyment. Instead, it's one that mirrors perfectly the person who holds it. And people do find, or invent, or create these jobs. They do it by working a process . . . that links who you are with what you do. The process involves developing a clarity about your talents, passions, and values—looking inside yourself to discover what you do best, what you're interested in, and the type of working environment that supports what you care about most. And then combining all three to develop a clear vision of the kind of work that links who you are with what you do. . . .

> The perfect job isn't a standard of living. It's a state of mind and state of being. In the perfect job, you're applying the talents you enjoy most to an interest you're passionate about, in an environment that fits who you are and what you value.

The romanticized dream of a successful career becomes even more problematic when it involves the fields within criminal justice. Many people are intrigued by such employment because they want to be like the TV undercover police officer or private investigator they watch week after week. You must enter your career search with a much more open mind. Realistically, what *is* the job you are seeking?

SELECTING AND DEVELOPING A CAREER

Carelessly pursuing a career can be costly. First, selecting a career is extremely important because the vast majority of your waking hours will be spent working—why spend so much time being unhappy and unfulfilled? Perhaps even worse is that job frustrations may manifest themselves in unpleasant, if not dangerous, ways. People who dislike their work show it. For people employed by the criminal justice system, job dissatisfaction could seriously affect job performance. At best, they may appear as unfeeling individuals, expressing little concern for anyone, including victims. At worst, inappropriate physical force, even brutality, could be evidence of something going on "inside." Such behavior can result in nationwide anti-police publicity as seen in the beating of Rodney King.

> Career dissatisfaction can lead to unhappiness, negativity and cynicism in the individual and to a decrease in productivity and morale for the unit in which the individual works. The impact may be felt by co-workers and may affect their work attitude as well.

The best ways to prevent career dissatisfaction is to research the field carefully before applying for employment, ask questions of those already in the field, and carefully evaluate the positive and negative aspects of the occupation *as they apply to your values and expectations.* Rather than jumping into a career you know little about, including how well suited to it *you* are, look objectively at the whole picture. Consider the job. Consider yourself. Is it a "match"? Or is it the frustrating pursuit of a fantasy? There is a story about a woman who loved everything about being an engine mechanic—except getting dirty. Absolutely nothing could prevent her from leaving work each night grimy and greasy, and it was causing her to consider a career change. The simple fact was that an inherent part of her work was to get dirty. Determining whether getting dirty was worth it was an issue that had to be addressed.

Similarly, facts about working in criminal justice and private security must be faced. The relatively mediocre pay, difficult hours, odd days off, public's perception of the job, limited opportunity for promotions and inherent danger are issues that may make the job unacceptable to some. For other job seekers, this field remains attractive for reasons that go far beyond the motivations for other fields of work, including the desire to play a helping role in society, to have an exciting career or to have a job with significant power over others (good or bad). Take a realistic look at these issues now, examining why you want to work in this field and what your true expectations are.

> The best way to avoid career dissatisfaction is to thoroughly research the field you are interested in and to carefully and realistically address issues concerning the nature of the work, the hours, the pay—any and all positives *and* negatives. Go in with your eyes wide open, free from unrealistic expectations.

While this text is specifically directed at helping you develop your own job-seeking strategy, there is much more to the process than merely learning to write a resume. If you are not heading in a direction that will really work for you, your work will not be fulfilling.

Career counselors help people develop the ability to examine their motivations, a skill which applies to people seeking to enter a certain career as well as those considering getting out. Nathan and Hill (1992, p.2) view career counseling as a process that enables clients to become more aware of their own resources to lead a more satisfying life as well as to "take into account the interdependence of career and non-career considerations" (p.3). They cite the approach advocated by Parsons (1909) nearly a century ago:

> In the wise choice of vocation, there are three factors:
> 1. A clear understanding of yourself
> 2. A knowledge of the requirements and prospects in different lines of work
> 3. True reasoning on the relations of these two groups of facts

In Figure 5-1, Krannich (1995, p.100) illustrates how the first two factors are critical to career development. The next section of this book focuses on steps 3 and 4.

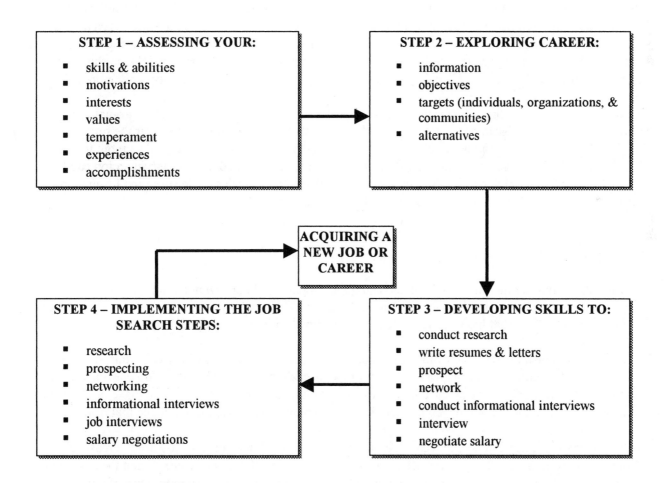

FIGURE 5-1   The Career Development Process

SOURCE: Ronald L. Krannich. *Change Your Job, Change Your Life.* 5th ed. Manassas Park, VA: Impact Publications, 1995, p.100. Reprinted by permission.

> Krannich identifies the four steps of the career development process as (1) self-assessment, (2) career exploration, (3) job search skill development and (4) implementation of the job search steps.

Interesting changes have occurred in what motivates job seekers. It is likely that as the baby boomers have become well-entrenched in the workforce, they have brought with them a degree of their "me-generation" mentality that includes a certain self-centeredness resulting in an expectation that everything should be perfect. . . at least for them! The question is, then, can work be . . . perfect?

Indeed, many Americans become encumbered by an ideal of the perfect job. But as Leider and Shapiro (p.93) note: "Every job has its good parts and its bad parts. It's hard to imagine any kind of work that would be enjoyable 100 percent of the time. Even sports heroes and movie stars have their bad days."

Unrealistic expectations of work may be a natural evolution of American society. Post-Depression work, followed by post–World War II work, really did help satisfy the American dream. The economy was strong and growing; opportunities were everywhere, and work itself provided so much to so many. Even as people expected more and more, the workplace was able to keep up . . . at least for a while. Increasing salaries, benefits and new types of jobs seemed limitless. But they weren't. And as time passed, jobs became more scarce, upward mobility more challenging and the seemingly "unlimited potential" noticeably more limited.

The world of work, including why people seek the jobs they do, has come back to where it arguably began: to provide for our more basic needs. Personal, perhaps selfish, needs take precedence over the broader things that work provides. The importance of the "whole person" in society has emerged as more important than the individual. The benefits a job directly provides is only one aspect of how satisfying a job can be. Now the important question that needs to be asked is whether a job provides the leisure time for individuals to achieve their goals beyond just being successful on the job.

Charting Your Future Course

It's difficult to consider the future without becoming philosophical. No one *knows* what the future will bring, so all you can do is speculate about what might occur. Of course, you can make some pretty darned good guesses based on what has occurred in the past combined with what is happening right now.

Here's what is known for sure: technology demands that successful job candidates have certain skill levels, and work affects your life to the degree that careful thought must be invested in future job considerations. The future of *your* work will be dictated by the decisions you make about it. Even if you make no decision and let yourself be blown about the job market like a tumbleweed, you have, indeed, made that decision.

Not only is the rapid development of technology influencing the working world, so too are the reasons people pursue certain jobs. The job you seek *does* influence how you feel about yourself and those around you. You must have a balance of interests and activities, a sense of identity, a realistic sense of your capabilities and reasonable goals for your life. It is also important to feel in control of your destiny. By examining yourself and your goals, together with a realistic idea of what expectations are truly important to you, you place yourself in control of your future.

One way to find out your true career interests *before* committing to a particular line of work is to volunteer with a potential employer, request a ride-along, or interview some officers or other employees. Visit agencies you think you'd like to work for and see what a typical workday is like. Local colleges and universities can often supply the names of recent grads working in your field. Call them to find out what they are doing and how they like it.

Career Counselors

A variety of tools exist to help you better understand your own aptitudes and interests. You are encouraged to take such interest inventories and aptitude tests to help highlight career areas that might satisfy your many needs. There may even be job options you have never heard about or considered. A great place to start is the counseling department at your school or career counselors in the private sector.

Messmer (1995, p.41) offers advice on selecting a counselor, beginning with the suggestion that "the most reliable way to choose a career counselor is to get a personal recommendation from someone whose opinion you trust." Other starting places include local schools and community organizations, where you may receive recommendations on qualified counselors. Once you've chosen a counselor, you should take the following steps to ensure you have picked the right person (p.41):

- Interview the counselor—Get a feel for how the counselor works. Don't be embarrassed to ask about fees and what you can reasonably expect. Trust your instincts. If anything about the counselor gives you the creeps (for example, a boa constrictor is sleeping on one of the office chairs), find someone else.

- Ask about the counselor's general approach—Find out how the counselor likes to work: whether the approach he or she uses relies heavily on testing or one-on-one interviewing and so forth. Don't be shy about asking what you can reasonably expect to derive from the overall experience. Ask for a description of the counselor's program—preferably in writing.

- Ask for references—You are a client buying a service and have rights to answers.

For more information about career counselors or a list of certified counselors in your area, contact one of the agencies listed at the end of this chapter.

Finally, don't overlook the resources readily at hand who already know you well: family and friends. Ask their opinions about what they think you'd be good at and whether they can see you in the work you're considering.

The steps to understanding yourself and your career goals have a beginning but never an end! Here's the beginning.

BRAINSTORMING POSSIBILITIES

Even if you are fairly certain about what you want to do with your life, it is worthwhile to consider other alternatives. These may be similar jobs, or they may be different altogether. Choices are what life is about, so start developing some.

Of all the exercises you will complete, this will be one of the easiest. Sit down with a clear mind and list in your journal the jobs that appeal to you. Don't analyze what you think you will or won't be qualified for. Simply write down the jobs that intrigue you.

> ➤   Do any general patterns emerge?
> ➤   Are the jobs you listed more in the service fields? The academic fields?
> ➤   Are they jobs which stress physical skills? Mental ability? Both equally?
> ➤   Do they stress working with people or alone? Indoors or outdoors?
> ➤   Why do you think you picked these jobs?

"JUST THE FACTS"

Having generated some career choices, next determine the facts about these alternatives.

> In deciding which career is best suited to you and your needs, you must consider age requirements, physical requirements, educational requirements, background limitations and experience requirements.

Age

A common question asked is "Am I too old" to consider law enforcement or criminal justice as a career? Frankly, a better question is "Am I too *young*?" More than ever, maturity is playing a very important part in who gets hired. Increased public scrutiny, increased liability concerns and the departure from the traditional paramilitary perspective make people with more life experience more attractive to employers.

Some jobs are better suited for young adults; others are ideal for retirees. Some positions, including certain law enforcement and security jobs, have age limitations. For example, most states require police officer recruits to be at least 21 years old. While the majority of policing jobs do not have an upward age limit for applicants, the federal system usually will not accept applicants older than 35. Some departments want very young recruits, while others may want more mature people.

Corrections and private security are open to an even greater variety of ages. On one hand, either field is exceptional for entry-level people seeking experience to help them eventually obtain jobs as police officers. On the other hand, corrections and security work can be great fields in their own right or ideal jobs for retired police officers or others.

Physical Requirements

The jobs you are interested in likely have physical requirements. Most agencies or companies set minimum vision and hearing requirements. One young man went through law school to be an FBI agent, only to learn later that his vision disqualified him from even taking the entrance test. Check with the agencies to find out what they require.

Most agencies want height and weight to be proportionate, even if they do not follow a specific chart. If you need to lose weight, start an exercise program now, preferably one you can continue throughout your career. An increasing number of agencies are requiring physical "stress tests" to assess candidates' vascular health. You can prepare for this by participating in a regular exercise program.

Most departments or companies will ask if you have any physical or health restrictions that will interfere with job performance. Be realistic with yourself and honest with the employer. While occasional back pain may not be a problem, an inability to lift heavy items might be. Various medical conditions will not necessarily eliminate you either. For instance, controllable diabetes should not be a problem for most jobs. Again, be honest with yourself and the employer regarding any health problems you have.

Education

Different states have different requirements regarding what schooling is needed. Similarly, different employers have different standards. Employers in either the private or public sectors may require at least a high school diploma or general equivalency diploma (GED). Some states, Minnesota for example, require at least two years of college. Some agencies, particularly in the federal system, may require graduate credits or even a graduate degree, such as a law degree.

The more education you have, the better. This can include specialized training such as first-aid courses, first-responder courses, CPR and the like. Knowing a foreign language, knowing how to "sign" to hearing-impaired people, having skills in photography—any specialized knowledge is likely to be a plus as you pursue your career. As one hiring agent for a law enforcement agency notes:

> When I receive job applications I place them into three piles: those with a high school education (minimum requirements); those with some college; and those with a bachelor's, master's or JD degree. I seldom, if ever, reach down into the pile of applications where the minimum requirement was the standard. Even if a person can get hired on just a high school diploma, the chances of advancement without at least some college are negligible. Yes, there are police departments out there that will hire a person with a high school diploma, but I don't think most people who are thinking in terms of a professional career want to work there.

According to the FBI's Web page, the agency is interested in people with the following backgrounds: law, accounting, foreign language and "generalist." Many believe getting a degree in a field besides criminal justice might "set them apart" from other applicants, since they will eventually learn what they need to know about being an officer by attending a police academy. However, the previously quoted hiring agent asserts:

> I believe there is a strong argument to be made for going ahead and getting that degree in criminal justice. First, not everybody going into criminal justice is going to be a cop and, therefore, will not go through an academy. Second, the training received at the academy is different than the education received at a college or university. Academies teach "how," whereas colleges teach "why." Both are needed to make a well-rounded criminal justice practitioner. Third, many students are going to end up in the private sector where they will need a criminal justice background in order to interface with the criminal justice system. Fourth, and finally, . . . would [you] go to an engineer if [you] needed brain surgery? As much as we are trying to make generalists out of our police officers these days, the skills, knowledge and abilities they need to do the job are not going to be picked up in a business college. Without a doubt, students in criminal justice need a strong background in liberal arts. . . , but a good solid core of criminal justice courses needs to be included in the student's/prospective employee's education.

It is further noted that a recent trend regarding hiring practices of the FBI and some other federal law enforcement agencies is to *not* hire students directly out of college, but rather to seek college graduates with two or three years of local law enforcement experience.

While it is possible to find an initial or entry-level job with the minimum-required high school diploma or some college courses, for those seeking promotions and other advancement, higher education becomes a "must have." According to Polk and Armstrong (2001, p.97): "Although the literature review revealed that there are inconclusive findings in prior studies about whether or not increased education caused an increase in the ability of law enforcement officers to perform their duties, this study showed no ambiguity in finding agencies are responding as if there are benefits if employees are more educated." From their research, Polk and Armstrong (p.97) conclude: "Those persons who hold higher levels of education, regardless of what other traits or personality characteristics they may possess, are more likely to hold higher rank and progress more quickly through their career path."

Background

Most private security companies, corrections facilities and certainly all law enforcement agencies will thoroughly investigate applicants' backgrounds. You should know what facts about your past will and won't affect your employment potential. Most police departments and security agencies will not accept an applicant with a felony conviction on their adult record. Depending on the nature of the crime, a misdemeanor may not automatically eliminate you. Be prepared to honestly explain the situation to the employer.

While it will be difficult to deal with any criminal record, it is much easier to explain a petty shoplifting charge when you were 18 than a conviction when you were 28. Unfortunately, some students make serious errors in judgment while studying to become police or security officers—errors that ruin their chances at a career in criminal justice. Act responsibly.

Traffic records, like lesser criminal records, may or may not be a hindrance. While they generally won't be grounds for automatic elimination from the application process, they will be strikes against you. Be up-front and honest about the circumstances. Many applicants make the mistake of saying they have no traffic record when, in fact, they do. It is easier to explain why you got a ticket 10 years ago than why you lied on your application. *Lying is justification to eliminate an applicant.* A traffic record may not be.

Juvenile records may also be a factor. Although the record may be sealed, an agency may likely find out about it during a background check. When police do a neighborhood check during the course of a background check, a neighbor may recall an incident involving the applicant and the police, where the applicant ended up leaving in the back seat of a patrol car.

Drug use is also considered. Experimental drug use within a year or so of applying may be cause for disqualification. Current drug use will most certainly eliminate you from the candidate pool.

Other situations need to be thought out honestly. Past counseling, or even institutionalization, may not be sufficient grounds for eliminating you from the running, but lying about it would be. Some agencies may be more likely to consider applicants who helped themselves by going through Alcoholics Anonymous or other self-help programs.

Most police departments and security agencies will not accept an applicant with a felony conviction on their adult record. A misdemeanor may not automatically eliminate you. Traffic records, like lesser criminal records, may or may not be a hindrance. Past counseling, or even institutionalization, may not be sufficient grounds for eliminating you from the running, but lying about it would be. *Always be honest* about such background circumstances.

Experience

Some agencies, such as the U.S. Bureau of Prisons and state probation and parole agencies, require previous experience in some related field. You should be aware of these requirements before applying for positions in these agencies. But remember, employers will be interested not only in direct experience (work similar to that you are applying for) but also "indirect" experience or *life experience*. Have you had some variety in your life, personally and professionally? Were you willing to take an entry-level job to work your way through school? Have you had jobs interacting with the public? Have you been enthusiastic enough to travel? Involved enough to participate in school activities and organizations? In other words, do you have some experience in life that contributes to you being unique enough to stand out from the competition? Experience is not just having held a job in that particular field; rather, it's the background you bring with you as an individual.

Develop a Positive Attitude

As Kennedy (1994, p.1E) advises:

> Recognize the things you cannot change. These include such things as you are out of work and need a job, and that you may be several inches shorter than you want to be. . . . Then recognize the things you can change. These include your attitude, your renewed vigor and your willingness to take a fresh look at what you really want to do.

Seeking employment can be frustrating. Be certain your attitude is not contributing to this frustration. Nathan and Hill (p.69) list several attitudes and beliefs that are often unconsciously held and may be self-defeating:

- I don't need anyone's help.
- "X" will sort it all out for me.
- I can't live on less than I earn now.
- It's undignified to have to promote yourself.
- Somewhere there's the perfect job.
- There's no point planning ahead when there's so much change afoot.
- Nobody will take me seriously.
- Life is so unfair to me.
- I won't be good enough.
- It's safer not to try than to risk failure.

- If I do well enough, Mum/Dad will love me.
- I'll fail.
- It's so competitive, I'd never get in.
- Everything will be okay when I get a new job.
- I can't change anything—I don't have any power.
- It's too late.
- If I wait long enough, things will change.
- I'm too old/young/overqualified/underqualified.
- Everyone else is better off than me.
- I can't help the way I am—it's just the way I'm made.

(Reproduced from Robert Nathan and Linda Hill, *Career Counseling*, p.69, copyright © 1992 by Sage Publications. Reprinted by permission of Sage Publications, Inc.)

WHAT DO YOU WANT FROM A CAREER?

A career is different from a job. A job is a short-term means to an end: money. High school and college students have jobs during the summer. People get jobs between careers to pay their bills. A career is more long-term, with more serious implications. Too many people find their jobs dull, laborious and repetitive—a necessity of life, like death and taxes. Most people are afraid to make changes—to take risks—and yet this is what is needed to be happy. One who risks nothing usually gains nothing.

Many people are trapped in jobs they dislike—even hate. This trapped feeling may be hard for younger job seekers to understand, especially those who are single. But as you get older, changing jobs becomes less attractive. The benefits associated with seniority—acquired sick time, vacation time, and preferential scheduling—can make it difficult to consider leaving an "old" job.

A primary reason people find themselves in a rut is that they fell into it. The deeper the rut, the easier it is to feel trapped. Rather than allowing yourself to fall into the job rut and become trapped, plan what you want out of life and then go after it. Nathan and Hill (p.129) describe several "career drivers" you may wish to consider:

- Material rewards—seeking possession, wealth and a high standard of living.
- Power and influence—seeking to be in control of people and resources.
- Search for meaning—seeking to do things believed to be valuable for their own sake.
- Expertise—seeking a high level of accomplishment in a specialised field.
- Creativity—seeking to innovate and be identified with original input.
- Affiliation—seeking nourishing relationships with others at work.
- Autonomy—seeking to be independent and make key decisions for oneself.
- Status—seeking to be recognised, admired and respected by the community at large.
- Security—seeking a solid and predictable future.

(Reproduced from Robert Nathan and Linda Hill, *Career Counseling*, p.129, copyright © 1992 by Sage Publications. Reprinted by permission of Sage Publications, Inc.)

In *The Inventurers*, Hagberg and Leider (1982, p.6) provide an "Excursion Map" to help people identify what is important to them and how to get there, thus enabling them to plan their own destiny rather than falling prey to a rut. They encourage readers to examine five important career issues (p.106).

 Take time to do so now. In your journal, record your answers to the following career issues:
  ➤ What are my present skills?
  ➤ What values are important to me?
  ➤ What lifestyle do I wish to lead?
  ➤ What work conditions are important to me?
  ➤ What interests do I have?

Take an introspective look at yourself and apply the information learned to answer this question: "Will this job allow me to get what I want from life?" By answering honestly, you are being an "inventurer, one of those special breed of people who take charge and create your own challenges to get yourself moving:"

You are an inventurer if you are willing to take a long look at yourself and consider new options, venture inward, and explore. You are an inventurer if you see life as a series of changes, changes as growth experiences, and growth as positive. You are inventuring on life's *excursions* and learning about yourself as a result. You may feel lonely at times, and get discouraged for a while. But you are willing to risk some disappointments and take some knocks in your quest because you are committed to a balanced lifestyle and to more than just making a living. You are part of a unique group of people who want to make a living at work. If you have these qualities, you are an inventurer.

Inventurers are people who choose to take a fresh look in the mirror to renew and perhaps recycle their lifestyle and careers. Some inventurers, seemingly snug in life and career patterns, are exploring their "greener pasture" . . . in search of their own personal Declaration of Independence: the pursuit of happiness. Other inventurers are planning second careers or early retirements. Some are underemployed and seeking careers more integrated with their abilities and lifestyle. They are female and male, old and young, and in between (Hagberg and Leider, pp.3–4).

According to Hagberg and Leider (p.6): "These inventurers prove what wise teachers have said for ages: *'The knowledge is right in us—all we have to do is clear our minds and open ourselves to see the obvious.'"*

Inventurers are people who take charge and create their own challenges to get themselves moving. They are willing to take a long look at themselves and consider new options, venture inward and explore. They see life as a series of changes, changes as growth experiences and growth as positive.

One important step is to look at what you love to do. As Mackay (1993, p.37) notes:

> Time and again I've observed that the people who stay happy and stimulated in careers for a lifetime are people who do what they love to do. George Allen was such a man. After retiring from coaching professional football for the Washington Redskins and the Los Angeles Rams, he became head coach for Long Beach State College. Was this a comedown from his glory days in the limelight? Hardly. George did it because he loved the young people and he loved coaching. When he died at the age of 72, the *Los Angeles Times* reported that he left several notes by his telephone. One note read:
>
> > 1) Win a championship.
> > 2) Have everybody graduate.
> > 3) Build a stadium.
> > 4) Then take a tough job.
>
> Do what you love and you'll never have to work a day in your life.

You might want to keep a "values journal" to help identify what is personally important and what is not. Write down how you spend your time. What problems do you encounter? What makes you happy, angry, sad, up, down? After keeping the journal for a while, review it, looking for patterns to such issues as the following:

➤ How do I, on an average day, generally spend my time?
➤ What are five or ten things that really interest me?
➤ What conflicts or problems do I have? Which ones did I create for myself, and which ones stemmed from outside factors?
➤ What short-range and long-range goals can I identify?
➤ What, ultimately, do I want to accomplish?

Also consider the "human equation" to answer the question, "How important is time with family and friends?" An involved family life may not be compatible with a career requiring 60-hour work weeks, a lot of traveling and hectic scheduling. Consider also where you want to live. Is climate important to you?

At this point in your self-inquiry, look at yourself and the world around you in relatively general terms. As you develop a sense of what is important to you, apply these ideas to the specific job choices that came out of the earlier brainstorming exercise. Ask: are my needs compatible with that particular job? Don't fool yourself. No one is watching to make certain you are honest. You will have only yourself to blame if you kid yourself now. Begin to apply some of your answers to the previous questions to the overall requirements of the jobs listed at the start of this chapter. Can you get what you need from the jobs that interest you? Consider the following:

➢ Am I old enough? Mature enough?
➢ Do I have a background that will prohibit me from any certain work?
➢ Am I healthy enough for such work?
➢ Does the job coincide with my personal values?
➢ Do I have the skills for this work?
➢ Will I be able to achieve my long-term goals (e.g., financial, promotional) through such work?
➢ Can my family goals be achieved with this job (considering such issues as travel and time commitments)?

Bolles (2001) encourages people to pursue their dream jobs, but realistically. According to Bolles, dreams about your "ideal work" have certain "essential parts" if they are to become realities.

 Consider each of these "essential parts" for your "ideal work" and record your responses:

➢ **Tasks**—What kinds of tasks, using what kinds of skills, do you see yourself doing? With what kind of style?
➢ **Tools or Means**—What do you need by way of information, things, or other people to be doing your ideal life's work?
➢ **Outcome**—What do you see your work producing, as its result? Immediately? Long-range?
➢ **Setting**—In what kind of setting do you see yourself working? "Setting" means both physical setting and also the invisible stuff: values and the like.
➢ **Compensation**—What kind of salary or other types of compensation do you want to have? What rewards do you hope your work will bring you?

Five essential parts for your ideal work are tasks, tools or means, outcome, setting and compensation. These parts must be considered if your dream job is to become a reality.

You might also consider taking an occupational preference test such as "Discovery II" to see how your interests and preferences match up with different occupations. Such tests are programmed so that computers can match your answers with answers given by representatives of different occupations. The computer compares your answers and indicates which occupational fields best match your interests.

MOVING TOWARD YOUR CAREER GOAL

Perhaps some jobs you considered in the brainstorming exercise were eliminated after you thought about what you need from a career to be fulfilled in life. Perhaps you are still considering whether the career field or a specific career is right for you.

Be honest in considering a career because, as stressed, the very nature of the work in many areas of criminal justice and security is disruptive to what many consider a "normal work routine." Scheduling; having days off in the middle of the week; working nights, holidays and weekends; seeing people at their worst; having your professionalism and honesty challenged in court—all are realities of the criminal justice and security fields. Also be aware of the areas on which the various levels of government are spending their resources. If you know you want to work in corrections but are unsure about where the majority of jobs are or how the payrolls compare, research the current available data.

In the final equation, do your goals, needs and desires balance with the realities of the job? Only you can make this determination. For example, if you were to enroll in an introductory course in law enforcement, where do you fit among the three groups of "typical" students enrolled in such classes?

➢ Students who have known since they were very young that they were destined to be police officers.
➢ Students who are considering the career, but have yet to make the commitment.
➢ Students who are fascinated by the subject, not the career.

If you have the chance to take an introductory course in law enforcement, corrections, private security or criminal justice, consider doing it. It's one good way to better understand what the careers involve and if they are right for you. Some students who have always wanted to go into law enforcement become troubled when they learn more about the field and begin to question whether or not it is right for them. This is an appropriate benefit of exposure to new knowledge and experiences, for it is far better to learn such things *before* you (and the agency that hires you) have spent the time and resources needed to get through the police academy. While many students end up feeling alone following this discovery, they are not. These fields are not for everyone.

Acquire What You Need

As you continue to assess whether your career goals are compatible with your needs and interests, you will also learn what else is required to get into the field. If you need college, register. If you need a physical fitness regime, begin one. If you need experience, get it.

As mentioned earlier, do some investigative research by visiting agencies and interviewing those working in the field(s) you are considering. Volunteer and get involved in short-term experiences with potential employers—step into the shoes and walk around in them for awhile to make sure they fit *before* you commit to buying them. Plodding along an uncharted path will get you, at best, nowhere, and at worst, somewhere you don't want to be. *NOW* is the time to develop your own realistic, exciting career map.

Internships

Internships are an excellent way to discover if a specific area of criminal justice is a good fit for you. An internship is an opportunity to receive supervised, practical, on-the-job training in a specific area. Many law enforcement agencies and correctional institutions offer internships, usually without pay, for those interested in learning about a specific area of employment while acquiring skills that make them more employable in that area. Often individuals who complete an internship with a specific police department are hired by that department when they have completed their formal education. Or, conversely, the intern or the department may find that the fit is not good and both are spared a difficult situation.

It is crucial for you to listen carefully to your internal responses to such internships. Many students ignore their reactions or discount their "gut feelings," writing off negative responses as merely a sign of their inexperience or their need to develop a tougher hide. Some students decide, in error, that the agency they interned with is not truly representative of the field as a whole—while the routine of their particular department seems boring, or the clientele is "yucky" and "rude," work in most other agencies is probably more exciting and the people are friendlier.

ALTERNATIVES

Look around and contemplate the almost infinite number of jobs that make up the criminal justice system and its related fields. It is truly amazing. Even if one job is not for you, another will be. Don't be afraid to change your mind, to take some risks. For many people, taking risks is more frightening than facing a gun. Facing a gun lasts only an instant—a wrong career choice lasts much longer!

Our culture does not encourage risk taking. Even during the 1960's and 70's, when a different cultural climate prevailed, a conservative work-ethic encouraged people to stay where they were. A successful career was often defined as a long career with one employer.

Then came a shift toward looking for a more satisfying career, which meant exploring work options and being open to changing employers and jobs. Even employers found benefits to hiring someone who had worked elsewhere. Rather than someone asking, "Why did you change jobs?" employees began wondering why someone didn't.

Today, change has become a fact of life in the world of work. Regardless of whether you ever want to change jobs, it is likely you will have to at some point. Change *is* intimidating. But stagnation is even more frightening. The greatest hazard in life is to risk nothing. It has often been said: "Those who risk nothing, do nothing, have nothing, are nothing." Don't let it be engraved on your headstone, *Here lies John Doe, his potential fully intact.*

> Risk-taking is important because it exposes you to challenges and prevents you from getting stuck in a rut. Ruts lead to stagnation, which leads to job dissatisfaction and other adverse effects.

A certain amount of risk taking is important because it exposes you to challenges, keeps you flexible and prevents personal and professional stagnation, which can lead to job dissatisfaction and burnout, which in turn affects one's personal life. As world-renowned counseling expert Richard Obershaw succinctly puts it, "A rut is a grave with the ends knocked out."

TO RISK OR NOT TO RISK—THAT IS THE QUESTION

Like everything else, risk carries with it a certain amount of . . . well, risk. Change is all well and good, but there isn't always a rainbow at the end of every trail. Particularly now, when job security isn't guaranteed, maintaining a job that meets your needs may prove to be every bit as important, if not more so, as leaving for the sake of leaving, or changing just for the sake of change. While staying in a job that makes you miserable and negatively affects all other aspects of your life makes no sense, leaving a secure job "just because" may not either.

In the first place, "dream jobs" often do not live up to the fantasy. A friend recently shared that his newly acquired dream job, one he'd worked all his career to achieve, was now ruining his life because of the associated demands and stress. Also, life has no guarantees. A colleague who quit a 17-year successful job to take a "calculated risk" with a startup venture found himself out of the new job after only three months because of the precarious financial times. In addition, it is wise to stay with a job for at least a minimum length of time to give yourself a chance to acclimate to a new environment and to avoid being thought of as a "job hopper."

Who Moved My Cheese? is a best seller about how people respond and react to change. You are encouraged to get this book and read it now, and reread it from time to time. It's straightforward and whimsical but sends a powerful message: whether you intend to change or not, you will find yourself confronting change, and so your strategy for dealing with it becomes as important as other life strategies you develop.

Is change always worth it? Probably not. Is change always an option? Absolutely! And it's nice to have options.

GET GOING!

An effective exercise for motivating yourself to change is the "last day of my life" test. Bolles suggests that you consider the statement "Before I die, I want to . . . ." and then list the things you would like to do before you die. Or write on the topic: "On the last day of my life, what must I have done or been so that my life will have been satisfying to me?"

 As the concluding exercise in this chapter, take time to write your feelings on one of these two topics.

Picking Daisies

If I had my life to live all over again, I would pick more Daisies.
If I had my life to live over, I would try to make more mistakes next time.
I would be sillier than I have been this trip.
I would relax. I would limber up.

I know very few things I would take seriously. I would be crazier;
I would be less hygienic; I would take more chances;
I would take more trips, I would climb more mountains,
Swim more rivers, and watch more sunsets.
I would burn more gasoline. I would eat more ice cream and less meals.

I would have more actual troubles, and fewer imaginary ones.
You see, I am one of those people who lives prophylactically
and sensibly and sanely, hour after hour, day after day.
Oh, I have had my mad moments, and if I had it to do all over again,
I would have more of them; in fact, I'd try to have nothing else,
just moments, one after another, instead of living so many years ahead.

I have been one of those people who never go anywhere without a thermometer,
a hot-water bottle, a gargle, a raincoat and a parachute.
If I had it to live all over again I would go places and travel lighter than I have.
If I had my life to live over again, I would start barefoot earlier in the spring,
and stay that way later in the fall. I would play hookey more,
I would ride on more merry-go-rounds. I'd pick more Daisies.

IT'S JUST A JOB . . .

Work and careers. Unquestionably important. But it is critical to bear in mind that this is only *part* of the balance that makes up anyone's life. Exploring careers should be an ongoing process that focuses on the questions: what am I doing now, and what do I want to do in the future? No law says you must stay in the same job or career forever. In fact, it's a crime when people do so to the detriment of themselves and their families, who then become casualties of the effects of work. And yet many people elect to stay in a job that is, quite literally, killing them.

This may sound extreme to a young person looking toward a career that can be as exciting as criminal justice. But things change, and so do priorities. It always pays to look ahead while assessing what's going on at the moment. Be prepared for change. It's going to happen. Control it, rather than letting it control you.

CONCLUSION

It is important to think carefully about what career you'd like to pursue *before* you jump into it. A hasty decision, or one based on rumor or television portrayals, will likely lead to disappointment and dissatisfaction. The four steps that comprise the career development process are (1) self-assessment, (2) career exploration, (3) job search skill development and (4) implementation of the job search steps. The first two steps are very important. In deciding which career is best suited to you and your needs, you *must* assess yourself and how your abilities and needs compare to the demands of the job.

Risk-taking is important because it exposes you to challenges and prevents you from getting stuck in a rut, which could lead to stagnation and job dissatisfaction. Become an *inventurer,* someone who takes charge and creates their own challenges to get themselves moving. Be willing to take a long look at yourself and consider new options. Venture inward and explore. See life as a series of changes, changes as growth experiences and growth as positive.

ADDITIONAL CONTACTS AND SOURCES OF INFORMATION

National Board of Certified Counselors (NBCC)
3 Terrace Way, Suite D
Greensboro, NC 27403
(910) 547-0607

National Career Development Association (NCDA)
5999 Stevenson Avenue
Alexandria, VA 22304
(703) 823-9800

? MIND STRETCHES

1.   What is your strategy for identifying a career path? Do you know anyone who just "floated along" whichever way the current carried them? Are they happy? Why or why not?

2.   Do you think American workers are cynical? Why?

3.   How important is job security to you? Can you see it changing in five years? Ten years?

4.   How important is money to you? Will you be satisfied with an officer's pay? Can you see this need changing for you?

5.   Have you ever worked nights, holidays or weekends? What can you imagine would be good about such a schedule? Bad?

6.   What prevents people from accepting change? What keeps people from taking risks? Why do you think many people stick with a less-than-satisfactory job?

7.   What five jobs within the criminal justice field interest you? Why? What jobs in the field do not appeal to you? Why?

8.   What elements of your personal history might be negative factors in pursuing your career goals? How can you deal with these at the interview?

9.   Why do you think more people don't take an active role in their career choices?

10.   What are the five most important things you will consider when selecting a job? Are these under your control?

INSIDERS' VIEWS

For this chapter, read the *Insiders' Views* by Bill B. Green ("The Private Security Alternative") and Kenneth S. Trump ("Searching Outside the 'Box' "), found on the Web site: http://www.wadsworth.com/criminaljustice_d/.

REFERENCES

Bolles, Richard Nelson. *The 2001 What Color Is Your Parachute? A Practical Manual for Job-Hunters & Career-Changers.* Berkeley, CA: Ten Speed Press, 2001.

Hagberg, Janet and Leider, Richard J. *The Inventurers: Excursions in Life and Career Renewal.* Reading, MA: Addison-Wesley Publishing Company, 1982.

Kennedy, Joyce Lain. "Going Back to the Basics Can Help Job Seekers of Any Age." (Minneapolis/St. Paul) *Star Tribune,* November 13, 1994, p.1E.

Krannich, Ronald L. *Change Your Job, Change Your Life,* 5th ed. Manassas Park, VA: Impact Publications, 1995.

Lande, Nathaniel. "Picking Daisies." *Mindstyles/Lifestyles.* Los Angeles: Price Stern Sloan, Inc., 1976.

Leider, Richard J. and Shapiro, David A. *Repacking Your Bags: Lighten Your Load for the Rest of Your Life.* San Francisco: Berrett-Koehler Publishers, 1996.

Mackay, Harvey. "Perfectly Positioned." *Successful Meetings,* February 1993, p.37.

Messmer, Max. *Job Hunting for Dummies.* Foster City, CA: IDG Books Worldwide, Inc., 1995.

Nathan, Robert and Hill, Linda. *Career Counseling.* Newbury Park, CA: Sage Publications, 1992.

Parsons, F. *Choosing a Vocation.* Boston, MA: Houghton-Mifflin, 1909.

Polk, O. Elmer and Armstrong, David A. "Higher Education and Law Enforcement Career Paths: Is the Road to Success Paved by Degree?" *Journal of Criminal Justice Education,* Spring 2001, pp.77–99.

SECTION TWO

MEETING THE CHALLENGE: PREPARING

Even if you are on the right track, you'll still get run over if you just sit there.

—Will Rogers

Most people don't plan to fail—they fail to plan.

—Anonymous

Before everything else, getting ready is the secret of success.

—Henry Ford

For every officer who is hired, there are 250 applicants who are not. The secret to accomplishing your dream comes down to one objective—preparation.

—Larry R. Frerkes

The normal process in seeking a job is to find where job openings exist, apply, submit a resume, undergo various kinds of testing, be interviewed and be hired! This section does not follow that order. Rather, it asks you to continue doing what you began in Chapter 5—looking at your own qualities, experiences and preferences and seeing how they fit with what criminal justice agencies and security departments are looking for. It also suggests ways to overcome any shortcomings you might find as you consider yourself in relation to the job requirements. This should be done *before* you actually begin looking for specific jobs. This section is written as though you were already actively engaged in testing and interviewing.

You'll begin by looking at the physical requirements of these fields and what tests you might have to pass (Chapter 6). One of the most important attributes of successful candidates is physical fitness—which doesn't happen overnight. Next you'll look at the educational and psychological requirements that might be considered and how they might be tested (Chapter 7).

This is followed by a discussion of the "beneficial attributes" of successful candidates in these fields, that is, who is most likely to be hired (Chapter 8), giving you a chance to realistically assess what attributes *you* have and how you might fare. The next chapter discusses how you can assemble the information you have collected about yourself thus far into that all-important document—your resume (Chapter 9). The section concludes with a critical part of the job hunting process—being prepared for rejection (Chapter 10). Each rejection must be seen as a learning situation, a chance to become better at presenting yourself and as being one step closer to that job you *will* eventually get.

These chapters should be reread at appropriate times during your actual job hunt. For example, if you are scheduled for a physical fitness test, reread Chapter 6 a few days before. If you don't even make it to the testing stage, reread Chapter 10. When you're ready, move on to Section Three, which presents specific job-seeking strategies to enhance your chances of getting a job in your chosen field.

CHAPTER 6

PHYSICAL FITNESS AND TESTING

Good physical condition not only adds years to your life, but life to your years.

—*Anonymous*

Do You Know:

➢ Why physical fitness is crucial for police, corrections or security officers?
➢ Why it is difficult for people in these fields to stay in shape?
➢ What five parameters are generally considered in evaluating physical fitness?
➢ What four things most physical fitness tests seek to measure?
➢ What three areas are of critical importance during the medical examination and what other tests might be conducted?
➢ What impact the ADA has had on medical examinations and inquiries about disabilities?
➢ How fitness and stress interrelate?
➢ How personality and stress interrelate?
➢ Why proper nutrition is important?
➢ What proportion of deaths in this country each year are due to an unhealthy lifestyle?

INTRODUCTION

One of the most critical criteria for obtaining a job in criminal justice, security and related areas is physical fitness. The importance of having physically fit personnel goes without saying. The job demands that those who pursue employment in these fields enter such work in shape and *remain* in shape. The work is physically and emotionally demanding and can lead to enormous amounts of stress. According to Blum (2000, p.13): "More than 2000 officers have heart attacks and die each year in the line of duty." Staying physically fit can help mitigate the negative impacts of such stress. Furthermore, as noted by Schultz and Acevedo (2000, p.34): "Individual officer fitness . . . can have a tremendous impact on how well a department functions. Studies have consistently demonstrated that healthy and fit officers improve work productivity, lower absenteeism rates, and reduce health risks."

Fitness can become a legal issue too. The people and property you are paid to protect will depend on your being able to do your job. If you cannot, you could be sued. In *Parker v. The District of Columbia* (1988), the jury awarded $425,046 to a man shot by a police officer who was arresting him. As part of the case, the court noted: "Officer Hayes simply was not in adequate physical shape. This condition posed a foreseeable risk of harm to others." Oldham (2001, p.77) notes: "Recent studies indicate officers who are in good physical condition are involved in far fewer uses of force than other, less fit officers." According to Heiskell (1996, p.33):

> Law enforcement requires a high degree of physical and mental fitness. The demands of a busy shift can be both mentally and physically exhausting. Physical fitness requires planning and regular exercise. Being physically fit means that you will not only be prepared for your busy shift, but will look and feel better, too.

Your future, your very life, may depend on your level of fitness. As noted by Slahor (1990, p.55): "The FBI emphasizes that physical fitness is 'often the factor that spells the difference between success and failure—even life and death.'" How much more important can it be?

Your future in criminal justice or security, your very life and the lives of the civilians you've sworn to protect depend on your physical fitness. Being "out of shape" can even become a legal issue.

As noted, these professions, while appearing to be full of exciting chases and confrontations, are more likely to consist of extended periods of idle waiting, punctuated by immediate demands for extreme activity. A shift, or maybe even an entire week, may go by without anything exciting occurring. Suddenly, you may be called on to exercise almost super-human strength—to drag a victim from a burning car, to carry a heart-attack victim from an upper-level apartment, to assist in carrying fire-fighting equipment up the stairs of a high-rise, or to fight for your life with a physically fit, drug-crazed criminal.

What is particularly critical about physical fitness for criminal justice and security personnel is that the nature of their jobs can actually contribute to keeping them *out* of shape. Most of these jobs involve a significant amount of inactivity. For example, sitting at a desk or driving all day provides little exercise. Combine this with odd working hours—often when only fast-food restaurants are open—and it becomes easy to understand why the stereotype of police, corrections and security officers is that of being overweight and out of shape.

Commenting on how the nature of police work often contributes to lack of fitness, Hoffman and Collingwood (1996, p.17) report: "Mortality statistics suggest that police officers have increased risk of premature death and may have a special vulnerability for certain diseases. Most studies indicate that officers die at earlier ages than expected for the general population for all causes of death, and in particular for diabetes, colon cancer, and cardiovascular disease." Strandberg (1997, p.38) adds: "There is a great disparity between the longevity in civilian population and in law enforcement. The average American male lives to be 72 years old, while the average law enforcement officer lives to be 59.5."

The very nature of police and security jobs can contribute a great deal to officers being out of shape. The often-sedentary duties, such as driving a car or sitting at a desk, and the need to eat quick meals on the go—often fast food high in calories and fat—all contribute to the deterioration of physical fitness.

Ignoring physical fitness is little different than carrying a malfunctioning gun or driving a defective squad car. It could kill you. Employers know it is a challenge to keep their officers in shape. It is difficult for everyone to keep in shape as the years pass. This is good reason for employers to seek applicants who are physically fit.

Think about what being physically fit says about you to an employer. It says you are concerned about yourself. It also says you can project a positive image of the agency or institution you represent. For obvious reasons, employers do not want employees who would make their agency or institution look bad.

WHAT IS FITNESS?

Fitness refers to a person's physical well-being or, to use the popular phrase, to being "in shape." Blum (pp.12–13) notes:

> Fitness is generally defined as the ability to carry out daily physical tasks or leisurely pursuits with vigor and alertness, but without undue fatigue. Fitness may also refer to individual, but measurable levels of ability when completing physically demanding tasks associated with aerobic (running) and muscular (bench press, sit ups) events. Wellness can be defined as a lifestyle encompassing health related habits to include proper nutrition, smoking cessation, cholesterol awareness, regular exercise, and stress reduction efforts. For example, heart disease is directly related to lifestyle wellness behaviors. It has become the number one killer of adult men and women, surpassing all types of cancer.

Frerkes (1998, p.54) lists five specific elements needed to make a well-balanced, comprehensive testing program:

➢ Cardiorespiratory endurance or aerobic capacity, measured by a 1.5-mile run
➢ Abdominal and lower back strength, measured by sit-ups
➢ Muscular strength and endurance, measured by push-ups
➢ Flexibility, measured by a controlled sit and reach test
➢ Body composition, or percentage of body fat

Physical fitness is being "in shape" and is often evaluated using five general parameters: cardiorespiratory endurance or aerobic capacity, abdominal and lower back strength, muscular strength and endurance, flexibility and body composition.

Regarding body composition, the trend is to look at the amount of body fat rather than weight as compared to height. The generally accepted percentage of fat for males is 14 to 16 percent of total body weight; for females, between 23 and 26 percent of body weight.

PHYSICAL FITNESS TESTING

Most candidates may undergo some sort of physical fitness testing. The test may take the form of maneuvering through an obstacle course within a set time limit. Marlowe (1995, p.14) notes the growing use of physical ability testing programs in applicant selection, such as the content-valid physical ability test developed by Stanard and Associates, Inc. (S&A), a nationwide public safety testing firm. According to Marlowe: "The job analysis process determined that the physical ability test should include such critical activities as crawling under low obstacles such as a porch, dragging an unconscious or uncooperative person a short distance, climbing through a window, sprinting to chase a suspect, and climbing stairs such as those commonly found in office and apartment buildings."

Pilant (1995, p.87) explains the significance of *content validity* in such tests: "The content of the test is the same as that specified by the job. For example, if an officer typically has to climb a 6-foot fence during foot pursuits, then the test would measure the officer's ability to climb a 6-foot fence." According to Pilant (p.88):

Fitness-standard testing, which has been found to be predictive of an officer's ability to perform [basic officer tasks], includes the following:

- Aerobic power/endurance (1.5-mile or 12-minute run): Pursuit tasks, use of force lasting one to two minutes.
- Anaerobic power (300-meter run): Sprints, use of force, any short intense burst of effort lasting less than 30 seconds to one minute.
- Absolute strength (1RM bench and leg press): Lifting, carrying, pushing and dragging heavy objects.
- Dynamic strength (one-minute sit-up and push-up): Use of force, lifting, carrying, dragging, pushing.
- Body composition (percentage of fat): Short and long pursuits, use of force, lifting, carrying. (. . . this test is not a strong predictor of fitness for duty. It has more recently been used as an appearance issue, not for making hiring or firing judgements.)
- Flexibility (sit and reach): Lifting, carrying, bending, pursuit with obstacles.

The Criminal Justice Institute at Broward Community College in Ft. Lauderdale, Florida, for example, uses the following physical agility obstacle course:

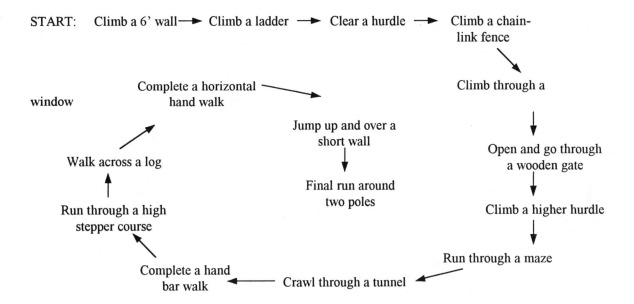

The Institute also tests strength and endurance using the following tests:

- Trigger pull (strong hand 18, weak hand 12)
- 10 push-ups
- Standing jump
- Vehicle push (20 feet, push from rear of vehicle)
- 3 pull-ups (from dead hang, palms facing away)
- ½-mile run (5 minutes maximum time)

Candidates who cannot perform up to the minimum standards are disqualified. The goal of most candidates is to "max out," giving them an edge over less physically fit candidates.

Another approach used by some departments is having candidates perform "events," such as a Back Yard Pursuit, a Stretcher Carry, a Body Drag and a 300-Yard Sprint.

> A wide variety of physical fitness tests may be administered, but they are all likely to measure the same things: endurance, agility, flexibility and strength.

Most police departments, correctional institutions or businesses hiring security personnel require that job applicants have a medical examination as well as a physical test of some sort to be certain they are physically fit.

THE MEDICAL EXAMINATION

Three areas of critical importance during the medical examination are vision, hearing and the condition of the cardiovascular-respiratory system. The vision test may include a test for colorblindness. Most agencies will accept applicants who have *corrected* vision and hearing problems, that is those who wear a hearing aid and/or eye glasses or contact lenses or who have had laser eye surgery. If you think you may have problems in any of these areas, get checked out before you apply for a position.

The cardiovascular and respiratory systems play a critical role in fitness. To a large extent endurance, the ability to continue exertion over a prolonged time, is directly related to the ability of the cardiovascular-respiratory system to deliver oxygen to the muscles.

The medical exam may also include tests for determining blood pressure, smoking status, drug use, blood sugar level (for diabetes) and the ratio of total cholesterol to HDL cholesterol (to identify cardiovascular risk factors). If a physician finds that you have a functional or organic disorder, the recommendation may be made to disqualify you.

> Three areas of critical importance during the medical examination are vision, hearing and the condition of the cardiovascular-respiratory system. The medical exam may also include a cholesterol check, blood pressure check, inquiries about smoking status or lung capacity checks, drug tests and blood sugar level check for diabetes.

The use of medical examinations in hiring is governed by the Americans with Disabilities Act (ADA). According to Rubin (1995, p.114):

> The Americans with Disabilities Act (ADA) is the most sweeping civil rights legislation enacted in the past 30 years. Inspired by a desire to integrate more than 43 million individuals with disabilities into the mainstream, this law affects virtually every segment of society. . . . The ADA has significant consequences on how corrections [and every other employer] hires personnel. The ADA prohibits administering medical exams or conducting any disability-related inquiries *prior to extending a conditional offer of employment* [italics added].

> The Americans with Disabilities Act (ADA) prohibits medical examinations or inquiries regarding mental or physical problems or disabilities *before* a conditional offer of employment has been made.

In other words, the employer makes the candidate a job offer provided the candidate passes the medical examination.

SELF-ASSESSMENT

It is important that you know how physically fit you really are. Just because you feel good does not necessarily mean that you are "in shape." The FBI's publication *Physical Fitness for Law Enforcement Officers* recommends the following:

- Feel your arms, shoulders, stomach, buttocks and legs. Are your muscles well-toned or are you soft and flabby?
- Give yourself the pinch test. Take hold of the skin just above your belt. Are your fingers separated by more than one-half inch?

This publication describes cardiovascular, balance, flexibility, agility, strength and power tests to assess your physical fitness. Their descriptions follow.

Cardiovascular Tests

Cureton's Breath-Holding Test. One simple way to test your respiratory capacity is to step onto and off a chair, bench or stool (approximately 17 inches high) for a period of one minute and then see how long you can hold your breath. You should be able to hold it for at least 30 seconds. If you can't, it indicates your cardiovascular function has deteriorated below a desirable level.

Kasch Pulse Recovery Test (3 min.). This test can be performed at almost any age. Only the infirm or the extremely unfit would find it too strenuous. You should not smoke for one hour or eat for two hours before taking the test. Also, rest for five minutes before taking the test.

EQUIPMENT
12" bench or stool
Clock or watch with a sweep second hand

PROCEDURE
a) Start stepping onto and off the bench when sweep second hand is at 11.
b) Step 24 times per minute, total 72.
c) Duration is three minutes.
d) Stop stepping when sweep second hand is again at 11, after three revolutions, and sit down.
e) Start counting the pulse rate when sweep second hand reaches 12 on the clock, using either the artery located inside the wrist or the carotid artery in the throat. Count every 10 seconds and record for one minute.
f) Total the six pulse counts for one minute and compare with the following scale:

Classification	0–1 Minute Pulse Rate after Exercise
Excellent	71–78
Very Good	79–83
Average	84–99
Below Average	100–107
Poor	108–118

Cooper's 12-Minute Walk/Run Test. Find a place where you can run/walk a measured distance of up to two miles. A quarter-mile track at a local school would be ideal; however, a nearby park, field or quiet stretch of road can be used. The test is quite simple—see how much of the two miles you can comfortably cover in 12 minutes. Try to run the entire time at a pace you can maintain without excessive strain. If your breath becomes short, walk until it returns to normal, then run again. Keep going for a full 12 minutes; then check your performance on the following scale:

Fitness Category (under age 30)	Distance Covered in 12 Minutes (in miles)
Very Poor	less than 1.0
Poor	1.00–1.24
Fair	1.25–1.49
Good	1.50–1.74
Excellent	1.75 +

(*NOTE*: People over age 30 should not take this test until they have had a complete medical examination and have completed approximately six weeks in a "starter physical fitness program.")

Balance Test

Stand on your toes, heels together, eyes closed, and your arms stretched forward at shoulder level. Maintain this position for 20 seconds without shifting your feet or opening your eyes.

Flexibility Tests

Trunk Flexion. Keep your legs together, your knees locked, bend at the waist and touch the floor with your fingers.

Trunk Extension. Lie flat on your stomach, face down, fingers laced behind your neck and your feet anchored to the floor. Now raise your chin until it is 18 inches off the floor. (Note: Average for male students at the University of Illinois is 12.5 inches.)

Agility Test

Squat Thrusts. Standing, drop down to squatting position, palms flat against floor, arms straight. Next, with weight supported on the hands, kick backward so that your legs are extended fully. Immediately kick forward to the squatting position and stand up. You should be able to perform four in eight seconds.

Strength Tests

Pull-ups. Hang from a bar, hands slightly wider than shoulders, palms turned away, arms fully extended. Pull up until your chin is over the bar. Lower yourself until your arms are fully extended and repeat. You should be able to perform four pull-ups.

Push-ups. From the front leaning rest position, hands slightly wider than the shoulders with fingers pointed straight ahead, lower your body until your chest barely touches the floor. Push up to the front leaning rest position, keeping your body straight. Standards from the Institute for Aerobics Research for push-ups done in one minute are:

> 60 and up, superior;
> 50–59, excellent;
> 35–49, good;
> 25–34, average;
> 18–24, below average; and
> 17 or less, poor.

Sit-ups. Lie on your back with your hands behind your neck, with your legs straight and free. Flex the trunk and sit up, and then return to the starting position. Standards from the Institute for Aerobics Research for sit-ups done in one minute are:

> 49 and up, superior;
> 46–48, excellent;
> 42–45, good;
> 40–41, average;
> 33–39, below average; and
> 32 or less, poor.

Power Tests

Standing Broad Jump. From a standing position, jump as far forward as you can, landing on both feet. Do not take a running start. The length of your jump should equal your height.

Vertical Jump. Stand facing a wall, feet and chin touching the wall, arms extended over your head. Using chalk, mark the height of your hands on the wall. Now jump up and touch the wall as high as you can with one hand. (Again, use chalk.) Note the difference between the two marks on the wall. You should be able to perform a vertical jump of 18 inches or more.

Even if you successfully pass all these tests, be sure you remain in good physical shape. Your lifestyle may be such that you do not require a formal physical fitness program. Many people who are active in sports such as swimming, tennis, jogging or running do not need to do much more to keep in shape. If, however, you have a relatively sedentary lifestyle, you may want to start a basic physical fitness program.

A BASIC PHYSICAL FITNESS PROGRAM

As noted by Hoffman (1993, p.25): "The majority of police work is done with a pad, pencil and radio, until the lid comes off and hell breaks loose, at which time the officer may need the physical attributes of an athlete to survive." Fay, a certified public safety physical fitness specialist and the program coordinator of the New York City Police Department's Cardiovascular Fitness Unit (1994, p.22), suggests this plan:

An exercise regimen which is time efficient, job specific, and physically sound can be completed in less than one hour. Begin with a two to three minute *warm-up* of mild walking, jogging or biking to prepare the heart and skeletal muscles for more vigorous activity. Three to five minutes of stretching exercises, emphasizing the lower back and hamstring regions will promote maintenance of good flexibility.

Twenty to 30 minutes of *aerobic training* using either treadmill, stair stepper, rowing and cross-country ski machines will reduce stress, improve body composition (weight loss), and strengthen the cardiovascular system. This should be followed by 15 to 20 minutes of *weight training and/or calisthenics* to develop upper body muscular strength and endurance. The abdomen and lower back regions are particular areas of concern and should not be neglected. Conclude with a five-minute *cool down* period of exercise of diminishing intensity, light stretching, adequate hydration and general relaxation.

Regular program adherence (three to five times per week) can have a significant impact on an officer's physical and emotional health as well as job performance.

An exercise program should start gradually and then build up. Oldham (p.76) suggests: "Walking is one of the easiest and most beneficial of all cardiovascular exercises. Recent studies have found little difference between walking and running." You should exercise at least three times a week. As you progress into your fitness program, you can increase the number of weekly workouts. Numerous books and articles outline fitness programs. Find one that suits you.

Tips

The following tips on exercising might be considered:

➢ Exercise to music.
➢ Vary your exercises to give yourself some variety.
➢ Drink water during your breaks.
➢ Plan your program to easily fit your daily routine. Exercise at the same time each day.
➢ Start small and work up to a full regime gradually to reduce your chance of injury.
➢ Record your efforts.
➢ Do not expect immediate benefits. It takes regular, long-term effort.
➢ Wait 10 minutes after your cool-down to take a warm shower. *A hot or cold shower can dangerously affect your blood pressure.*
➢ If you stop exercising for a while—even a week or two—start at a lower level and gradually work your way up again.

(*NOTE:* Never pursue an exercise program without consulting with your physician.)

Sticking to Your Fitness Program

We are creatures of habit. And if your previous habit has been to skip the bike ride in favor of watching highlights of the Tour de France from the comfort of your sofa, you may find it difficult to stick to a fitness program. Creating a new habit, no matter how beneficial to you, takes a sustained effort. The key to long-term success with an exercise routine is to stay motivated. Rod Dishman, Ph.D., director of the exercise psychology laboratory at the University of Georgia offers five strategies to keep your fitness program afloat (Kallen, 2001, p.72):

1. Give yourself plenty of support. Work out with an encouraging partner, join an exercise group, or frequently remind yourself that putting time and effort into your exercise program is worthwhile.

2. Tell yourself you're getting benefits beyond a better-looking body. Keep in mind that regular workouts help you feel better about yourself, reduce stress, help you sleep, and improve your overall health.

3. Set both idealistic long-term goals—so you'll have something to look forward to—and flexible short-term goals that will help you chart your progress without demanding too much from yourself.

4. Put your workouts into your weekly schedule, and stick to them just as you would any social engagement or business appointment.

5. Offer yourself extra rewards by arranging to do things you enjoy, but only after you've had your workout.

Exercise is a powerful tool in managing stress, a common element of employment in the criminal justice and security fields.

FITNESS AND STRESS

Careers in criminal justice and security can be highly stressful—and so can seeking employment in these fields. An important part of being physically and mentally fit is managing stress.

> Physically fit bodies are better able to cope with stress, and stress is abundant in the professions of criminal justice and private security. Keep fit to ward off stress.

Some personality types tend to be more susceptible to stress, particularly those identified as *Type A*:

> Individuals with a Type A personality typically speak and move rapidly, hold feelings in, have few outside interests, are precise and numbers-oriented, find it difficult to relax, are excessively time conscious, seek approval from others, are usually engaged in multiple tasks with impossible deadlines and are continually hurried and overscheduled. Due to the release of artery-damaging stress hormones associated with Type A behavior, the greatest health risk of having a Type A personality is heart disease. . . .
>
> Current research indicates that the Type A personality traits most responsible for increased heart disease risk may be hostility and anger (Hawks et al. 1989, p.49).

If you are a Type A personality, which many people drawn to criminal justice and security are, be aware of these risks. Exercise and relaxation techniques can help reduce them.

> People with Type A personalities are more susceptible to stress and are at increased risk for heart disease. It is vital for such people to learn and use exercise and relaxation techniques.

In addition, three personality traits, called the *3 C's*, help protect against the negative stress everyone experiences as part of living in our fast-moving, complex society: control, commitment and challenge. *Control* means taking charge of your life, being confident in your ability to direct your own life rather than letting it be directed by outside forces. *Commitment* means being actively involved and caring about your family, friends, job, hobbies and the like. *Challenge* means accepting setbacks as something to be overcome and change as something to be adapted to.

The Upside of Stress

Not all stress is negative. Most people need a certain amount of stress to keep them sharp. Think of the last time you had a deadline to meet. It was the stress of the deadline that probably finally got you moving. As noted by Hanson (1985, p. xviii):

> Stress can be *fantastic*. Or it can be *fatal*. It's all up to you. As well as respecting the dangers of stress, you can learn to harness its benefits.
>
> Olympic records are not set on the quiet training tracks, but only with the stress of competition—in front of huge crowds. . . .
>
> Serious poker players will play only if significant amounts of money are bet on each hand . . . . Many people with sedate working lives actively seek stress in the form of parachuting, cliff climbing, downhill skiing, horror movies, or simply riding a roller coaster. Such stresses bring more joy into their lives.

The key is to keep stress from becoming *distress*.

FITNESS AND NUTRITION

The U.S. Army's total fitness program emphasizes nutrition. Among the concepts it stresses are the following:

➤ Drink 6 to 8 glasses of water a day.
➤ Avoid too much sugar.
➤ Avoid too much sodium (salt).
➤ Include fiber in your daily diet.
➤ Cut down on protein and fats.

Obesity

Many police officers are obese. Recall that the average life span of officers in the United States is 59 years, compared to 73 years for the general population. Obesity may be an important risk factor in this death rate. High blood pressure, common among police officers, is also related to obesity.

The same is true for related professions. The key to losing weight is a sensible diet and exercise. Physicians and health club consultants can suggest what diet might be best for you if you have a weight problem.

Proper nutrition is an important part of fitness and avoiding obesity, believed to increase the risk of certain diseases and to shorten the life span.

FITNESS AND LIFESTYLE

Hawks et al. (p.51) suggest that the following simple lifestyle habits can add significantly to longevity:

- Sleeping for seven to eight hours each night.
- Eating breakfast every day.
- Not eating between meals.
- Maintaining an ideal weight.
- Exercising regularly.
- Drinking only moderate amounts of alcohol (or none at all).
- Not smoking cigarettes.

About half of the deaths in the United States every year occur because of an unhealthy lifestyle.

Hawks et al. (p.48) suggest that individuals assess their lifestyle and general fitness in terms of risk factors they can control:

> The three most significant risk factors that can be controlled include hypertension (above 140/90), elevated blood cholesterol (over 220) and smoking. Additional contributing factors include obesity, lack of exercise, diet, stress, diabetes, and personality type. All of these factors are interrelated and have a multiplying effect when two or more are present.

Smoking, Alcohol and Other Drugs

These substances are harmful to your health and your career. Keep in mind that an increasing number of both public and private agencies are limiting candidates to those who are nonsmokers. So if you smoke, quit. If you use controlled substances, stop. And if you drink alcoholic beverages, do so in moderation. Other people's lives, not to mention your own, depend on you having a clear head and quick reflexes.

To understand how drug use could seriously affect your employment potential, consider this scenario:

> A few months ago, Grace was in the middle of looking for a security job. She had been on over a dozen interviews, but no job offers had been made and she was beginning to lose hope. One weekend, her friends suggested going to an outdoor concert to help lift her spirits, and she agreed it might help take her mind off her unemployment.
>
> Early into the concert, Grace noticed one of her friends take something from her jacket pocket, light it, take a hit off it and pass it to the friend next to her. When it got to Grace, she hesitated. Her best friend leaned over and whispered, "C'mon, Gracie. You need to lighten up a little. It won't kill you."
>
> A second later, Grace felt her lungs filling with smoke, and as she held it in she thought, "Yeah, I do need to relax." After a second hit, she passed the joint on to her friend. The rest of the evening was spent swaying to the music and getting high.
>
> On Monday, Grace got a phone call from one of the security firms, wanting her to come in for a second interview. At first she was thrilled . . . then panic set in when she realized there might be a drug test.

Increasingly, companies are conducting random drug tests on current and prospective employees.

BENEFITS OF BEING PHYSICALLY FIT

Some benefits of being physically fit are:

- More personal energy
- Increased ability to handle job-related stress
- Less depression, hypochondria and anxiety
- Fewer aches, pains and other physical complaints
- More efficient digestion
- Stronger bones
- Slowing of the aging process
- A better self-image and more self-confidence
- A more attractive body
- More restful sleep
- Better concentration at work

Several of these benefits would also be advantageous to the job seeker.

CONCLUSION

Your future in criminal justice or security, your very life and the lives of the civilians you're sworn to protect depend on your physical fitness. Being "out of shape" can even become a legal issue. Fortunately, fitness is one area you *can* control. Once you get in shape, *stay there.* This may not be easy because the very nature of criminal justice and security jobs can contribute a great deal to being out of shape. However physically fit bodies are better able to cope with stress, and stress is abundant in the professions of criminal justice and private security.

Everyone has made decisions they later wish they had not. It is what we are doing now that makes a difference. Some decisions may be countermanded by what we have done with them. For example, paying off debt shows an ability to be accountable for oneself. Fitness is different, in that "what you see is what you get," at least at interview time. For the most part, preparing yourself by getting into shape for the job-seeking process gives you the opportunity to present yourself in the best possible light. This is a significant opportunity, particularly in professions that understandably demand fitness.

MIND STRETCHES

1. How would you judge your current level of physical fitness?

2. Are you currently working out? What is your fitness program?

3. Why do you imagine the stereotype of the overweight, donut-eating cop exists?

4. How do law enforcement and security careers tend to prevent fitness?

5. Is being overweight and out of shape possibly part of the "macho" image of being a cop or security guard? If so, is this changing?

6. What does an out-of-shape officer communicate to the public by appearance alone?

7. Why do you think so few Americans exercise regularly?

8. Recognizing that perhaps working night shift would make keeping in shape difficult, in what creative ways could an officer working such a shift exercise?

9. Are criminal justice and private security more stressful than other careers? Why or why not?

10. How would you define *physically fit*?

INSIDERS' VIEWS

For this chapter, read the *Insiders' Views* by Capt. Richard W. Stanek ("Pre-Employment Physical Fitness") and Dr. Sheldon T. Hess ("What Physical Fitness Really Means: Everyone Talks About It, But Not Many Understand"), found on the Web site: http://www.wadsworth.com/criminaljustice_d/.

REFERENCES

Blum, Jon. "Physical Training for Law Enforcement . . . A New Approach?" *The Law Enforcement Trainer*, July/August 2000, pp.12–15, 48.

Fay, Michael. "Sedentary Lifestyle: Putting Officers at Risk." *Law and Order*, June 1994, p. 22.

Frerkes, Larry R. *Becoming a Police Officer: A Guide to Successful Entry Level Testing*. Incline Village, NV: Copperhouse Publishing Company, 1998.

Hanson, Peter G. *The Joy of Stress*. Kansas City, MO: Universal Press Syndicate Company, 1985.

Hawks, Steven R.; Hafen, Brent Q. and Karren, Keith J. "How Does Your Health Rate?" *Journal of Emergency Medical Services,* March 1989, pp. 46–51.

Heiskell, Lawrence E. "The Road to Wellness." *Police*, November 1996, pp.32–35, 71, 74.

Hoffman, Art. "Add Muscle to Your Fitness Programs." *Law Enforcement Technology,* August 1993, pp.24–27.

Hoffman, Robert and Collingwood, Thomas R. "Fit for Duty." *Law and Order*, July 1996, pp.17–18.

Kallen, Ben. "How to Stick to Your Fitness Plan." *Men's Fitness*, August 2001, pp.68–73.

Marlowe, Carolyn. "Ongoing Physical Ability Testing." *Law and Order*, August 1995, pp.14–15.

Oldham, Scott. "Physical Fitness Training for Police Officers." *Law and Order*, June 2001, pp.75–77.

Physical Fitness for Law Enforcement Officers. Washington, DC: Federal Bureau of Investigation, U.S. Department of Justice.

Pilant, Lois. "Physical Fitness." *The Police Chief*, August 1995, pp.85–90.

Rubin, Paula. "The Americans with Disabilities Act's Impact on Corrections." *Corrections Today*, April 1995, pp.114–116.

Schultz, Ray and Acevedo, Art. "Ensuring the Physical Success of a Department." *Law and Order*, 2000, pp.34–37.

Slahor, Stephenie. "Focus on Fitness: The FBI Way." *Law and Order,* May 1990, pp.52–55.

Strandberg, Keith W. "Health and Fitness for Law Enforcement." *Law Enforcement Technology*, August 1997, pp.34–40.

CHAPTER 7

OTHER FORMS OF TESTING

===

Experience is not what happens to you; it is what you do with what happens to you.

—*Aldous Huxley*

Do You Know:

➢ What test anxiety is and how common it is?
➢ How you can improve your test-taking performance?
➢ What areas of general knowledge you might be tested on?
➢ What other kind of knowledge you might be tested on?
➢ What the most common kinds of tests are and what you should know about each?
➢ What assessment centers are and what purpose they serve?
➢ What psychological tests measure and if you can prepare for such tests?
➢ What integrity tests try to determine?
➢ What polygraph tests try to determine, how accurate they are and what law governs their use in pre-employment screening?

INTRODUCTION

The tests used in the hiring process are likely to include the following:

➢ Knowledge
➢ Psychological
➢ Polygraph

This chapter reviews areas commonly tested to help you understand what the tests are and what purpose they serve. You will not be given "suggested" answers. In fact, for some tests, preparing for or trying to "out-psych" them can be a mistake. It's important to know what to expect and what aspects of the testing you can prepare for. Before considering the specific areas, however, take a few minutes to look at a very common phenomenon: *test anxiety*.

TEST ANXIETY

Test anxiety is a general uneasiness or dread characterized by heightened self-awareness and perceived helplessness that frequently leads to diminished performance on tests. It includes the psychological, physiological and behavioral responses to stimuli associated with the experience of testing. In other words, it is the worry, concern and stress commonly associated with any circumstance in which individuals find themselves being evaluated.

Test anxiety is a reality for most people. Recognize its existence and take control of it. How? By being as prepared as possible. The fewer surprises a test-taker encounters, the less anxiety is felt. You probably can recall walking into a test and being pleasantly surprised to find an essay question you knew the answer to "cold." Conversely, you can also probably recall walking into a test and being confronted with a question that was indecipherable.

> Test anxiety is the worry, concern and stress commonly associated with any circumstance in which individuals find themselves being evaluated. It is a reality for most people.

Frerkes (1998, p.42) notes that most written pre-police service tests are made up of multiple-choice questions and that it is possible for applicants to prepare for such tests, and consequently improve their scores, by *practicing*. Many books are available that contain hundreds of practice multiple-choice questions typical of those found in written police tests. Arco and Monarch publish general intelligence study references to help you prepare for the written tests used by many criminal justice agencies and departments. Two specific books are listed at the end of the chapter to help officer applicants prepare for such exams. Frerkes concludes (p.42): "Successful test taking is often determined by repetition. The more opportunities you have to take written tests, the better you will do." And as you gain confidence in your test-taking abilities, you will also likely notice a decrease in test anxiety.

> Test performance can be improved through practice and repetition. The more practice you have with such written tests, the better you are likely to do.

In addition to being as prepared as possible, the following will help reduce test anxiety:

➢ Get a good night's sleep before the test.
➢ Eat.
➢ Take at least two pens, two #2 pencils and a large eraser.
➢ Know exactly where the test is to be given and how to get there. (You might make a practice run to the site.)
➢ Arrive with time to spare so parking or other hassles do not make you anxious.

TESTING KNOWLEDGE

It is hard to imagine that only a few years ago a person could become a law enforcement officer by merely responding to an advertisement. In fact, many fine officers today applied for their jobs rather spontaneously one day and were handed a gun and badge the next. Even today, many security jobs, some involving immense responsibility, require little, if any, knowledge of the applicant.

As appealing as this may sound at this stage of your job search, it is easy to see the many problems associated with what is quickly becoming a practice of the past. As these fields strive to become recognized professions and respond to the increasing demands and potential liability created by our complex society, employing agencies are having to take their hiring practices much more seriously. Whether the job for which you are applying requires certification or licensure or just requires applicants to be responsible individuals, almost all employers will want to determine what the applicant knows.

General Knowledge

Some tests are designed to assess certain basic levels of ability in areas such as math, English, grammar and composition. Because communication skills are vitally important, employers want assurance that the people they are considering hiring (for *any* level job) can express themselves well. According to Rafilson (1997, p.100): "Basic skills tests measure ability. This can be broken down into things like problem-solving (cognitive ability), inter-personal communications and specific skills. These ability tests will all be predictive of what an employee is capable of doing on the job. It is the 'can do' component of testing."

Many large departments, particularly those sensitive to minorities, focus more on general knowledge, such as reading comprehension, vocabulary, analogies and general math. Computer literacy is also becoming more critical.

> General knowledge that is commonly tested includes reading comprehension, vocabulary, analogies and general math—basic reading, writing and arithmetic. Computer literacy is also becoming more important.

While different tests can be used to examine these basic areas, they will all look at the same basic abilities. Ask yourself if you possess the necessary reading, writing and math skills required of any employee (usually a college freshman level). If you are not at this level, immediately start a plan to improve your skills. Many community colleges have a policy of open admission. As part of the process, the student is tested in reading, writing and math skills. The college offers remedial courses for the underprepared student.

Once on the job, lack of basic reading, writing and math skills can't be hidden long from an employer. To avoid wasting everyone's time, many job applications include some basic questions to let the hiring agency know if you have these basic academic abilities. An increasing number of application forms have a section that requires a brief essay to test your writing, spelling, grammar and organizational abilities.

For example, the Minnesota Police Corps requires applicants to submit a personal essay *and* be prepared to write three short essays during testing:

Part VI. Personal Statement and Essays
Attach a personal statement to this application. Word limit: 500–700 words.

Tell us something about yourself. Why do you think you would be a great candidate for the Police Corps? What do you consider your greatest strength and why? What do you consider your greatest weakness and why? If you feel that you have faced difficult circumstances in your life, please write about how you have overcome these obstacles.

Although you are not required to write about any specific topic, an essay that shows growth, maturity, leadership, courage and commitment could be particularly helpful to your application. We are looking for a demonstrated interest in law enforcement and dedication to public service. (**5 points**)

Be prepared to write several essays when you are called in for testing.

You will be required to write a short (200–300 word) essay on each of the following topics. Your written statements should be concise and should reflect your true feelings and beliefs. Please give some thought to each topic ahead of time. Your writing must be legible. Illegible answers will not be graded and you will lose those points.

- Why are you applying to the Police Corps? (**5 points**)
- What do you see as the primary challenges confronting children growing up today in the communities of Minnesota? What role do you see for the police in addressing those challenges? (**5 points**)
- List three books that have influenced your thinking or contributed to your development. Briefly explain how and why. (**5 points**)

The essays are evaluated by the following standards:

- A clear main idea that fulfills the assignment.
- Adequate, specific support.
- Organized into logical paragraphs with coherent transitions.
- A concise style.
- Appropriate word choice.
- Sentences that are complete, varied and effective.
- Standard grammar: correct use of pronouns, adjectives and adverbs, negation, articles and subject/verb agreement.
- Mechanically correct: spelling, abbreviations, numbers, capitalization and punctuation.

Because writing is a skill you will need for the rest of your life, regardless of your professional pursuits, do not overlook this all-important area now. Take advantage of classes during your education, and if you have already completed any degree-seeking program, do not hesitate to return to school to become an adequate writer. There is no getting around it—you must be able to write well. Even if you somehow obtain a job without having adequate writing skills, this is an area you will be evaluated on during your probationary period when you will write, literally, constantly.

If you need remedial help in any area, get it *now*. Many opportunities exist to improve yourself. Often the only thing stopping someone from improving themselves is that they feel too embarrassed to ask for help. The help you need may be in a review book available from a library or bookstore, or you may want to enroll in a class at a community college or in an adult learning program.

Specific Knowledge

Applicants may be required to know specific information for certain jobs. In states requiring certification or licensure, successful completion of requisite levels of training or education will be evidence of such knowledge. Certainly such required knowledge will indicate the areas of specific knowledge you will be expected to know. For example, in Minnesota, which requires a minimum of two years of college to be eligible to be licensed as a police officer, areas of required knowledge include:

• Administration of justice	• Firearms	• Report writing
• Criminal investigation	• Human behavior	• Statutes
• Criminal procedure	• Juvenile justice	• Testifying in court
• Cultural awareness	• Patrol functions	• Traffic law enforcement
• Defensive tactics	• Police operations and procedures	

Less specific knowledge is required to be a private investigator in Minnesota, but in addition to passing a strict background investigation, a minimum of three years' experience in security work is required.

Even if the areas of specific knowledge are not set forth clearly, you should be able to foresee what may be asked during an oral interview. Basic statutes that apply to public or private officers would be likely questions. Often, such questions are intertwined with the "What would you do if . . . ?" question. This allows employers to test not only specific knowledge, but the application of it using problem-solving techniques and communications skills.

> Applicants should expect to be tested on some specific knowledge in areas pertaining to the field, such as relevant statutes and procedures.

It's your responsibility to be prepared to the best of your ability. If you do not know what you might be tested on, it does no harm to call ahead to ask. The worst that could happen is that they won't say. But it is much more likely you will be told, putting you a giant step ahead of applicants who haven't a clue as to what will be asked.

It's also a good idea to learn as much as possible about the department or agency you are applying to. If it is a law enforcement position, maybe you can arrange for a ride-along, thus providing an opportunity to ask questions about the department. If it is a corrections position, arrange to visit the institution if possible. If it is a private security position, visit the facility and talk with a security officer.

Do what you can to learn and review what you think will be asked. Remember, no one can know everything. Sometimes you will be able to immediately give the exact answer, maybe even amazing yourself. Sometimes you may give a wrong answer. Sometimes you may draw a complete mental blank. You are likely to experience all these reactions at one time or another during testing.

Keep in mind the purpose of the testing process. If the only thing employers wanted were accurate answers, they would replace their employees with computers. Employers want someone who can think and act human. Part of being human is to *not* know it all and yet to keep functioning. In fact, tests might include an "off-the-wall" question just to see how you respond. In all probability, you will look a lot better admitting you are nervous and forgot or don't know the answer (but know where to find it), than to fake it. In short:

➤ Be as prepared as you can be.
➤ Seek remedial help if necessary.
➤ Know as much as you can.
➤ Know how to find what you don't know.
➤ Don't be afraid to admit what you don't know.
➤ Don't make up answers.

Memory and Observation Tests

Many police departments use tests to determine applicants' ability to recall information. For example, pictures of several "bad guys" may be flashed on a screen and personal information given about each of the individuals, such as names, ages, criminal activity, etc. The test then continues by flashing a picture on the screen and requiring the applicant to recall all the information about the subject, or recall a nickname, or match a crime with a face.

STRATEGIES FOR TAKING TESTS

No matter whether the tests cover general information, specific knowledge, memory and observation skills, or a combination, the successful candidate knows how to approach the specific type of test given.

> The most common tests are multiple choice, true/false and essay, and each type of test has its own guidelines and strategies to follow.

Olson (1990, pp.S-17–19) offers practical advice for approaching such tests.

 Taking the Test [1]

When you are given the test, look it over so you can plan how to allocate your time. Answer the questions you know best first. Then come back to the harder questions. Always read directions very carefully. *The number one cause of errors on tests is the failure to read and follow directions.*

For *MULTIPLE-CHOICE TESTS,* follow these guidelines:

- If you are asked to read long passages and answer questions about the material, read the question stems before you read the material. This will help you find what you are looking for faster and easier.
- Do not be afraid to change your answer if you have a good reason. It's a myth that you should stick to your original choice. Research studies show that most students are at least twice as likely to change an incorrect answer to a correct one.
- Read the stem of the question. Try to answer the question before you read the possible answers. Then skim all the answer choices and select the one most like your initial answer.
- Absolute words such as *a, none, always, constantly, never, entirely, every, only* and *best* often make the answer false and can usually be eliminated as possible answers.
- Make a complete sentence from the stem and each choice and ask yourself, "Is the statement I made true or false?" A true statement is probably the correct answer.
- Think logically. If the options are dates or numbers, you can usually eliminate the lowest and highest numbers. The option "all of the above" is usually the correct answer. And the longest statement is usually the correct answer.
- Don't spend too much time on questions you can't answer. Leave them and come back later if you have time.

For *TRUE/FALSE QUESTIONS,* follow these suggestions:

- Assume the question is true unless you can establish that it's false.
- It is usually easier to write a true question than a false one.
- A statement is false if any part of it is false.
- Absolute statements tend to be false. Be aware of the words *never, always, none, all, best, invariably, entirely, every.* These statements are usually false. However, words such as *many, most, generally, frequently, sometimes* and *often* are most often used in true statements.

---

[1] From *Study Skills: The Parent Connection,* 2nd ed. by Patricia S. Olson. © 1990 by Reading Consulting, Inc., Burnsville, MN. All rights reserved. Reprinted by permission.

- The word *not* completely changes the meaning of a statement. Be careful in answering a question containing *not*.
- If you are not sure what the question is asking, ask your teacher to explain it.
- It is all right to guess on a true/false question. You have a 50–50 chance of guessing the right answer.

For *ESSAY QUESTIONS*, follow these steps:

- Read over the essay question and jot down in the margin any ideas that immediately come to mind.
- Briefly outline your main points in the margin before you begin to write. This will help you stay on track.
- Restate and answer the question in the first sentence of the essay. This serves as your introduction. For example, the question is, "Discuss the three main causes for the Revolutionary War." Your answer should begin: "The three main causes for the Revolutionary War were _____, _____ and _____."
- Support each main point with specific examples. Show your reader why you think your answer is valid.
- Don't forget to write a conclusion. ("In summary, _____, _____ and _____ were the three main causes of the Revolutionary War.")
- Proofread your essay before turning it in. Composition errors make a poor impression on the reader and may affect your grade.

GENERAL RULE: Never skip an item or leave an answer blank *unless* it is stated that mistakes count against you.

ASSESSMENT CENTERS

According to Garner (1998, p.77): "Assessment Center Testing has been around for the last 60 or 70 years. Both the Allies and the Axis used it during World War II to train their spies. The technique involved putting the candidates in a situation where they must role-play the position they are seeking." Rachlin (1995, p.29) states:

> The assessment center is a process (not a facility) that uses a variety of techniques to evaluate performance skills. . . . [It] is usually administered near the end of the selection process—after the resume and applications have been reviewed, the candidates screened and interviewed, preliminary background checks have been conducted, and possibly a battery of psychological tests have been given. . . . It is used to identify candidates' strengths and weaknesses in areas critical to successful performance of the job. . . . The essential elements of an assessment center include a job analysis which identifies the dimensions (abilities) needed for the position; multiple assessment techniques which must include simulation-type exercises; multiple assessors who must be properly trained; and scores that must be derived by using a consensus process.

> Assessment centers are processes that identify a candidate's strengths and weaknesses to evaluate how well that candidate is likely to perform on the job. Situational tests are a common part of such assessment centers.

Rachlin (p.30) also notes: "A typical selection process may include other exercises or tests that are not simulations, such as paper and pencil tests, multiple choice tests, intelligence tests, personality inventories, and management type indicators."

PSYCHOLOGICAL TESTING

Psychological testing is a cause of anxiety for applicants because so much of it is out of their control. What should I say? How should I answer? What are they looking for? Psychological testing is an immense and complex subject about which hundreds of texts have been written. So what do you need to know? First, such tests should not and probably could not be prepared for through such traditional means as memorization. It is better to understand what these tests are meant to do, how they are administered and what they can show.

Purposes of Psychological Testing

Although psychological testing is a relatively new practice, no doubt you have taken some form of psychological test, probably at some point in your school career. According to Ho (2001, p.319): "Psychological testing has become a crucial element in the police officer recruiting process since the President's Commission on Law Enforcement and the Administration of Justice (1967) aggressively promoted the necessity of psychologically screening police applicants' emotional stability." Furthermore (p.337): "Psychological evaluation and psychologists' recommendations of hiring have demonstrated a unique measure in assisting the police department to screen out those applicants who are mentally and psychologically unfit." Most people would agree that law enforcement officers should be mentally and emotionally stable. But defining and assessing what this consists of is a complex, challenging task.

> Most psychological tests measure differences between individuals or between the reactions of the same individual on different occasions. Preparing for such tests is very different from preparing for more traditional "knowledge-based" tests, but you *can* prepare for them.

Sergeant Dennis Conroy, St. Paul (Minnesota) Police Department, also a clinical psychologist, gives the following advice concerning psychological tests administered to police/security candidates:

> To prepare for a psychological evaluation, applicants must begin to get psychologically "fit" several months before the examination. Preparation for a psychological evaluation *cannot* be rushed.
>
> Applicants must begin preparation early enough so they can make changes to assure that they are as psychologically healthy as possible. This includes looking at relationships, mature behavior and ways to deal with tension.
>
> Frequently applicants take psychological evaluations just after finishing school. Their lives have been hectic. They have not taken time to relax for months. They are wound tighter than a $2.00 watch. This stress affects their entire being. It determines how they see the world. It is crucial for applicants to take time to relax before a psychological examination. This requires more than a 15-minute process the day before the evaluation. Some practical suggestions after you have taken time for yourself are as follows:
>
> - Don't fight with your wife or husband, boyfriend or girlfriend or parents the night before the evaluation.
> - Get plenty of sleep the night before. Make sure you are at your best.
> - Get up early the morning of the evaluation so you have time for yourself. Take a walk and relax.
> - Leave early for the evaluation. Get there with about 15 minutes to spare. Take time to relax when you get there. Read the paper or something.
> - During the exam, *be honest*. You have honestly worked toward entering this profession for a long time. Don't change now. Copy from the person next to you only if you are *absolutely sure* you want his or her personality and are willing to bet your career on it.

According to Frerkes (p.87): "Research data indicates that psychological testing disqualifies 40 to 60 percent of applicants." Ho (p.334) adds: "All else being equal, . . . applicants were almost 8.4 times more likely to be recruited by the police department if they had a positive recommendation by psychologists relative to those applicants who were not recommended by psychologists." Nonetheless, as Champion (1994, p.3) asserts, honesty cannot be stressed enough:

> Attempting to outwit the testers is one of the worst mistakes job applicants can make. I have had more students come to me and say, "How should I answer this or that scenario?" My answer is, "Use your best judgment." If they say, "How should I respond to personal questions—masturbation, thoughts best kept to one's self, etc., what should I say?" I always advise them to tell the truth, no matter what.

Testing Methods

Methods vary greatly from test to test. Personality tests are of two main types: objective and projective. Objective personality tests, such as the California Personality Inventory (CPI) and Inwald Personality Inventory (IPI), ask objective true/false or multiple-choice questions. These questions are then grouped into scales to measure different aspects of personality. Projective tests involve ambiguous stimuli that the subject must interpret by "projecting" into the interpretation aspects of his or her own personality. Common projective tests are the Rorschach Inkblot Test and the Thematic Apperception Test (TAT).

Specific Psychological Tests

In attempting to anticipate how an applicant might perform on the job, evaluators look at both the past (grades, job references, traffic and police records, etc.) and the present. Psychological tests are tools employers use to learn about the applicant's present state of mind, what is important to that person and how that person is likely to respond to certain stimuli. An applicant's answers form patterns that are evaluated by psychologists, who compare the patterns with past studies to determine a psychological profile of the applicant. Tests frequently given include:

- California Personality Inventory (CPI)
- Wonderlic Personnel Test (WPT)
- Inwald Personality Inventory (IWI)
- Myers-Briggs Type Indicator™
- Minnesota Multiphasic Personality Inventory (MMPI)
- Watson-Glaser Critical Thinking Appraisal
- Strong Interest Inventory
- Behavioral Personal Assessment Device (B-PAD)
- Rorschach Inkblot Test
- Thematic Apperception Test (TAT)

The *California Personality Inventory* (CPI), one of the most popular personality test, is a "multi-level self-administering questionnaire designed to identify the status of highly important factors in personality and social adjustment. Each scale forecasts what a person will say or do under defined conditions. The test identifies individuals who will be described in characteristic ways by others who know them well. The CPI is designed to assess normal personality characteristics important to everyday life.

The *Wonderlic Personnel Test* (WPT) is a timed (12 minutes), 50-item paper-and-pencil test that can be taken individually or in groups. This test predicts success in learning situations and is a very accurate estimate of intelligence that serves as a quick assessment of cognitive skills or as a screening device to determine the need for more detailed evaluations.

The *Inwald Personality Inventory* (IPI) is a 310-question test in which an applicant has to respond to a statement as either "true" or "false," based on experience, attitude or feeling toward the content of the statement. As Ho (p.325) notes: "The IPI is designed to measure 26 behavioral characteristics, such as job difficulties or hyperactivity, which are presumably relevant to police-related functioning. . . . [Researchers] have proclaimed that the practical values of the IPI psychological measurement are critical to predict applicants' job performances as police officers in the future."

The *Myers-Briggs Type Indicator*™ is a widely used measure of people's disposition and preferences. Millions of people in a wide variety of occupations have taken the Myers-Briggs. The test describes 16 easily understood personality types based on individuals' stated preferences on four indexes:

➢   Extroversion-Introversion
➢   Sensing-Intuition
➢   Thinking-Feeling
➢   Judgment-Perception

The *Minnesota Multiphasic Personality Inventory* (MMPI) is used primarily for emotional stability screening and frequently for entry-level psychological screening. This self-report questionnaire is the most widely used paper-and-pencil personality test being used (in all fields). Respondents are asked to indicate "true," "false," or "cannot say" to 680 statements covering a variety of psychological characteristics such as health, social, political, sexual and religious values; attitudes about family, education and occupation; emotional moods; and typical neurotic or psychotic displays such as obsessive-compulsive behavior, phobias, hallucinations and delusions.

Conroy asserts the MMPI is virtually impossible to study for. Its validity scales have cross-indexed questions and, in most cases, applicants who try to "fool" the test "fool" themselves out of a job instead. The MMPI has numerous sufficiently similar items so that it is difficult to lie consistently. The best advice here, again, is to tell the truth. One candidate tried to beat the MMPI and was denied a federal job. When the same candidate took the test again a year later and told the truth, he got the job.

The *Watson-Glaser Critical Thinking Appraisal* has five subtests: (1) Inference, (2) Recognition of Assumptions, (3) Deduction, (4) Interpretation and (5) Evaluation of Arguments. The test has 80 items, including problems, statements, arguments and interpretations of data like those encountered daily at work and in the classroom, and is to be completed within 40 minutes.

The *Strong Interest Inventory* has 325 items covering a wide range of occupations, occupational activities, hobbies, leisure activities, school subjects and types of people. It compares a person's interests with the interests of people happily employed in a wide variety of occupations. It measures *interests,* not aptitude or intelligence.

The *Behavioral Personal Assessment Device* (B-PAD) is one of the most progressive testing instruments in police recruiting and is used to measure problem-solving ability, judgment under pressure, decisiveness, diplomacy and an applicant's genuine interest in people. The test is presented in video format. The applicant views numerous video screens and must respond as if he or she was the officer at the scene. The B-PAD was designed not as a test of police procedure but rather to assess an applicant's ability to effectively evaluate a variety of situations typically encountered by police officers (Frerkes, p.89).

The *Rorschach Inkblot Test* consists of 10 inkblot patterns of various shades and colors. The applicant is shown a pattern and asked what it might be. Frerkes (p.92) states: "The test is effective in assessing an applicant's objectivity, values, and emotional tendencies as well as revealing neuroses, psychosis, character disorders, addictions, and psychosomatic disorders."

The *Thematic Apperception Test* (TAT) is a projective instrument similar in context to the Rorschach Test but with no quantitative scoring technique. The test consists of 10 picture cards for women, 10 for men and 10 for both sexes. The purpose of the TAT is to provide insight into an applicant's self-image, relative strengths and various needs by inducing thoughts, attitudes and feelings about a subject depicted on the picture cards.

Integrity Tests

One type of psychological test commonly used by employers is the paper-and-pencil honesty questionnaire. The first test of this type was developed in 1951 by John E. Reid and was called the Reid Report. This test, described by Inbau (1994, p.34), consists of "a questionnaire with approximately eighty questions that are answered by a yes or no response, accompanied by biographical data questions, and by a list of thefts or theft-related acts that the candidate may have committed."

The questionnaire has four parts. Part 1 determines trustworthiness by asking a series of questions, such as, "Do you believe a person should be fired by a company if it is found that he helped another employee take a little merchandise from the company?" Part 2 is a criminal admissions questionnaire. Part 3 elicits information about recent drug use, and Part 4 examines work history.

Integrity tests are psychological tests commonly used by employers to determine trustworthiness. The test asks questions about the candidate's ethics, criminal record, recent drug use and work history.

COMPUTERIZED SCREENING

You should also be prepared to be assessed by computer. As Clede (1995, p.16) describes:

> Candidate Officer Preliminary Screen ("COPS") is a psychological test that candidates can take by keyboard-selecting best answers to multiple-choice questions on the computer monitor. Designed by two psychologists with more than 15 years' experience of police candidate testing, "COPS" evaluates basic honesty, domination desire, ability to handle stress, and also looks at basic personality features.

POLYGRAPH TESTING

In 1892 Dr. James MacKensie invented the "Ink Polygraph," which recorded heartbeat, venous pulse and arterial pulse. A clock spring mechanism drove a paper ribbon with time markers every fifth of a second. Three decades later the Larson Polygraph, credited as the original "lie detector," was built for Berkeley Police Chief August Vollmer. Bulky and complicated, the device took half an hour to set up.

The modern polygraph is much more compact, about the size of a briefcase. It measures changes in:

➤ Relative blood pressure and pulse rate with a standard medical blood-pressure cuff
➤ Galvanic skin resistance (GSR), or perspiration, with two electrodes attached to the fingertips
➤ Stomach and chest breathing patterns with hollow, corrugated-rubber tubes, one placed around the abdomen and one around the upper thorax

Activity in each of these physiological measurements is monitored by either electronic or mechanical means and is permanently recorded on a paper chart by a pen-and-ink system. Dees (1995, p.53) states:

> The most recent innovations in polygraph technology occurred in the last few years with the advent of computerized polygraphy. In computerized polygraphy, much of the mechanical equipment (streaming graph paper, mechanical pens, wet ink) that led to many glitches during the process of the exam is done away with in favor of a "virtual" graph on the computer monitor.

According to Clede (1998, p.91): "Computerized models use the POLYSCORE mathematical algorithm developed at Johns Hopkins University by the Applied Physics Lab (APL) . . . [which] claims an interpretation accuracy of over 95%." Yet despite such claims of high accuracy, the Supreme Court has held there is simply no consensus that polygraph evidence is reliable. An opinion written by Justice Clarence Thomas ("Supreme Court Finds . . .," 1998, p.3) states:

> To this day, the scientific community remains extremely polarized about the reliability of polygraph techniques . . . . There is simply no way to know in a particular case whether a polygraph examiner's conclusion is accurate, because certain doubts and uncertainties plague even the best polygraph exams.

Use of the polygraph in pre-employment is so controversial that it has become strictly regulated through the Employee Polygraph Protection Act (EPPA), signed into law by President Reagan in 1988. This law prohibits the use of all mechanical lie detector tests in the workplace, including polygraphs, deceptographs, psychological stress evaluators and voice stress analyzers. The EPPA does, however, allow for the polygraph to be used by private sector employers for certain types of pre-employment screening, such as companies who provide certain types of security services. Furthermore, the EPPA does not apply when the particular employer is the United States government or any state or local government. Government employers may use any lie detector test without complying with any of EPPA's procedures or restrictions. However, not every state requires a polygraph for law enforcement and security jobs.

In other words, although using the polygraph during pre-employment is prohibited in most fields, it is *not* prohibited in law enforcement or in many private security jobs. Therefore, make no objections if you are asked to take such an exam. The employer probably has the right to request this. Just be yourself. Relax, and tell the truth.

Polygraph tests are used to determine a candidate's honesty and, according to field practitioners, are 90 to 95 percent accurate. Use of the polygraph during pre-employment screening is *not* prohibited in government jobs, including law enforcement.

The primary use of the polygraph is to substantiate the information gathered during the background investigation.

BACKGROUND CHECKS

Another type of test candidates must pass is the background check, also referred to as pre-employment screening. Chiaramonte (1995, p.72) notes: "The use of pre-employment screening programs has become more important in recent years as companies are increasingly being held liable by the courts for the actions of employees. Liability is often based on the employer's failure to perform reference checks or to verify past employment."

The background check typically includes checking with past employers and references listed on your application form. It may also include checking your credit history, driving record, academic background, criminal record and if you possess any and all required professional licenses. Nelson (2000, p.87) states:

> The background investigation is not merely a tool to determine if an applicant is honest but also a tool to measure the applicant's judgment and suitability to be a police officer. One measure of judgment is the care and wisdom used in selecting references.
>
> Applicants should be instructed to select individuals who know a broad spectrum of their life, usually peers, as opposed to selecting individuals for their prestige or likelihood to supply a favorable reference based upon limited knowledge of the applicant. References should not be, as a general rule, teachers, coaches, doctors, pastors, politicians, or friends of the applicant's parents who know an applicant typically at only a superficial level. If an applicant's references do not meet the criteria, it is an indication of the applicant's ability to make judgments and decisions. . . .
>
> Another area that must be examined is work history. The greatest predictor of future behavior is past behavior. If the applicant has an established pattern of poor work history, it is unlikely to improve.

Candidates for most jobs in criminal justice and security should anticipate a rigorous background check conducted by investigators trained in this specialty area. Do not try to hide anything. Today's background investigators will find it. They know who to ask, what to ask, and how to look for any indications of problem behavior that might later cause someone to allege the hiring agency "should have known" the potential risks posed by an employee. Furthermore, in addition to whatever it was you were hiding, you will now be viewed as dishonest, a trait no agency wishes to deal with. Also bear in mind that most background investigators will want to know where else you have applied. If you have been dishonest during the application process in the past, it will follow you.

While you may be able to change your level of physical fitness, you cannot change your background. In addition to certain actions that will statutorily prohibit people from entering professions, some past acts will at least be of concern to potential employers. You will have the opportunity to address these issues, and maybe even turn some indiscretions around to your advantage (proving how you addressed a problem and have learned and improved as a result), but be assured lying in any manner about your background will be a legitimate reason for disqualification.

THE PREVALENCE OF OTHER TESTS AND SCREENING TECHNIQUES

Hogue et al. (1994, p.120) collected data regarding how common various screening procedures were with law enforcement candidates, including those discussed in this chapter. The results are shown in Table 7-1.

TABLE 7-1   Reported Use of Selected Screening Techniques

Technique	Presently Used	Would Use if Budget Permitted	Not Worth the Time and Cost
References	96.7%	2.8%	0.5%
Arrest records check	96.4	2.7	0.9
Driving record check	96.4	3.2	0.5
Educational record check	89.6	8.0	2.4
Fingerprint check	87.6	10.9	1.5
Oral board review	78.2	13.0	7.8
Field investigation (background)	76.7	19.8	3.5
Screening interview	70.4	13.0	6.0
Military records check	69.5	23.5	7.0
Financial records check	49.7	34.1	16.2
Mental health records check	49.4	44.3	6.3
Psychological evaluation:			
intelligence/ability	41.7	52.9	5.3
emotional stability	37.6	56.6	5.8
Written exam	29.6	56.2	13.0
Polygraph examination	12.6	67.1	19.8

SOURCE: Mark C. Hogue, Tommie Black and Robert T. Sigler. "The Differential Use of Screening Techniques in the Recruitment of Police Officers." *American Journal of Police,* Vol. 13, No. 2, 1994, p.120.

CONCLUSION

The testing process is another opportunity to prove to a prospective employer that *you* are the one to hire. Present yourself as you are. If you do not feel you would test well now, improve yourself by developing a rigorous plan to increase both your fitness level, your knowledge and your writing skills. Take some practice tests. Be *realistic* about who you are and what you can be. Be honest with yourself. Because work greatly influences *all* aspects of your life, you do not want to pursue any career that will be a dead end. View the testing phase of the application process as a positive experience for both the employer and you, to both determine if there is a match. If not, it is best for everyone to learn this while there is time for you to find a different niche in the world of work.

ADDITIONAL CONTACTS AND SOURCES OF INFORMATION

Two recommended test preparation books:

How to Prepare for the Police Officer Examination,
  by Donald J. Schroeder and Frank A. Lombardo,
  Barron's

Police Officer
  ARCO Publishing, MacMillan General Reference,
  A Prentice Hall MacMillan Company

MIND STRETCHES

1. Does your field require proof of certain levels of knowledge? How will you prepare for this?

2. What do you anticipate a battery of psychological tests will say about you? Are there factors in your life that need to be attended to before you pursue your chosen career?

3. How do you feel about taking a polygraph examination? Are there skeletons in your closet that you need to honestly confront?

4. As part of your job search strategy, have you taken into account what you can and cannot prepare yourself for?

5. What areas of the hiring process do you have such limited control over that you can't prepare for them? Is there any area of the hiring process that you have absolutely *no* control over, or is there always something you can do to give yourself an edge over the competition?

6. Is what you have done in the past a realistic indicator of how you will perform in the future?

7. Have you ever taken a psychological test? If so, how did you feel: positive, neutral or negative? If negative, what can you do to reduce these feelings?

8. If you suffer from test anxiety, what can you do to reduce it?

9. How well do you write? How can you know for sure?

INSIDERS' VIEWS

For this chapter, read the *Insiders' Views* by Dennis L. Conroy, Ph.D. ("Getting Set") and Russell M. Anderson ("Learning Should Never Stop"), found on the Web site: http://www.wadsworth.com/criminaljustice_d/.

REFERENCES

Champion, Dean J. Review of *Seeking Employment in Law Enforcement, Private Security, and Related Fields*, 1st ed. October 11, 1994, p.3.

Chiaramonte, Joe. "Background Checks: Past as Prologue." *Security Management,* May 1995, pp.72–77.

Clede, Bill. "Screening Officer Candidates." *Law and Order,* March 1995, p.16.

Clede, Bill. "Technology—It Helps Find the Truth." *Law and Order*, July 1998, pp.91–93.

Dees, Timothy M. "Polygraph Technology." *Law Enforcement Technology*, July 1995, pp.52–54.

Frerkes, Larry R. *Becoming a Police Officer: A Guide to Successful Entry Level Testing.* Incline Village, NV: Copperhouse Publishing Company, 1998.

Garner, Kenneth. "Assessment Center Testing." *Law and Order*, November 1998, pp.77–82.

Ho, Taiping. "The Interrelationships of Psychological Testing, Psychologists' Recommendations, and Police Departments' Recruitment Decisions." *Police Quarterly*, September 2001, pp.318–342.

Hogue, Mark C.; Black, Tommie and Sigler, Robert T. "The Differential Use of Screening Techniques in the Recruitment of Police Officers." *American Journal of Police,* Vol. 13, No. 2, 1994, pp.113–124.

Inbau, Fred E. "Integrity Tests and the Law." *Security Management,* January 1994, pp.34–41.

Nelson, Kurt R. "A Tale of Two Cities: A Comparison of Background Investigations." *Law and Order*, May 2000, pp.85–88.

Olson, Patricia S. *Study Skills: The Parent Connection*, 2nd ed. Burnsville, MN: Reading Consulting, Inc., 1990.

Rachlin, Harvey. "Assessment Centers." Part of "The Hiring of a Police Chief." *Law and Order,* March 1995, pp.29–31.

Rafilson, Fred M. "Everything You Always Wanted to Know About Written Exams . . . but Were Afraid (Really) to Ask!" *Law and Order*, September 1997, pp.100–102.

"Supreme Court Finds No Violation in Ban on Polygraph Evidence." *Criminal Justice Newsletter*, March 3, 1998, p.3.

CHAPTER 8

ATTRIBUTES OF SUCCESSFUL CANDIDATES

It's not your aptitude, it's your attitude that determines your altitude.

—*Anonymous*

Do You Know:

➤ If a lack of law-related experiences seriously hurts your chances of obtaining employment in the fields of criminal justice or private security?

➤ What your past is a good predictor of?

➤ What past employment says about you?

➤ What the benefits of volunteering are?

➤ Where you might look to gain some work-related experience in criminal justice or security?

➤ If military experience is beneficial or detrimental to one seeking a job as a police, corrections or security officer?

➤ What advanced education says about an applicant?

➤ How important communication skills are?

➤ What the benefits of internships are?

➤ How you should handle past mistakes when applying for a new job?

➤ What role ethics plays in law enforcement and security?

INTRODUCTION

 Imagine yourself as an employer responsible for selecting the best candidate from a number of applicants. What criteria would you use to make this decision, which is sure to have important consequences? What positive attributes or characteristics would you, as an employer, look for? List these in your journal.

 What negative attributes would influence you *not* to hire a candidate? Again, write them down.

Employers are not just selecting employees; they are selecting people who will often directly influence other people's lives and who will also be representing their department or agency.

Police officers routinely deal with the most private business of the public for whom they work. Officers bandage wounds, intervene in disputes, guard property, search homes and offices and educate children. Officers may bring victims back to life or have to watch them die. They uphold the law, which not only benefits the public, but also holds the guilty responsible by drawing them into the criminal justice system in a way that will alter that defendant's life forever. Being a police officer is an *awesome* responsibility.

Correctional officers perform a vital function in guarding those sentenced to any of the variety of corrections facilities throughout our country. They deal with our nation's offenders daily and have the power to make positive changes in inmates' lives. Correctional officers are also tasked with protecting society from these offenders by making sure those they are guarding do not escape. Some correctional positions involve counseling inmates while others consist of an armed position in a watchtower.

Security officers also have great responsibility. Most security directors have complete access to every part of a company's assets—its secrets, its property, its cash—all are literally under the protection of the security manager and the security officers.

Other professionals in criminal justice and public safety fields are equally entrusted with important issues. Whether social workers, psychologists or others in the helping professions, *all* employees in criminal justice are truly professionals.

What criteria are used when hiring criminal justice and security personnel? These criteria range from how you present yourself to who you really are.

HOW DO YOU APPEAR ON PAPER?

Impressions are important. Initial contacts, resumes and follow-ups are critical. Employers *will* look at both what you have done and how you have done it. If you are determined to get the job, take control of your future by establishing a solid background of knowledge and experience. Many opportunities are available to acquire those attributes employees seek in candidates.

PERSONAL ATTRIBUTES

What kind of background will help you get that entry-level job? Recognize that employers are often as interested in non-law-related experience and attributes as they are in law-related ones.

Most employers are more interested in the type of a person you are than in what you know about law enforcement, corrections or security work, especially for entry-level positions. A more general background helps anyone broaden the perspective of their world. Those doing the hiring want to know how you can relate your past experience to law enforcement, even if all you've done is flip burgers. Did you deal with customers? Did you have to solve problems? Did you do public relations? Did you have to communicate with people? These things will help the candidate get the job even if there has been no "police experience."

Many candidates have difficulty recognizing the positive traits implied by past jobs. For example, the student who has worked for the same grocery store for three years but is now managing it while the owner is away, making the bank deposits, handling stock and supply issues, opening and closing—these tasks demonstrate the respect in which he or she is held by the employer. Similarly, some students are embarrassed by their experience as bartenders and are reluctant to mention this part of their work history to a prospective employer. However, such students are failing to recognize that these jobs require the ability to handle unruly customers and demonstrate the applicant's ability to handle aggression and respond well under pressure—some of the same traits required of law enforcement officers, correctional officers and security professionals.

A lack of law-related experience by no means disqualifies you as a candidate for work in criminal justice or security. In fact, most employers are more interested in the type of a person you are than in what you know about law enforcement, corrections or security work.

Hogue et al. (1994, p.121) state: "There appears to be considerable agreement among those who make screening decisions in law enforcement about the characteristics that are desirable for police officers. The candidate should be honest, reliable, emotionally stable, patient, and of good character." The desired characteristics for law enforcement officers are summarized in Table 8-1.

TABLE 8-1 Desirability of Selected Characteristics for Police Officers

Characteristic	Essential	Desirable	Not Desirable	Not Acceptable
Honest	96.8%	3.2%	--	--
Truthful	94.1	5.9	--	--
Emotionally stable	92.8	7.2	--	--
Good character	90.1	9.5	0.5%	--
Reliable	88.6	11.4	--	--
U.S. citizen	88.4	10.6	0.9	--
Law abiding	87.7	11.9	0.5	--
GED certificate	75.5	15.1	8.5	0.9%
Loyal	73.4	26.6	--	--
Fair	70.4	29.2	0.5	--
High school diploma	60.7	37.9	1.4	--
Careful	60.2	38.7	0.5	--
Skillful driver	49.5	48.6	1.9	--
Slow to anger	48.6	50.9	--	--
Patient	47.8	50.5	--	--
Firm	43.1	55.6	1.4	--
Past job performance	41.7	58.3	--	--
Consistent	41.1	57.5	0.5	--
Good physical appearance	35.6	63.5	0.9	--
Ambitious	28.4	68.4	3.3	--
Assertive	24.9	73.2	1.9	--
Authoritarian	19.5	55.7	23.3	1.4
High intelligence	16.2	81.0	2.8	--
Aggressive	16.1	66.4	15.6	1.9
Rigid	13.0	38.6	45.4	2.9
Good financial management	12.3	79.2	4.7	3.8
Vision without glasses	10.2	77.7	11.6	0.5
Appearance of strength	9.2	78.8	12.0	--
College education	4.7	80.5	14.4	--
Social alcohol use	3.9	7.8	73.7	14.6
Social drug use	1.4	1.9	11.7	85.0

SOURCE: Adapted from Mark C. Hogue, Tommie Black and Robert T. Sigler. "The Differential Use of Screening Techniques in the Recruitment of Police Officers." *American Journal of Police,* Vol. 13, No. 2, 1994, p.119.

Slahor (1998, p.60) examined how one department selects the best-qualified candidates for police work:

> The department . . . [makes] sure it finds people who are problem solvers and who can make judgments under pressure. Willingness to confront problems, devise solutions and work not only with colleagues, but with the community are also key to the selection process.
>
> Successful candidates must have an interest in people and be sensitive to the best steps to take in a situation. Integrity and dependability are essential . . . not only for the daily work and for testifying in court but also in the wider scope of the officer's role in the neighborhood and community.

Weiss and Dresser (1998, p.48) add: "The two most important abilities required of a police officer are communication skills and common sense." Furthermore (p.50): "Departments are looking for people who are flexible but also determined and able to assume control under pressure." Desirable characteristics include maturity, openness, flexibility, cheerfulness, judgment, congeniality, the ability to handle social situations, the ability to deal with people at their worst, and tolerance for other opinions.

These same traits are vital if you're considering a career in corrections or private security. These traits are not genetic; they're learned. The more general life experiences you have, the better your chance of acquiring these traits. Broad experience also helps you better understand human behavior, a valuable attribute.

Other important attributes are ego strength and anger control. Ego strength is essential and comes from having good self-esteem and a good self-valuing system. Anger control is especially important because of the nature of the work. An empathetic attitude toward those who come to your attention because they are violating the law or a company policy is highly desirable. True professionals do not take client behaviors personally. They keep emotion out of decisions that affect other's lives through *intellectualization*—that is, they think before they act.

In addition to having the preceding characteristics, successful candidates have also performed well in the past.

> A good predictor of how candidates will perform in the future is how they performed in the past.

Experiences that can reflect positively on a candidate include:

- Past general employment
- Volunteer community experience
- Work-related experience
- Military service
- Education
- Communication skills/experience
- Computer, typing and word processing skills
- Interning

Past General Employment

While some employers may be looking for specific experience, those hiring entry-level personnel are usually more interested in a person's general background. Past employment says a lot about a person. The simple fact that a person was successfully employed says that someone wanted to hire that person and that they were responsible enough to stay on the job. Keeping a job says that the person could operate on a schedule, complete assigned tasks, not take advantage of the basic trust placed in all employees and get along with others.

It might also be said that the more remote a person's past jobs were from the position being applied for, the more favorable the experience would be viewed. Many employers would rather hire entry-level personnel and train them "from scratch." Also, more general backgrounds provide a broader view of the world and opportunities to have developed varied experiences.

Don't worry if the only work experience you have is flipping burgers or stocking shelves. It says you chose to work. The more and varied experiences you have, the better you'll look—at least on paper. What previous jobs say about you is important enough that career counselors frequently advise students, particularly younger ones, that it will enhance their ability to be hired if they get a responsible job for a few years. Employers, especially those in such critical fields as criminal justice and security, would prefer not to be the first employer a person has.

Past employment, regardless of the setting, says a lot about a person, such as the person was responsible enough to stay on the job, could operate on a schedule, complete assigned tasks, not take advantage of the basic trust placed in all employees and get along with others.

Volunteer Community Service

Volunteering speaks highly of the way we view our neighbors, reaching out to help when needed. Those who give of themselves make the statement, "I am willing to help." Because a fundamental role of criminal justice and security professionals is interacting with and helping people, any volunteer community service will reflect positively on you.

Many people looking for work, especially younger people, are frustrated that most employers want some experience. The dilemma: How do you get a job without experience? How do you get experience without a job? Volunteering in any way in your community is an exceptional opportunity to gain experience. Furthermore, the trend in modern professional law enforcement is to emphasize *community policing*. Many police agencies want to know you are able to work in the community in something other than an enforcement capacity and that you genuinely want to be a contributing community member. For example, an interviewer might ask prospective candidates, "What do you do for your community?"

Volunteering is an exceptional opportunity to gain experience and reflects positively on you by telling a prospective employer you are willing to help your community.

Work-Related Experience

While experience not directly related to your career goals has many benefits associated with it, you may be eager to become involved in your chosen field. Opportunities for such experiences are abundant and provide a strong base from which to seek employment. Explorer posts, for example, provide opportunities to combine social and learning experiences. Similar to Boy Scouts and Girl Scouts, law enforcement explorer groups have a great deal of fun while learning about the profession. Generally sponsored by a community law enforcement agency, explorers learn such skills as shooting, first aid, defensive tactics and crime scene investigation. Good-hearted competition helps to hone these valuable skills.

Police reserve units also serve several valuable functions. Not only do such units provide backup to the paid officers in such situations as crowd control and crime scene searches, but it is yet another chance to gain experience in the field while serving the community. Participating in a reserve unit says you can work as part of a team and not abuse this association.

Volunteer and paid-on-call fire departments offer another opportunity to do more than "get your feet wet" (literally). Firefighting, recognized as an extraordinarily dangerous activity, demands the same attributes required of police, corrections and security officers: a cool head, the ability to work on a team and the ability to confront dangerous obstacles. Because police officers may answer fire calls, too, it helps to know how to respond.

Other agencies have opportunities that provide valuable experience. For example, some sheriffs' departments have special rescue squads, water patrol units and even mounted posses—all staffed by volunteers. Some departments have opportunities available for qualified individuals to provide patrol services to supplement their paid officers. In addition, some colleges have security departments staffed by students, another excellent opportunity to acquire experience in private "policing."

Work-related experience may be gained by becoming involved in an explorer post, police reserve unit, volunteer fire department, special rescue squad, water patrol unit or mounted posse.

A note: Do not strive exclusively for work-related experience. If the only experiences you have include police reserves, police explorers, playing in the police band and volunteering with the police holiday food drive, you will be viewed as a candidate with a shallow experience from which to draw. Many employers will place greater emphasis on the *non*-police related experiences candidates have made for themselves.

Military Service

Military service has many advantages for people considering work in security and criminal justice. First, military service provides an opportunity to enter an admirable field of work with absolutely no previous experience. It allows you to gain valuable experience while enhancing your reputation and developing maturity—not to mention drawing a paycheck. Military service is a great chance to spend some time serving your country, even if you aren't sure about what your final career goals will be. Rather than wasting the time after high school or college by drifting, you could demonstrate your ability to develop in a professional field by joining the service.

Employers recognize that law enforcement, corrections and security are paramilitary and that successful military service is a very good indication of potential success in such civilian service. If you know early enough that you seek involvement in security or criminal justice, getting into a military policing unit can give you valuable experience.

On the other hand, the trend is toward a more humanistic, less authoritarian style of policing in both the public and private sectors. Because the military trains its officers to follow military law rather than the U.S. Constitution, such training may be a detriment to civilian policing. According to one employer, those who had been in the military drew more citizen complaints than their non-veteran counterparts. Furthermore, military veterans tended to be less flexible and less problem-solving oriented than their non-military comrades in police work. Veterans tended to look for "by-the-book" answers. Rigidity and by-the-book responses are out of sync with the current objectives of community policing and problem solving. Additionally, bear in mind that the military teaches interdependence and teamwork, and while both are important parts of policing, the majority of police work is done by the officer acting alone.

A significant benefit employers recognize from military experience is discipline. Because, right or wrong, some think today's young people lack discipline. Military training makes a strong statement to the hiring authority. Some employers assert that individuals having military experience combined with advanced education make excellent officers.

> Military experience can be beneficial to those seeking employment in police, corrections or security work because it develops discipline and allows the individual to mature. However, military training may also be a detriment because civilian policing strives for a more humanistic, less authoritarian approach and reversing the military training may be difficult.

Education

Education is more important today than ever in many fields, including criminal justice and private security. If these fields are to be considered professions, which they are striving to do, then education plays an important role.

New focus has been placed on how well our schools are preparing young adults for life in the working world. To examine this issue, the U.S. Department of Labor formed, in 1990, a committee known as the Secretary's Commission on Achieving Necessary Skills, or SCANS. According to a 1992 SCANS report titled "Learning a Living: A Blueprint for High Performance" (1992, p.ix): "[SCANS] was asked to define the know-how needed in the workplace and to consider how this know-how is best assessed." The Commission's first report, issued in 1991 and titled "What Work Requires of Schools," identified the need for schools to help students develop a foundation of basic academic skills, thinking skills and personal qualities necessary to achieve competency in the workplace, as shown in Figure 8-1. The 1992 report (p.xiv) also revealed:

> The time when a high school diploma was a sure ticket to a job is within the memory of workers who have not yet retired; yet in many places today a high school diploma is little more than a certificate of attendance. As a result, employers discount the value of all diplomas, and many students do not work hard in high school.

More than a decade later, the fundamental skills and competencies detailed in Figure 8-1 remain the focus of SCANS, as stated on their Web site: "The central theme in all our work is creating a workforce development system that properly prepares workers to compete in the international economy of the 21st century." For more detailed definitions of these competencies and skills, or to learn more about school-to-work programs and education reform, visit SCANS 2000 Workforce Skills Web site: http://www.scans.jhu.edu/

Education says something about those who obtain it. It says the person can identify, pursue and accomplish important goals. It shows patience, drive and self-determination. It shows the ability to commit to both short- and long-range goals. It says those seeking education are interested in both themselves and the world in which they live.

The know-how identified by SCANS is made up of five competencies and a three-part foundation of skills and personal qualities that are needed for solid job performance. These are:

WORKPLACE COMPETENCIES: Effective workers can productively use:

- **Resources**—They know how to allocate time, money, materials, space and staff.

- **Interpersonal Skills**—They can work on teams, teach others, serve customers, lead, negotiate and work well with people from culturally diverse backgrounds.

- **Information**—They can acquire and evaluate data, organize and maintain files, interpret and communicate and use computers to process information.

- **Systems**—They understand social, organizational and technological systems; they can monitor and correct performance and they can design or improve systems.

- **Technology**—They can select equipment and tools, apply technology to specific tasks and maintain and troubleshoot equipment.

FOUNDATION SKILLS: Competent workers in the high-performance workplace need:

- **Basic Skills**—reading, writing, arithmetic and mathematics, speaking and listening.

- **Thinking Skills**—the ability to learn, to reason, to think creatively, to make decisions and to solve problems.

- **Personal Qualities**—individual responsibility, self-esteem and self-management, sociability and integrity.

FIGURE 8-1   Workplace Know-How

SOURCE: "Learning a Living: A Blueprint for High Performance. A SCANS Report for America 2000." The Secretary's Commission on Achieving Necessary Skills, U.S. Department of Labor, April 1992, p.xiv.

Education *does* make you view the world differently. Education expands horizons, helping you better understand the differences that make our diverse society not a threat, but a challenge. In addition, many agencies now *require* some college. According to Sharp (1997, p.27):

> Some 69% of the respondents to a recent poll acknowledged a trend in law enforcement work that requires college degrees as a condition of employment. Only 14% did not see the trend. (The rest were not sure.)

> And 53% answered that college degrees should be required for police officers as conditions of new or continued employment for *all* departments. Significantly, 91% stated that college degrees were important in departments of all sizes.

For the past three decades, every national commission on violence and crime in America has concluded that college education can improve police performance. More than 25 years ago the National Advisory Committee on CCommittee on Criminal Justice Stals warned: "There are few professions today that do not require a college degree. Police, in their quest for greater professionalism should take notice." Vodicka (1994, p.91) asserts:

> In this highly technical age, police officers must be able to perform a myriad of duties with skill and success—information processor, community organizer, crime analyst, counselor, street corner politician, arresting officer, school liaison, and community lead. Any of these actions, taken individually, would generally warrant a higher education requirement. Yet, the idea of college for police officers evokes much emotion and debate.

Mahan (1991, pp.285–286) likewise urges that departments establish a policy regarding educational requirements and that several arguments support a requirement for college credits for those pursuing employment in law enforcement:

- It develops a broader base of information for decision making;
- It allows for additional years and experiences for maturity;
- Course requirements . . . [instill] responsibility in the individual;
- It permits the individual to learn more about the history of the country, the democratic process and an appreciation for constitutional rights, values and the democratic form of government;
- College education engenders the ability to flexibly handle difficult or ambiguous situations with greater creativity or innovation;
- It permits a better view of the "big picture" of the criminal justice system and both a better understanding and appreciation for the prosecutorial, courts and correctional roles;
- Higher education develops a greater empathy for minorities and their discriminatory experiences through both course work and interaction within the academic environment;
- It permits a greater understanding and tolerance for persons with differing lifestyles and ideologies, which can translate into more efficient communications;
- The college-educated officer is assumed to be less rigid in decision-making . . . with a greater tendency to wisely use discretion to deal with the individual case;
- The college experience will help officers communicate and respond to crime and service needs of the public in a competent manner with civility and humanity.

These same arguments apply to other positions within criminal justice and security.

No longer do legal barriers stand in the way of police departments requiring college education. In *Davis v. Dallas* (1986), a U.S. Court of Appeals upheld a requirement by the City of Dallas that entry-level police recruits have completed 45 college credits with a C average.

Advanced education is valuable to anyone seeking employment in criminal justice or private security not only because of the actual knowledge gained but also because of what pursuing such education says about you to a prospective employer—that you can identify, pursue and accomplish important goals; that you have patience, drive and self-determination; that you possess the ability to commit to both short- and long-range goals and that you are interested in both yourself and the world in which you live.

You should keep a personal training log or journal documenting any training or educational programs in which you participate. Such a journal may be useful in preparing your resume or in answering any questions prospective employers may ask about your training and/or education.

Can You Be Over-Educated? In all honesty, the answer might be "yes," at least in some employers' eyes. Particularly for employers who may have achieved their position in the more traditional way of coming "up through the ranks" and at a time when higher education was considered less important for officers' career development than it is today, they may not regard advanced education as a necessary or desirable attribute. Some might see it as an outright threat to them.

While it is not as much a problem as it might have been once, candidates with a master's degree, for example, will want to be prepared to answer any similar questions to "Why did you pursue your education at the graduate level?" Those holding law degrees, Ph.D.'s or other doctoral-level degrees will undoubtedly be asked about this, especially those applying for an entry-level position. You will have no difficulty pointing out the benefits the degree will have for the department if you are hired, but hiring authorities may have a legitimate concern whether you will be bored at the job you are applying for. Even if not asked directly, you will want to address this because they are probably, albeit silently, wondering about it.

Communication Skills

Communication skills are critical for public and private officers, for they communicate orally and in writing every day. How well you communicate will, to a great extent, determine how far you advance. Writing skills are especially important because once something is in writing, it is *permanent*. In addition:

➤ The police reports are often the first impression a judge or defense attorney has of an officer's competence, both generally and in regard to the specific elements of the offense charged.
➤ The decision to charge someone with a crime is based upon the police reports, usually alone.
➤ Complete and well-written police reports help to speed up the entire system. Delays in prosecution often occur because of incomplete reports.
➤ A well-written report alone can settle a case.

Unfortunately, most schools do not teach what the workplace requires. Any experiences you can have that enhance your ability to communicate, both orally and in writing, are extremely important.

Communication skills—oral and written—are critically important for public and private officers and may determine how far you will advance in your career.

Computer, Typing and Word Processing Skills

You may be thinking, "I'm not applying for a secretarial job. Why do I need to know how to type?" But face it—we've gone techno. With today's reliance on the computer to generate reports and manage casework, typing, keyboarding and computer skills are essential for entering the fields of criminal justice and security. For example, it is estimated that probation and parole officers spend approximately 75 percent of their workday *typing* pre-sentence investigation reports. Clearly, knowing your way around the keyboard is a must for this job.

You will be expected, to one degree or another, to be comfortable with computers. Your first sign of this to a prospective employer is the appearance of your application materials. There is no question which comes off an old manual typewriter and which comes off a word processor.

Also, many agencies (private and public) are going to computerized report writing and making an effort toward the "paperless office." More and more police departments are giving their officers laptop computers or mobile data terminals (MDTs) in their squad cars, expecting them to write their reports, possibly at the scene, and send them wirelessly to headquarters. The old-fashioned "hunt and peck" typist isn't going to be as strong at the job, or in applying for it, as one who is even moderately proficient in typing and computers.

A practical example of how such skills are required to perform the everyday duties of police work is given by Pilant (1999). An officer responding to an accident scene involving six vehicles and multiple injuries needed to, among other things, write several DWI tickets and send seven people to three different hospitals. Pilant (p.12) states: "The paperwork alone would have generated at least 35 forms, all of which required filling in the same information—for example, name, date of birth, and driver's license number." Instead of doing this all "by hand," however, the officer was able to use the Advanced Law Enforcement Response Technology, or ALERT, to enter the basic information once and assign it to as many forms as needed. ALERT is an on-board computer that performs numerous vital functions, including controlling patrol car devices (lights, sirens, radar) and enabling officers to write and transmit reports.

Strandberg (1998, p.82) notes:

> Writing is a constant fact of life for law enforcement. Reports, memos, updates, evaluations—all of these and more have to be written to drive the information machine that is law enforcement. Unfortunately, a great deal of law enforcement writing is mired in stilted language, unclear reporting, inconsistencies and mistakes, jargon and inappropriate word choice. This directly impacts how the justice system works.

Hess (1999, p.44) offers the following caution regarding the accuracy of spelling in reports:

> A misspelled name, for example, might cause serious problems for the reporting officer. And although spell-checkers are great—you can't rely on them completely. Consider the following examples—all of which would get past a spell-check:
>
> - He was arrested for a mister meaner.
> - She was a drug attic.
> - The victim was over rot.
> - After the accident he went into a comma.
> - She was a cereal killer.

The importance of and reliance on computers is constantly increasing. Computer skills are no longer something you can add to a resume; they are something expected of a viable candidate. It's difficult to contemplate a job in criminal justice or security that doesn't involve the routine use of computers. If you aren't comfortable with or knowledgeable about computer basics, become so.

Interning

A great way to break into the real world of work while still learning is by interning. As an intern, you get to work on the job as an educational experience. Many criminal justice programs across the nation are implementing internship programs and courses to help prepare their students for future careers. And while internships are seldom paid positions, the experience itself is priceless.

Interning serves a number of purposes. Some will be to the agency's benefit, but most will be to yours. Not only will you get an opportunity to see if this work, in general, suits you, but you will get a view of the profession that only an insider can attain. You may be expected to merely observe or to take a very active part in all aspects of the job. Be it helping to investigate a homicide at the crime scene or helping a probation officer interview a client, interning provides an excellent chance to combine experiential learning with academic learning—a true educational experience. It also provides a means to determine if this is the profession for you.

Internships provide a unique opportunity to look into a field to determine if it's the right profession for you while allowing you to gain some valuable experience.

Taylor (1999, p.3) asserts:

> Internships will help [students] determine the most desirable areas for their future careers or indeed, decide whether they want to remain in the discipline at all. . . . Furthermore, student interactions with agency supervisors, clients, and the agency staff constitute a comprehensive instructional experience that will prove invaluable and will aid in cultivating alliances that may be beneficial in obtaining employment in the future. In some instances, students may be employed by the agencies after the internships end.

Taylor (p.95) also notes interns are expected to follow certain ethical guidelines for the benefit and protection of themselves, as well as for that of clients, internship supervisors and agencies, and the internship coordinator and educational institution. Ethical standards interns must adhere to involve confidentiality, competency, avoidance of corruption and building interpersonal relationships.

A word of caution to those considering taking advantage of internship opportunities: be careful! If you behave in a way that causes you to be asked to leave, this will *not* look good for you in the future. If you anticipate scheduling problems or any other issues that might cause you to receive a less-than-favorable report on your internship, you are better off to wait until you can perform at your best. Interning is about as close to actually having the job as you can get.

This may sound easy, but it isn't necessarily so. You will certainly have less training than those who are actually employed in the profession. And you may not be provided with absolutely clear expectations or guidelines. You are going to have to use excellent judgment; they will be watching how you perform. More and more agencies use their interns as a pool from which to consider actual job applicants, so you simply can't afford to blow it here. You can be sure that when the background investigator checks on your internship performance, he or she will be told how you did. So the most important advice for interns is: don't be a know-it-all. I actually witnessed an intern tell a senior officer how she could do her job better! Needless to say, that intern didn't even get considered for full-time employment. Keep quiet, ask appropriate questions, and don't expect to be accepted as "one of the gang," at least not at first. And don't take this personally. Again, your time will come . . . if you allow it to happen.

PAINTING A PICTURE

Consider your job application, in all respects, as a painting—a unique painting. It is not going to be like that of anyone else. Yours will be made up of the experiences you have developed for yourself and will have aspects others do not. You will have strengths where others have weaknesses, and there will be areas where you are building skills and improving. There may even be areas you have to clarify or explain to the person viewing it. Yet everything you have done and are doing will contribute to this picture that is uniquely you.

 What experiences do you have that make a statement, and what do they say about you? Write them in your journal.

Impress in a job interview

MAKING THE BEST OF BAD SITUATIONS

How many people can honestly say they have absolutely no blemishes on their records? If you're like most people, you learn more by making mistakes than by doing it right the first time. Did you really believe your mother when she said the stove was hot? Honestly? Or did you have to see for yourself?

A popular poster reads: *When life gives you lemons, make lemonade.* However you say it, if you have made a mistake—which everyone has—it does not mean you have forfeited your future in security or criminal justice. Granted, *some* mistakes will bar you from certain positions in these fields. For example, no state will permit you to be a police officer if you have a felony on your record. They may, however, allow a misdemeanor or traffic offense.

Know in advance how you will deal with past mistakes, and accept that they do not automatically make you an outcast from society or from your chosen profession. Most professions accept mistakes, but they do *not* accept people who cannot change their ways, nor do they accept dishonesty. To lie on an application says nothing less than that you can't be trusted. It may even be a crime.

How do you deal with blemishes such as traffic citations or misdemeanor criminal charges? Approach them upfront and honestly. Since the best defense is often a good offense, you will usually want to confront these issues head on. It looks better if you bring them up rather than having the employer learn about them during the background check. If they dredge up one questionable issue from your past, they may wonder what else might be hidden.

Once you have admitted you made a mistake (or two, or three), take it one step further. Share what you learned from the experience. If you have a less-than-perfect traffic record or a shoplifting charge from your youth, it would sound better to explain how that experience influenced you to want to become a police officer or a security officer. Consider how a hiring board would react to being told you were so influenced by the professionalism shown by the police officer who gave you that ticket that you wanted to become a police officer and positively influence others in the same way. What about a DWI conviction? Rather than eliminating you from the running, it could result in your taking subsequent steps to get your life together. To admit any shortcoming and prove you took advantage of an opportunity to grow and change does not make you an undesirable person. It makes you exceptional.

Imagine, for example, that you had a questionable driving record and were in competition with one other applicant. Other than the driving record, you have identical attributes. Would the hiring board use your driving record to decide against you? Or maybe even for you? They might if you accept that you are what you are. Present yourself in the best light—honestly. While you might have made some admittedly questionable decisions in the past, you want them to fully understand that that was then and you learned from it. To do otherwise makes you look, at best, on the defensive and, at worst, a liar.

Judge for yourself—which sounds best in response to an interviewer's question: "How is your driving record?"

> **Candidate #1.** Fine. (If this is true, great. But it will take about 10 seconds to verify this on the computer. If you lied, you're out.)

> **Candidate #2.** Well, I've had a few tickets. But I was only a kid, and the cops in my town had it in for me because of that. I think they just had to meet their quotas and it was easier to do by picking on us kids.

> **Candidate #3.** As a matter of fact, I got some traffic tickets when I was a teenager. I can't say I didn't deserve them because I did. I learned about obeying traffic regulations the hard way— having to work summer jobs to pay for the tickets and the increased car insurance premiums. But it taught me a valuable lesson. *I* was accountable for my actions. It wasn't the fault of the officers who gave me the tickets or my parents for not picking up the tab. It was my own fault. It worked for me. This is one reason I want to be a police officer—to help others learn.

You get the picture. Consider another situation, this time with candidates responding to an interviewer's question: "Have you ever used illegal substances?"

> **Candidate #1.** No. I would never do anything illegal. (Again, if this is true, great. But if the background investigation proves you to be a liar, you are out.)

> **Candidate #2.** To be honest, as a teenager I did experiment with marijuana. Most of my friends smoked pot, and I gave in to their pressure. It didn't do a thing for me, and I was forced to think about who was running my life—my friends or me. I knew it was time to stand up for myself, and it was a good learning experience. In fact, most of my friends quit too. We each thought the others expected it of us. What an eye-opener that was!

To take care of minor problems that would generally bar employment, consider interviewing with a mid-sized agency that has hired applicants with minor problems. And remember, you can't change the past, but you *can* present it so it looks positive rather than negative.

Although some mistakes will bar you from certain positions in these fields, most employers accept mistakes *if* you are open and up front about them during the pre-employment interview, share what you learned from the experience, and express honestly how you have changed your ways.

This is not to suggest you will be able to justify or "explain away" every indiscretion in your background. For example, a pattern of alcohol-related problems or financial difficulties are sure to concern those considering your application. Having chronic problems or an abundance of unresolved issues may well eliminate you from consideration. You must be realistic in this area, particularly if it continues happening as you apply for positions.

CRIMINAL JUSTICE, PRIVATE SECURITY AND ETHICS

Ethics has become a buzzword in almost every profession. Certainly criminal justice and private security demand the highest ethics. You can anticipate having to deal with this issue. In fact, ethics is a favorite topic of interview boards, so carefully consider your values and what you believe ethical behavior to be.

To develop and maintain a professional reputation, codes of ethics have been adopted in both law enforcement and private security. The Law Enforcement Code of Ethics is shown in Figure 8-2.

As a law enforcement officer, my fundamental duty is to serve the community; to safeguard lives and property; to protect the innocent against deception, the weak against oppression or intimidation, and the peaceful against violence or disorder; and to respect the constitutional rights of all to liberty, equality and justice.

I will keep my private life unsullied as an example to all and will behave in a manner that does not bring discredit to me or my agency. I will maintain courageous calm in the face of danger, scorn or ridicule; develop self-restraint; and be constantly mindful of the welfare of others. Honest in thought and deed both in my personal and official life, I will be exemplary in obeying the law and the regulations of my department. Whatever I see or hear of a confidential nature or that is confided to me in my official capacity will be kept ever secret unless revelation is necessary in the performance of my duty.

I will never act officiously or permit personal feelings, prejudices, political beliefs, aspirations, animosities or friendships to influence my decisions. With no compromise for crime and with relentless prosecution of criminals, I will enforce the law courteously and appropriately without fear or favor, malice or ill will, never employing unnecessary force or violence and never accepting gratuities.

I recognize the badge of my office as a symbol of public faith, and I accept it as a public trust to be held so long as I am true to the ethics of the police service. I will never engage in acts of corruption or bribery, nor will I condone such acts by other police officers. I will cooperate with all legally authorized agencies and their representatives in the pursuit of justice.

I know that I alone am responsible for my own standard of professional performance and will take every reasonable opportunity to enhance and improve my level of knowledge and competence.

I will constantly strive to achieve these objectives and ideals, dedicating myself before God to my chosen profession . . . law enforcement.

FIGURE 8-2   Law Enforcement Code of Ethics

SOURCE: Reprinted with permission from the International Association of Chiefs of Police, Alexandria, Virginia. Further reproduction without express written permission from IACP is strictly prohibited.

The International Association of Chiefs of Police (IACP) has also developed a Police Code of Conduct that covers primary responsibilities of a police officer, performance of the duties of a police officer, discretion, use of force, confidentiality, integrity, cooperation with other officers and agencies, personal/professional capabilities and private life. See Appendix A for the entire IACP Police Code of Conduct. The security profession has also developed a similar code of ethics, which is presented in Appendix B.

The ethics of police, corrections and security officers play a large role in whether these fields are viewed as true professions. In fact, ethics is a favorite topic of interview boards, so you should thoughtfully consider your values and what you consider to be ethical behavior.

According to Smotzer (1999, p.32): "Ethics isn't a written code, it's about what we do." He cites "the six pillars of character" as trustworthiness, respect, responsibility, justice and fairness, caring, and civil virtue and citizenship. He also stresses five principles of ethical policing: fair access, public trust, safety and security, teamwork, and objectivity.

The importance of ethics is also emphasized by the Ethics Training Subcommittee of the IACP Ad Hoc Committee on Police Image and Ethics (1998, p.14): "Ethics is our greatest training and leadership need today and into the next century." The IACP has recommended a Law Enforcement Oath of Honor as a symbolic statement to ethical behavior (p.19):

> On my honor,
> I will never betray my badge,
> my integrity, my character,
> or the public trust.
> I will always have
> the courage to hold myself
> and others accountable for our actions.
> I will always uphold the constitution
> and community I serve.

Values

To a potential employer, a person's values say a great deal about who they are and what kind of employee they will prove to be. Values are more than just having ethics or a positive background. Values are what's important to an individual. In fact, many consider one's values the best overall statement of *who* they really are. For example, the core values of the Minnesota State Patrol, which their cadets learn, are the essence of this organization. They provide a strong basis for the group and for the individual.

> The mission of the Minnesota State Patrol is
> working together to ensure a safe environment
> on Minnesota's roadways.
>
> The Minnesota State Patrol has adopted
> the following core values as part of its training curriculum:
>
> **Core Values**
> Pride
> Preservation of Life
> Pursuit of Excellence
> Ethics
> Loyalty
> Professionalism
> Trustworthiness

As an organization has basic values, written or unwritten, so does every individual. The picture you paint of yourself will reflect the values you hold to be important. Obviously, your values will make an impression on a prospective employer.

CONCLUSION

Your life is like a painting being continuously worked on. It will be developed, refined, altered and improved. It is never completed. Although the canvas may occasionally be briefly set aside, the paint is never completely dried—unless you allow it to be. At every phase of your life, you will appear to others as you have developed yourself. How will you appear to prospective employers? How can you add to your "life's painting" to be as appealing as possible? If you need more substance to your picture, get it. You have the control, the opportunity. Do you have the ambition and foresight?

   MIND STRETCHES

1.   Do you believe your past is an accurate assessment of your employment potential?

2.   Who would be a better risk as an employee: candidates who tested the system as juveniles, occasionally having run-ins with the law, or candidates who walked the "straight and narrow," never doing anything "wrong," but also never testing their own limitations?

3.   What are important benefits of attending college?

4.   What volunteer opportunities exist in your community?

5.   What do good writing skills say about you? How can you develop them?

6.   Name five important attributes an employer might seek from applicants, regardless of the job. How can you develop these attributes?

7.   Why is ethics of particular importance to criminal justice and private security?

8.   As you look at your past, are there facts that could hurt you as a job applicant? How will you address them to put them in the most positive light?

9.   What are your personal and professional strengths?

10.   Is it possible to be "overqualified"? Why or why not?

INSIDERS' VIEWS

For this chapter, read the *Insiders' Views* by Chief Michael P. Stein ("Getting Your Foot in the Door") and Special Agent Monte D. Zillinger ("Out of the Ordinary"), found on the Web site: http://www.wadsworth.com/criminaljustice_d/.

REFERENCES

Hess, Kären M. "The ABCs of Effective Reports: Observe the Basics." *Police*, March 1999, pp.43–44.

Hogue, Mark C.; Black, Tommie and Sigler, Robert T. "The Differential Use of Screening Techniques in the Recruitment of Police Officers." *American Journal of Police,* 1994, pp.113–124.

IACP Ad Hoc Committee on Police Image and Ethics, Ethics Training Subcommittee. "Ethics Training in Law Enforcement." *The Police Chief*, January 1998, pp.14–24.

"Learning a Living: A Blueprint for High Performance. A SCANS Report for America 2000." The Secretary's Commission on Achieving Necessary Skills, U.S. Department of Labor, April 1992.

Mahan, R. "Personnel Selection in Police Agencies: Educational Requirements for Entry Level." *Law and Order,* January 1991, pp.282–286.

Pilant, Lois. "Going Mobile in Law Enforcement Technology." *National Institute of Justice Journal*, January 1999, pp.11–16.

Sharp, Arthur G. "The Forecast for Police Employment Is a Matter of Degrees." *Law and Order*, May 1997, pp.27–32.

Slahor, Stephenie. "How One Department Gets the Best." *Law and Order*, May 1998, p.60.

Smotzer, Andrew A. "Ethics Training for Law Enforcement." *Law and Order*, February 1999, p.32.

Strandberg, Keith W. "Toward Better Report Writing." *Law Enforcement Technology*, June 1998, pp.82–84.

Taylor, Dorothy. *Jumpstarting Your Career: An Internship Guide for Criminal Justice.* Upper Saddle River, NJ: Prentice Hall, Inc., 1999.

Vodicka, Alan T. "Educational Requirements for Police Recruits: Higher Education Benefits Officers, Agency." *Law and Order,*
March 1994, pp. 91–94.

Weiss, Jim and Dresser, Mary. "Job Hunt Karate." *Law and Order*, May 1998, pp. 47–52.

CHAPTER 9

THE RESUME: SELLING YOURSELF ON PAPER

Writing a Resume: Spend time on self-assessment first. Identify all the achievements of your past that illustrate skills. Describe them in active verbs and look for consistencies. That's the clue as to what you should emphasize. A resume is scanned, not read. It's a sales tool that should give someone a sampling, not details in full.

—*Jean Clarkson*

Do You Know:

➢ What a resume is?
➢ What purposes a resume serves?
➢ What seven steps are involved in creating a resume?
➢ . What items to include in your resume?
➢ What is best left off your resume?
➢ What three basic types of resumes are commonly used and how they differ?
➢ What is important about the format of your resume?
➢ What the key to writing an effective resume is?
➢ What to keep in mind when printing your resume?
➢ When to send a cover letter and what elements are essential?
➢ The best way to deliver your resume and what to do after the delivery?
➢ How to make your resume computer compatible?

INTRODUCTION

You've spent a lot of time thinking about your goals and yourself, your fitness, education and attributes. Now it's time to pull all this information together into one of your most important job-seeking tools—the resume.

You probably know what a resume is. But that's a little like saying you know what surgery is. A vast amount of territory exists between recognizing a concept and grasping its true meaning. To have a working understanding of such a concept is even more involved. This chapter gives a working knowledge of the resume. *Resume* is a French word (pronounced *REZ-oo-may*) that means "summary."

What is a resume? Webster's defines *resume* as: "A short account of one's career and qualifications prepared typically by an applicant for a position." A resume is a capsulized account highlighting and describing *significant* aspects of your background and qualifications for a given job—a promotional tool designed to *sell* you.

A resume is a brief, well-documented account of your career achievements, which highlights significant aspects of your background and identifies your qualifications for a given job. Its purpose is to *sell* you to a prospective employer.

Wendleton and Dauten (1999b, p.D4) state: "The average resume is looked at for only 10 seconds!" They add: "Ten seconds is plenty of time, if you remember that your goal isn't to answer every possible question, but to arouse enough interest to make a manager want to interview you." The competition to attract an employer's attention is keen, bitter and brutal. A well-prepared resume can be the determining factor in whether an employer calls you for an interview, allowing you a "foot in the door." Your resume may be your first contact with a potential employer. It may also be the last. The choice is yours.

In some cases, however, particularly in larger agencies and institutions, resumes are not used. Instead, the agency goes through a civil service commission. Applicants fill in only the commission's paperwork and can add nothing to it. A resume can backfire if you include it and it is *not* asked for or wanted.

THE PURPOSES OF THE RESUME

The resume is important to the *employer* because it helps weed out unqualified candidates. For most employers, this is the most important function of a resume. Employers will use *any* flaw in a resume to cut down the number of individuals to be interviewed. Resumes help employers cut through a lot of preliminary questioning about applicants' qualifications and help employers structure their interviews.

The resume is important to *you* because it can help get you in the door for an interview. It serves other purposes as well. Preparing your resume will force you to take a hard look at your skills, qualifications, past experiences and accomplishments. It will force you to recall (or look up) dates and addresses. It will force you to organize your past clearly and concisely. This will help you present yourself in an organized manner during the interview as well. In addition, you can approach the interview confident that you have the qualities and background the employer is looking for, or why would you be called in?

> Resumes serve a variety of purposes for both the employer and the applicant. A resume helps an employer by weeding out unqualified candidates, answering preliminary questions about an applicant's qualifications and structuring an interview. A resume helps applicants obtain interviews and organize their experiences, accomplishments, present skills and qualifications so they may be coherently discussed during an interview.

During the interview, the resume will save time by providing a common ground to start from. It will also keep you honest. The temptation to exaggerate your experience or accomplishments will be removed when you know the employer has seen your resume. Now that you know how important your resume is, look at the specific steps in creating one.

STEPS IN CREATING A RESUME

Creating a resume is like painting a picture of yourself. From the conception of the idea to the completion of the masterpiece, you need to take seven specific steps.

> The seven specific steps to creating a resume are:
>
> 1. Compile all relevant information.
> 2. Select the most appropriate type of resume.
> 3. Select a format.
> 4. Write the first draft.
> 5. Polish the first draft.
> 6. Evaluate the resume and revise if necessary.
> 7. Print the resume.

Creating an effective resume is *hard work*, but the results will be well worth it. Without an effective resume, you are wasting your time applying for most jobs. You won't get to first base. Even if an agency does not require a resume, they will expect you to be a "living resume" at the interview. Get yourself organized before that. Make up your mind to devote several hours to this important document.

COMPILE INFORMATION

Gather all the information that could possibly be included in your resume. Some will be used; some won't. Painters gather all of their brushes and paints before they begin to work so they aren't interrupted during the creative process. Likewise, you will want to gather all the information you *might* decide to include. You don't want to interrupt the creative writing flow to look up a phone number or address.

 Use the worksheets in Appendix C to organize your resume information. Flip to the back of the book and place a paper clip at the top of Appendix C to help you locate it quickly while working through this section. Don't cut corners during this first step. Your background makes a great deal of difference. As you compile information, you may be amazed at how much data an employer will need to even consider you.

You'll look at three kinds of information: (1) data you must include, (2) data you might include and (3) data you should probably not include but should be prepared to discuss. Don't guess at dates. Verify them. Don't guess at addresses. Check them out if it's been awhile since you worked or lived somewhere.

Look first at what *MUST* be included: personal identifying information, your educational background and your work experience.

Personal Identifying Information

Name. Obvious? Yes. But believe it or not, some people actually forget to include their name. In addition, think carefully about how you want your name to appear. Do you want to include your middle name? An initial? A nickname? A title? If you include a nickname, put it following your first name with quotation marks around it, like this: *Robert "Bob" T. Jones*. This lets the employer know what you prefer to be called. Avoid extreme or inappropriate nicknames such as "Killer."

 How do you want your name to appear in your resume? Write it on the worksheet.

Address. It is usually best to give only your home address. Put the street address on one line. Do not abbreviate. Put a comma between a street address and an apartment number. Put the city and state on the next line and separate them with a comma. Use the two-letter state abbreviation—both letters capitalized and NO period. Include your zip code. Do *not* put a comma between the state and zip code.

Example: 123 Third Avenue South, #401
My Town, MN 55437

 How should your address appear? Write it on the worksheet.

If you move frequently, you may want to include a permanent address in addition to your present address.

 E-mail address: Include your e-mail address *only* if you check your e-mail daily.

Phone Number. *Always* include a phone number. Busy employers often prefer to call rather than write. Make it easy for them. Give the area code, followed by a hyphen and then your phone number. Indicate if it is a home or a work number. Many people prefer to *not* include a work phone to avoid being called at work. Would getting job-search-related phone calls at work cause you any problems? If so, do *not* include your work number. Some people also include the hours they can be reached at a given number. Others put this information in their cover letter.

Example: Work Phone   612-555-9929 (9 a.m. to 5 p.m.)
              Home Phone   612-555-8818 (6 p.m. to 10 p.m.)

 Enter your phone number(s) on the appropriate line on the worksheet.

Did you know there was so much to think about in simply giving your name, address and phone number?

Education

Information about your education is crucial to your resume.

 College. List each college attended, city and state, number of years completed, major/minor, unique areas of study and degree(s) earned. Start with the most recent and work backwards. Include any honors, awards or leadership positions. Include grade point average *if* outstanding.

 Professional Schools. Include the same information as for colleges. Include academies here also.

 Internships. Include the place and length of the internship.

 Certificates. Relevant certificates would include first aid, CPR and the like. Give the year the certificates were awarded and expiration dates, if relevant.

 Other Educational Experiences. Include any relevant seminars, workshops, correspondence courses and the like.

 High School. Include name, city and state, year of graduation, and grade point average if it is outstanding. Include your high school *only* if you graduated within the last 10 years or if you have no other education to include.

Work Experience

Recall from Chapter 8 that past general employment of any type is valuable in the job search, even if not related to your field. Volunteer experience, work-related or not, should also be included on your resume. Of special importance are the qualifications and skills you bring to the job. You may want to refer to Chapter 8 for attributes most employers are looking for. Your resume should stress achievements more than education and experience.

 Begin with your present job, or your most recent job if you are not currently employed. Work back in time. Use the worksheet in Appendix C. Make a copy of this worksheet for each job you have had. Use the work experience section to describe your qualities and skills wherever and however you can. If applicable, you might also demonstrate these qualities and skills in the education portion of your resume as well.

Several other areas of information might also be included in your resume, depending on your background. Even if you decide *not* to include much or most of the following information, it is important for you to think about it and have it clear in your mind because it could come up during the interview.

Position Desired or Employment Objective

What specific job do you have in mind? Are you open to *any* position in your chosen field? This information can be very helpful to busy employers as they skim through stacks of resumes. An attractive job candidate is one who knows what he wants to do.

 In Appendix C, write down the position desired and, if relevant, your employment objective. An example might be: *Position desired: Entry-level officer with opportunity to provide* _____.

Tell what you can do for the employer—not what the employer can do for you.

Other Information

Other information that may be put in your resume includes the following:

 Birth date, height, weight, health, willingness to travel, willingness to relocate, military experience, professional memberships, knowledge of foreign language(s), foreign travel, awards, publications, community service or involvement, interests and hobbies. Also, list your accomplishments and don't be modest.

Many job-search consultants suggest giving a glimpse of your personal side: marital status, spouse's occupation, ages of your children, family interests and hobbies. It gives a more well-rounded impression of you.

 You might also want to include your availability—can you start immediately or do you need a certain amount of time to give notice to your present employer? Can your present employer be contacted?

Your resume should also include the statement: "References are available on request." And be sure they are.

References

If you get to the point in the hiring process where you are being considered, most employers will want to check your references.

 Choose references *now* and fill in that portion of the worksheet in Appendix C. Try to have business, professional and academic references as well as personal references.

Choose your references carefully. Recall from Chapter 7 the advice on selecting references for the background check. *Always* ask your references if they are willing to provide you with a *positive* reference. Most people do *not* include the references in their resumes. You can simply state: "References available on request," and prepare a separate sheet of references to make available to employers who request them. This also keeps your references confidential until a request is made for them.

Photograph

Some books on resumes suggest that a photograph should never be included with a resume. Other books highly recommend it. Those who are against it suggest that it violates anti-discrimination laws by providing information an employer cannot legally ask about. For example, race, sex and approximate age are revealed in a photograph. If you feel these factors may work in your favor, you may decide to include a photograph.

One advantage of including a photo is that it will probably make your resume stand out from the rest, always a primary goal. However, unless it represents you in a way the employer will appreciate, the photo could detract from your resume. If you do include a photo, be certain it is recent, professional and puts you in a favorable light. You should be neatly groomed, and the reproduction should be clear and crisp.

Items you *must* include in your resume are personal identifying information (name, address and phone number), educational experience and work experience. You might also include the position you desire, your employment objectives, personal information (birth date, health status, marital status, etc.), your willingness to travel or relocate, military experience, professional memberships, knowledge of foreign language(s), awards, publications, any community service or involvement and your availability. You should include a statement that references are available upon request. Whether to include a photograph is debatable. Include a photograph only if it is recent, professional and presents you in a favorable light.

What *Not* to Include

What not to include is a matter of opinion. You obviously want to present yourself as positively as possible. While you will *never* lie on a resume, you will want to present yourself so that even negative occurrences look good for you. If you have to explain them in depth during an interview, that's fine, as long as you *get* to the interview. What *not* to include depends to a great extent on your particular circumstances.

Including too much data is the *number one* fault on resumes. Not only does it present a document that won't get read, but you can harm yourself by saying too much. For example, you will usually have no need to state in a resume why you left past jobs. If the reason was somewhat spectacular, for example a series of promotions, put it in. The presumption will be that you moved upward and onward to better positions. Also, the resume is not the place to explain difficulties you've had. It is a chance to provide a *brief* overview of yourself, to be expanded on once it has gotten you an interview. Be certain everything you include is relevant and cannot in any way detract.

Exceptionally personal data can also detract from the emphasis that should be on your skills and qualifications. If you want to state your family status, fine. But don't give the names and ages of everyone in your family. Does the employer really care? Could it work against you? What if you have very young children and the employer thinks you should be at home with them? What if the employer sees your children are all grown and concludes you are too old for the position? Don't include anything that could work against you. Individual circumstances will determine whether including children's ages allows a glimpse of your personal side or detracts from the more important elements of your resume.

Including too much data is the *number one* fault on resumes. Don't overdo it. Avoid including these items in your resume:

> ➤ Reasons for leaving your current or previous job.
> ➤ Salary (previous or desired).
> ➤ Religious or church affiliations.
> ➤ Race, ethnic background, nationality.
> ➤ Political affiliations/preferences.
> ➤ Anything that negatively dates your resume.

SELECT THE TYPE OF RESUME

When you go fishing you select the bait that will best serve your purpose based on the specific conditions at that particular time and the fish you're after. Likewise, you should have all the "bait" you need to land an interview in the form of the data you have just put together. Now decide how to present it. Three basic types of resumes are commonly used:

> ➤ Historical or chronological
> ➤ Functional
> ➤ Analytical

Each type has a specific format, specific content and a specific purpose.

Historical/Chronological Resume

The historical/chronological resume is the most traditional and is often considered the most effective. As implied by the name, this style presents information in reverse chronological order, starting with your most recent work experience and moving back in time to your past work experience. The educational and employment information worksheets in Appendix C are organized this way. Both education and employment lend themselves to this style. Always include dates and explain any gaps in the chronology.

The historical/chronological resume is easy to read and gives busy employers a familiar form that can be quickly read. It is the best format to use when staying in the same field. It is not the best format if you have little related experience. Use a chronological resume if:

➢ You have spent three or more years with previous employers and have not changed jobs frequently.
➢ You are seeking a position in the same field in which you have been employed.
➢ You have worked for well-known, prestigious companies.
➢ You can show steady growth in responsibilities.

See Appendix D for a sample chronological resume.

Functional Resume

The functional resume emphasizes your qualifications and abilities as they relate to the job you are applying for. After each job is a brief description of your duties and expertise. Dates do not receive as much attention. This style is most applicable if you have had only a few jobs or have been with a particular company or department for a long time. Such a resume stresses experiences and abilities rather than a chronological listing of jobs. It minimizes irrelevant jobs, employment gaps and reversals while maximizing scant work experience. Use a functional resume if:

➢ You are seeking a job in a field new to you.
➢ You have been unemployed for more than three months.
➢ Your responsibilities are complicated and require explanation.
➢ You can point to specific accomplishments on your last job.
➢ You are competing with younger applicants.

See Appendix D for a sample functional resume.

Analytical Resume

The analytical resume stresses your particular skills. It is especially helpful if you are changing career goals but you have obtained necessary skills and qualifications from your present and past jobs. It lets you stress those *skills* and *talents* instead of your work history. Dates are usually omitted, but past jobs and experiences are referred to at some point. Again, you must determine if this approach can best reflect your particular abilities.

See Appendix D for a sample analytical resume.

The three basic types of resumes commonly used are the historical or chronological resume, the functional resume and the analytical resume.

➢ The *historical/chronological resume*, the most traditional and often considered the most effective, presents information by beginning with the most recent experience and going backward in time.
➢ The *functional resume* emphasizes your qualifications and abilities; minimizes irrelevant jobs, employment gaps and reversals; and maximizes scant work experience.
➢ The *analytical resume* is appropriate if you are changing career goals and stresses *skills* and *talents* instead of past jobs.

What About Creativity?

You may be wondering if these three styles are rather boring. You may want to be somewhat more creative. Think carefully about it. An imaginative or creative approach may be of great benefit, or it may burn you. The positive side of such an approach is that it may set your resume apart from the dozens, hundreds, even thousands of others, thus receiving the attention it deserves. The negative side of a creative resume is that it might be the reason the employer is looking for to jettison your resume, along with any others that do not appear "normal." Remember, many employers feel a resume is a business matter and should be presented in a businesslike manner.

If you decide to use an imaginative/creative resume, be sure to include all the information any other style would present. If you can do so, you just might be on to something. For example, what could possibly catch a police department's eye quicker than a resume that takes on the appearance of a "Wanted" poster? It might work, but give very serious consideration to such an idea at an entry-level position.

FORMAT THE RESUME

The format is the layout of the information—what comes first, second and third. *Block* your material and use *headings* to guide the reader. If you have recently graduated, your educational background is probably most important and should come first. If you decide to include hobbies and other personal information, this is usually tucked in at the end. Plan for margins at the top, bottom and sides. Use white space freely. The format should be attractive, businesslike and professional. Actually *design* your format on a sheet of paper. Will you center your identifying information? Have it flush left? Will you use one or two columns for the bulk of the information? Try to fit all the information on *one* page. However, if you need two pages, use them. Keep in mind: If your resume is too long, you risk it not being read; too short, and you risk leaving out relevant information. data

---
The format of your resume should be attractive, businesslike and professional. Not too long; not too short.

Note: Formatting considerations for e-mailed resumes and other computer compatibility issues are discussed later in this chapter.

WRITE THE RESUME

If possible, use a word processor to write your resume. This will make editing it much easier and will also make updating less painful. The key to writing an effective resume is to use short, action-packed *phrases.*

Short. Omit all unnecessary words. This includes:

> ➤ Personal pronouns: *I, me* and *my.*
> ➤ Articles: *a, an* and *the.*

Action-Packed. Write with *verbs,* not with *nouns.* For example, don't say *conducted an investigation,* say *investigated.* Writing with verbs is also shorter than writing with nouns. Look at the following:

> I conducted an analysis of all the incoming calls to the dispatcher, and I compiled detailed analytical reports based on my analysis.

Twenty-two words. Eliminate the pronouns (*I, my*) and articles (*an, the*) and use verbs instead of nouns. What you'll get is something like the following:

> Analyzed all incoming calls and wrote detailed reports.

Which statement would you rather read? Which conveys an image of the writer as focused and authoritative?

Phrases.   Phrase your writing. Watch where lines end. Avoid hyphenating words at the end of the line. For example, read the following:

> It was a difficult job because my boss was a rat-
> her rigid person.

The key to writing an effective resume is to use short, action-packed *phrases.*

Get the idea? Pay attention to effective ads on television and in print. Notice how the words are strung together for maximum effect. You can do the same in your resume. Try using short "bullet" phrases that begin with active verbs. Strive for variety in your verbs. Here are some that might fit your experience:

achieved	consulted	guided	organized	scheduled
adapted	controlled	hired	planned	selected
administered	coordinated	identified	presented	served
analyzed	decided	improved	produced	set up
applied	delegated	increased	proved	solved
approved	designed	inspected	provided	spoke
arranged	developed	invented	published	supervised
assessed	edited	investigated	recorded	surveyed
assisted	educated	led	re-designed	taught
built	encouraged	managed	represented	trained
chaired	established	modified	researched	updated
completed	evaluated	monitored	reviewed	wrote
conducted	examined	operated	revised	

A final suggestion: tailor your resume to fit the job. Dauten and Nelson (1996, p.D3) recommend: "Have at least three or four [resume] versions, each with a different length and emphasis. Then . . . match the version with the preferences of the reader. There is one rule: 'The reader rules.' " They explain how a simple phone call to the company can help you find out which style the reader prefers:

> Picking up a copy of the employment ads from our local newspaper, Mark took the first ad he came to—a job for an accounting clerk. He got human resources and asked for the person who screens resumes. A pleasant, young-sounding man named Glen took the call. He explained that he usually is the one who looks at resumes but that for this job they would be screened by the company's accountant, Karin.
>
> "What kind of resume does Karin like to see?" my partner asked. "Oh, she likes them really short. No baloney. Crisp." Before long, Glen recommended that Mark send a resume directly to Karin and say Glen suggested it. So, in less than [15 minutes], Mark was in a position to send a custom resume directly to the person doing the hiring. He could say in a cover letter that her coworker asked him to do so and mention that his resume is short because that's what he heard she likes.

Once you have written your first draft, let it sit overnight. You will then be ready to edit and polish it.

EDIT AND POLISH YOUR FIRST DRAFT

First drafts simply don't cut it. Continue to work with it until it has the punch you want. Because employers are busy, say as much as you can with as few words as possible. Spend time refining each phrase. Work at developing brief statements that explain clearly and strongly what your education and experience are, what opportunities you've taken advantage of and what qualifications and skills you would bring to the job.

You might consider hiring a professional editor or even a professional resume writer at this point. Using such services will be less expensive if you have completed all the background research, designed a format and written the first draft. Razek (2001, p.12) states: "For a fee, Vault.com's career experts evaluate your resume and provide career coaching by phone. Prices range from $39 to $319." The Web address is: Vault.com/careerservices

Proofread your draft. Check the spelling of every word. Check every capital letter and punctuation mark. Then check it again. Better yet, have a friend whose writing skills you respect check it for you. It is very hard to see your own writing errors. Some people find it helpful to proofread by going from right to left in each line, looking at each word.

EVALUATE AND REVISE

 Use the form in Appendix C to evaluate your resume. Consider both appearance and content. Grade each category as Excellent, Average or Poor. If a category is Poor, decide how to improve it.

PRINT YOUR RESUME

You are at the final step. Don't blow it now. Have your resume professionally printed or use a high-quality laser printer. Consider the following:

➢ Use 8½-by-11-inch white bond paper and print on only one side.
➢ Buy a quantity of blank paper and matching 9 x 12 envelopes.
➢ Have it printed using black ink.
➢ If necessary, have it slightly reduced in size to assure adequate margins.
➢ Use a type that is easy to read, at least 10-point size.
➢ Do NOT use all capital letters, script, bold or italic print. Use such graphics sparingly or, better yet, not at all.
➢ Most people prefer a *serif* typestyle. Serifs are the little curves or feet added to the edges of letters to make them more readable. This book uses a serif typestyle. *Sans serif* typestyles do give a crisp, clean appearance, but are much harder to read. (Example: Arial Typeface—compare p and p, or A and A.)

Have your resume professionally printed in black ink, on 8½ x 11 inch white bond paper. If necessary, reduce it slightly to assure adequate margins, and use capital letters, script, bold and italic print sparingly.

MAKING IT A "10"

Your resume is a direct reflection of you on paper. Be sure it depicts you as you want—a professional for a professional job. Everything about your resume will say something about *you*. Because employers have to start cutting back the number of finalists, they look for reasons *not* to pursue you as a candidate. For example, typos on a resume have served as a legitimate reason for disregarding an application for any number of positions. Sometimes, when there are a lot of very good applicants, reasons for getting rid of one resume and keeping another become, at best, arbitrary.

Put your resume in an attractive binder or enclose it in an attractive envelope with the name and address of the prospective employer typed. This may say that this particular applicant put that extra effort into the process and should, therefore, be given consideration—an interview. Do not, however, use anything slippery or difficult to file. You don't want your resume to stand out because it is hard to handle.

THE COVER LETTER

Never send a resume without a cover letter, even if the employer has asked you to send a resume. Cover letters should be individually typed, addressed to a specific person and company or department, and signed. Anything less will be ineffective.

Keep your cover letter short and to the point. It is a brief personal introduction of the "you" embodied in your resume. Don't repeat resume information. Entice the reader to want to find out more about you. Make clear in your opening paragraph the type of resume submission:

➢ Unsolicited. If so, give a reason for selecting this particular employer.
➢ Written as a referral or from personal contact, for example, "My mechanic told me your department was looking for qualified security officers."
➢ Written in response to a job advertisement.

Send the letter to a specific person and use that individual's title. You can usually get this information by calling the agency or department, asking who is in charge of hiring and asking for the spelling of that person's name and official title. The little time this takes can pay big dividends. Wilbers (1994, p.D2) notes:

> [The] most personal and crucial of documents [is] the letter of application. . . . your opportunity to breathe some life and personality into the cut-and-dry outline format of your resume. To treat it as nothing more than a cursory note or transmittal letter is to miss an important opportunity to make a statement that sets you apart from the crowd. . . .
>
> - Open by clearly identifying the job you are applying for and stating where you learned about it.
> - Highlight especially pertinent qualifications.
> - Anticipate and address questions raised by your resume.
> - Convey a sense of your personality.
> - Offer a positive reason for leaving your present position.
> - Consider using an attention-getting opening.
> - Make your letter an example of your professionalism and competence.
> - Close by asking for an interview and stating where you can be reached. . . . don't say you'll call to schedule [an interview].
> - Avoid gimmicks or clumsy attempts at humor.

Always send a resume with a cover letter. Cover letters should be individually typed, short and to the point, addressed to a specific person (including his or her title) and a specific company or department and signed.

An effective format for a cover letter is the full-block style—everything begins at the left margin. The parts of the letter should be as follows:

Your name
Your address (street number, street name, and apartment number, if applicable)
Your city, state and zip code

The date you are writing

The name of the person you are writing to
That person's title
The name of the company/department
The address of the employer

Salutation (Dear . . .):

Opening paragraph—why you are writing.

Second paragraph—provide some intriguing fact about yourself as a lead into your resume.

Concluding paragraph—ask for an interview and state where you can be reached.

Complimentary closing (Sincerely, or Yours truly),

(Skip four lines—sign in this space)

Typed name

Encl: Resume

Notice the spacing between the various sections. Notice the capitalization and the colon following the salutation and the comma following the complimentary closing.

Avoid starting every sentence with "I." *Never* start with: "I am writing this letter to apply for the job I saw advertised in the paper." BORING! Focus on the reader. More effective would be something like this: "Your opening for a police officer advertised in the *Gazette* is of great interest to me." Keep your letter short—one page. Be direct in requesting an interview. A sample cover letter is given in Appendix E.

SENDING YOUR RESUME

Mail your cover letter and resume unfolded in a 9 x 12 envelope. Everybody else's is going to be folded and crinkled. Resumes that travel flat are going to look better than all the others. As one employer commented: "When I looked for resumes, the easy ones to find are the flat ones. They stand out in the pile of folded resumes." Also, mail your letter and resume to arrive in the employer's office on a Tuesday, Wednesday or Thursday.

One final suggestion—consider using certified mail, with a return receipt requested. Not only will you eliminate those nagging doubts about if it got delivered, but again, it says something to the employer about the kind of person you are. Here is a candidate concerned enough to make *sure* it arrived. That's the kind of a detail a lot of employers are looking for.

HAND DELIVERING YOUR RESUME

It's always a good idea to hand deliver a resume if possible because it allows the employer to associate your name with a face. Dress well and look professional when you deliver your resume. Even if you don't get to the boss, you will make a good impression on the staff person accepting it. These people can have a great deal of influence on their bosses. Don't let your guard down because you aren't dealing directly with upper management. When you drop your material off, it is another opportunity for you to emphasize that you really want the job. Keep in mind many secretaries and receptionists are gatekeepers. Establishing a positive contact with the person taking your resume (or answering the phone) may also help you get that interview.

FOLLOWING UP

Be sure to follow up. The follow-up is another opportunity to prove what kind of person you are—the kind they should hire! A day or two after you have mailed or hand delivered your resume, write a brief letter to the employer. Recognize that the employer will be busy and only a short letter stands a chance of being read.

Confirm that you delivered your resume and thank the employer for the opportunity to participate in the hiring process. Even if this merely gets stapled to your resume without getting read initially by the employer, or gets forgotten by the employer who might read it, it is something that just might catch the attention of the interview committee when your resume surfaces. If they are looking for reasons to keep some and get rid of others, this could be the reason yours stays in the running. See Appendix E for a sample follow-up letter.

Wendleton and Dauten (1999a, p.J1) assert: "A follow-up letter should sell you, separate you from your competition and state a next step—such as 'I have a few ideas for the job I'd like to discuss with you.'. . . The goal is to keep the dialogue going. . . . Follow-up is one way that employees 'self-select' themselves into jobs."

Hand deliver your resume if possible to enable the employer to match your name with a face. Dress well and look professional when you deliver your resume. A day or two after you have delivered your resume, be sure to follow up by writing a brief letter to the employer confirming the delivery of your resume and thanking the employer for the chance to participate in the hiring process.

But *don't* become a pest. Too many letters or calls can just as easily land you in the "no" pile, identified as overly eager or unable to exercise enough common sense to know when it's "too much."

PREPARING AN E-RESUME FOR CYBERSPACE

To e-mail your resume, prepare it to be compatible with electronic data bases. These data bases match key words from a job description with key words in a resume, enabling an employer to rapidly scan hundreds of e-resumes and search for particular skills, qualities or experience. Use a common typeface, such as Courier, for ready recognition by scanning programs; a font size 12 points or higher; and avoid italic and boldface type. Hayes (2000, p.15) adds: "Instead of avoiding jargon, *use it often*—computers target words specific to an industry and are likely to select resumes containing those words multiple times."

As more companies go online, newer and more immediate ways of submitting resumes are becoming available. "Please e-mail your resume in ASCII format" is becoming an increasingly common statement in job listings. As noted in one article, "Launching Your Resume into Cyberspace" (1998, p.30): "ASCII text (pronounced "askee") is the standard, common text language that allows different word-processing applications to read and display the same text information. . . . To create an ASCII resume, type your resume using any word-processing application and then save it as a text-only document." ASCII files or text-only documents do not retain special formatting commands, so to make your resume easy to follow by the recruiter, you need to follow several guidelines (p.30):

➢ Do not use special characters such as mathematical symbols.
➢ Use your spacebar rather than tabs.
➢ To indent a character or center a heading, use the spacebar.
➢ Use hard carriage returns to insert line breaks, not the word-wrap feature.
➢ Font size and type face will be whatever your computer uses as its default, so boldface, italics and various sizes will not appear in the ASCII version.
➢ Always run a spell check on your document before you save it as a text-only file.
➢ Instead of bullets, use asterisks or plus signs at the beginning of lines.
➢ Instead of lines, use a series of dashes to separate sections. Don't try to underline text.

A basic rule of thumb is to keep it simple, as if you were using an ancient typewriter with no function keys or fancy formatting devices.

> Make your resume computer compatible by using a common typeface, avoiding use of italic and boldface type and saving the document as a "text only" file.

It is common practice in many companies to scan resumes received via regular mail so they may easily search for keywords and transmit the document to any and all interested parties. Fancy graphics, complicated formatting and general clutter typically do not scan readily, and the resume that will appear on the recruiter's monitor may simply look too messy and unappealing to even warrant a read-through. Potter (1996, p.22) cautions:

> There is an acronym from the computer industry that is worth considering when you are developing your resume: "GIGO." It stands for "garbage in = garbage out." If your resume is disorganized, difficult to read, filled with misspellings, or just plain unimpressive, it won't get any better (or any more impressive) when it is scanned into a computer! If your resume doesn't represent you well on paper, it won't represent you well on a computer screen.

If you are e-mailing your resume, the rule about sticking to one page becomes more flexible. The sophisticated programs used to scan resumes, searching for specific words and phrases to single out the most desirable candidates, can comb through a two-page resume just as easily as one on a single page. Challenger (2000, p.6) states: "E-resumes that are too short are less likely to contain the magic phrases."

He also advises, since business is changing so rapidly, your resume need not cover your entire career but should focus on the most recent five to ten years. Finally, Challenger suggests expanding the dimensions of your resume, perhaps by including the Web address for your personal home page. Should employers be interested enough in your resume to want to learn more about you before committing to an interview, they could simply sign on to the site. Things to place on your home page might include work samples, an audio or video of a major work presentation, etc.

Faxing Your Resume

In the search for ways to get your resume to prospective employers faster, it may be tempting to use a fax machine. And while fax and e-mail submissions are routine and acceptable for many employers, do not assume it is acceptable for all of them. You must ask first before you submit your resume via fax machine. Here is a tip from a human resources specialist concerning this:

> *Don't fax your resume.* Since you know that there is a chance, with almost any available job, that your resume will be scanned and stored in a computer, don't take chances. If you have ever received a fax, you know how bad the printing can be. There are many reasons why a fax can be degraded during transmission, but the point is that a faxed copy is never as good as the original (Potter, p.20).

FOR MORE HELP

Bookstores and libraries have dozens of texts on resume writing, each with its own particular advice. Other sources of information and assistance may be found online—search under the keyword "resume." The references at the end of this chapter provide a start if you want to go into this topic in more detail or from other perspectives. If you are in college, your computer career center can be of help.

CONCLUSION

One of your most important job-seeking tools is the resume. A resume is a brief, well-documented account of your career achievements, which highlights significant aspects of your background and identifies your qualifications for a given job. Its main purpose is to *sell* you to a prospective employer. But don't overdo it. Including too much data is the *number one* fault on resumes. And remember, *always* include a cover letter with your resume, even when delivering the resume in person.

 MIND STRETCHES

1.   Imagine you have been assigned the task of reducing an extremely large pile of resumes to a more workable number. Regardless of the position, what are five reasons you can think of to get rid of applications right away?

2.   What are three things you might look for that would make a resume stand out as being worth taking time to look at further?

3.   Paint with words the picture you want your resume to make. Use three words. Use six words.

4.   How can you liven up your resume?

5.   What might be dangerous about preparing a resume that is too creative? What benefits might result?

6.   What attributes do you have that will impress an employer?

7.   What concerns do you have about your qualifications that you will need to consider in preparing your resume?

8.   What are five power verbs you associate with yourself?

9.   Which resume style could work best for you? Why?

10.   What unique ways can you present your resume?

INSIDERS' VIEWS

For this chapter, read the *Insiders' Views* by Chief Jim Clark ("Three Key Opportunities") and Commissioner Gil Kerlikowske ("The Resume: A Balance of Modesty and Self-Confidence"), found on the Web site: http://www.wadsworth.com/criminaljustice_d/.

REFERENCES

Challenger, John A. "Surprise! Resume Rules Have Changed." *Bottom Line Personal*, March 15, 2000, p.6.

Dauten, Dale and Nelson, Mark. "A Little Research by Phone May Reveal How to Tailor Your Resume to the Job." (Minneapolis/St. Paul) *Star Tribune*, July 14, 1996, p.D3.

Hayes, Kit Harrington. "Scannable Resumes." *Bottom Line Personal*, September 15, 2000, p.15.

"Launching Your Resume into Cyberspace." *Successful Meetings*, July 1998, pp.30–31.

Potter, Ray. *Electronic Resumes That Get Jobs*. New York: MacMillan, 1996.

Razek, Rula. "Setting Your Sites on Finding a New Job." *USA Weekend*, August 31–September 2, 2001, p.12.

Wendleton, Kate and Dauten, Dale. "Good Follow-Up Ensures a Successful Hunt." (Minneapolis/St. Paul) *Star Tribune*, April 18, 1999a, p J1.

Wendleton, Kate and Dauten, Dale. "Tailor Resume to Highlight Skills You Want Noticed, Not Red Flags." (Minneapolis/St. Paul) *Star Tribune*, January 31, 1999b, p. D4.

Wilbers, Stephen. "Effective Writing: Well-Written Letter Can Open Door to Interview." (Minneapolis/St. Paul) *Star Tribune*, September 23, 1994, p. D2.

CHAPTER 10

PREPARING FOR NOT GETTING THE JOB

Accept that some days you're the pigeon and some days you're the statue.

—Roger C. Anderson

Do You Know:

➢ What you can do to prepare for and effectively handle rejection in your job search?
➢ Why a support system is beneficial?
➢ The importance of maintaining a positive attitude?
➢ What emotions are part of the sequential reaction to loss and change?
➢ What feelings follow the transition curve?

INTRODUCTION

It's hard to get a job in these fields! It is most unusual for a person to get the first job they apply for. And because the job market today is changing so rapidly and downsizing is more prevalent than ever, you will find an increasing number of people competing for work. You should gain comfort in knowing that the vast majority of successful applicants were eventually successful because they had a lot of experience in the application process. In a negative situation, many people fail to take advantage of a great opportunity to gain from it. Energy *is* present, albeit uncomfortable, and can be rechanneled in a positive direction.

While the majority of this book deals with how to get a job, this brief but important chapter deals with *not* getting a job—a realistic part of any job search. You need to know how to deal with failure in order to continue on. You may want to reread this chapter when you get that first, almost inevitable, rejection. It should assure you to know that your feelings are normal and that you need to go forward.

HANDLING REJECTION

Many adages apply to not obtaining something . . . and with good reason. We all experience rejection. Think about it: for every individual hired, many more did not get hired for that job. Everyone in the job search market will face rejection, and the adages reflect this reality:

> *Failure is not falling down; it is remaining there when you have fallen.*
> *Our greatest glory is not in never falling, but rising every time we fall. —Confucius*
> *He who dares nothing need hope for nothing.*
> *The only time you mustn't fall is the last time you try. —Charles F. Kettering*

You may hear similar sentiments following a less-than-successful interview:

> There must be something better around the corner.
> They didn't deserve you. Besides, they're probably all jerks anyway.
> You can do better than that place.

These statements may be true, and you will no doubt hear them from your friends and family. After all, they want to support you. You will agree, of course, but inside you may be thinking things like:

> I knew I could never get that job.
> I'm no good.
> Everyone else is better than me.
> I'll never get a job.
> I should never have gone into this profession.
> Etc., etc., etc. . . .

If you are not careful, this negative "self-talk" might overwhelm you and become a self-fulfilling prophecy. If you get to the point that *you* don't believe in yourself, why should a *potential employer* believe in you? Remember, success comes in "cans"—failure comes in "can'ts."

Tell yourself everyone must take their share of rejection. Sure, some take a little more, some take a little less, but everyone takes it. It's simply part of looking for a job. If you understand ahead of time the reality of rejection and are prepared for it, when the first one hits you, it's not likely to knock you down so hard. And if you're one of those fortunate few who hears "yes" on the first try, way to go! You beat the odds on this one. For the rest of us, each "no" we hear brings us one step closer to that "yes". . . as long as we don't give up. Keep in mind: It takes an average of two years to land an entry-level job in law enforcement.

It has been said the average job seeker must send out ten resumes to get one interview, and that it takes an average of ten interviews to get one job offer. If you do the math, you'll see that it takes the average person 100 resumes to receive one job offer. That's 99 "nos" for every one "yes"! So don't get discouraged—the "yes" will come.

 Try this exercise: Take a deck of standard playing cards and shuffle them well. Pretend every face card is a job interview and that one of them, say the queen of hearts, is a job *offer* following a dynamite interview. The rest of the deck (aces through tens) are flat-out "nos." With the deck facedown and starting with the top card, flip over cards until you get an interview. How many flips did it take? Flip again until your next interview. Try this several times and you'll get the picture. Sometimes you get an interview on the first flip; sometimes it takes seventeen flips and then you get four interviews in a row—and the queen of hearts is one of them! Or she could be at the bottom of the deck, under 51 rejections. But she's there. If you stop flipping after the fourth, fourteenth or even forty-fourth "no," you'll never get to her.

No one ever said job hunting was easy. For all practical purposes, job hunting will have to be a full-time job itself, at least for a while. If it isn't full-time timewise, it will be energywise. But, in the beginning, you'll probably believe rejection could never happen to you.

It's similar to the "It Can Never Happen to Me" syndrome frequently heard in discussions of officer safety. The idea is that an officer's daily existence would be too difficult if he or she thought that harm or perhaps death was lurking around every corner. Officers instinctively develop the "It Can Never Happen to Me" attitude in order to continue on with their day-to-day lives. To a certain degree it helps prevent them from becoming hopelessly paranoid. Problems arise, however, when all caution is thrown to the wind. Police, corrections and security officers must accept the natural risks associated with their jobs, but they must also be prepared. They must be realistic. Similarly, job applicants must balance the risks. If you know you're going to be rejected, why even try? This is what happens to some job seekers who start out feeling they will never be rejected. Two or three rejections turn them into defeatists who simply go through the motions.

Part of life is competing for what you want. No one can always be number one. The top doesn't have that much room. Accept this and decide that doing your best is what it's all about. Eventually this *will* pay off. You will get where you want to be. Accepting the facts of job seeking from the start will keep you from getting overwhelmed when rejections are received. Goulston and Goldberg (1998, p.45) suggest: "Take things seriously, not personally."

Consider the applicant who had become so defeated after several "thanks but no thanks" letters that when he woke up on the morning of an interview and found that it was raining, the weather became the last straw. He decided to stay in bed. This would-be police officer made it easy for the employer to weed out one more applicant. Who does this applicant really have to blame for this failure?

Success is getting up one more time than you fall down. Make up your mind right now to accept the facts of job seeking.

➤   Fact #1: Criminal justice and security are *very* popular, sought-after, competitive jobs.
➤   Fact #2: You're up against many, many applicants.
➤   Fact #3: Eventually you will get hired *IF* you're right for the job.

The benefit of having to repeat the application process is that you will improve each time. The downside is that it can get you down. The choice is *yours*.

To prepare for and effectively handle rejection in your job search, be aware that it does happen to just about everyone and that the only ones who fail are the ones who stop trying. Avoid negative self-talk and never lose faith in yourself. Each "no" brings you closer to a "yes."

REMAINING POSITIVE

You can and, in fact, must turn the negative energy from rejection into positive momentum. Rather than giving up, become determined to strive that much harder, knowing you are stronger and more polished. How does that saying go? *That which doesn't kill me makes me stronger.* It's what makes a boxer or any other professional athlete more determined—what's often referred to as "having the heart of a champion." No one likes to be turned down, especially for a desperately wanted job. But it is bound to happen, and it is going to sting. It does not get any easier the second, third or sixth time. In fact, the more you are turned down, the heavier it may weigh on you.

Maintain a positive attitude. To deal most effectively with that most common part of job hunting—the rejection—keep the following basics in mind:

➤ Go into the process understanding you probably will have to try for several jobs. With so many applicants, the odds are against you.

➤ Not getting this job does not mean you deserve to be banished from the planet. It simply means you did not get this one job.

➤ Another job is just around the corner (trite, but true). Avoid the temptation to believe that a particular job is your one-and-only dream job.

➤ If you need help, *ask for it!* No law says you must go it alone. If you are not confident about your job-seeking skills, seek help. If you get depressed, seek help. Just ask—not always easy for officer-types!

➤ Most important—keep trying. You've come this far. It is no time to give up. *Listen* when everyone tells you that you can get a job. You can. Just give yourself time.

Take advantage of everyone else's understanding of rejection and build a support system from the start. It really helps to talk, and you might be surprised by how many people have experienced similar rejection. Besides, there *is* strength in numbers.

Support systems are valuable because they allow you to talk out your frustrations and realize you are not the only one who has ever felt rejection—everyone else has experienced it too. People in your support system may be able to share what worked for them in getting past their rejection.

Do not be afraid to get support and help if you need it—professional or otherwise. Frustration and disappointment is normal. Do not let it get the best of you. Negative feelings can become overwhelming, and they can also be self-perpetuating. Feeling depressed and gloomy often leads to deeper feelings of depression and gloominess. Besides not feeling good, they can sap so much of your energy that your interview skills become less than adequate, and you will not perform as you need to.

Employers are very aware of how much competition you have—they have to sit through all those interviews! What would happen if you went into your tenth interview all worn out and depressed and the next person after you was upbeat and positive because it was only their first interview? Presenting the same energy and freshness during your tenth interview that you possessed at your first one will not only leave a positive impression on the interviewer but will help fuel positive feelings in yourself. You have a choice: You can come out of the interview feeling even worse because you *knew* you were mopey and unenthusiastic, or you can come out feeling great because you gave it your best shot. In short, if you do not deal with the uncomfortable feelings that go along with rejection, you will eventually come to believe that you do not deserve to be hired, and it will show. Pick up and press on.

Remaining positive is crucial to a successful job search. A positive attitude leaves a favorable impression on an employer, and it helps fuel positive feelings in yourself.

LEARNING FROM THE PROCESS

Ask prospective employers who turned you down what could have made a difference. If approached in a non-threatening way, people will usually be honest and open. As one employer states: "I was impressed several times by young applicants who, after being turned down for a job, called and made an appointment to visit with me to discuss their job-hunting strategies. I even ended up hiring a couple of them."

NORMAL REACTION TO LOSS

The fear of the unknown is always the worst. Since it helps to know what to expect, here's a brief explanation of what many people experience when they lose something (such as a death in the family, a ruined relationship or a lost job opportunity). Called the *sequential reaction to loss and change,* it describes how many people *normally* act when they lose something important. If you get a rejection, you may feel the following, in roughly this order:

➢ Denial
➢ Anger
➢ Sadness
➢ Hopelessness
➢ Disorganization
➢ Withdrawal
➢ Reorganization

This sequential reaction to loss and change is illustrated in Figure 10-1.

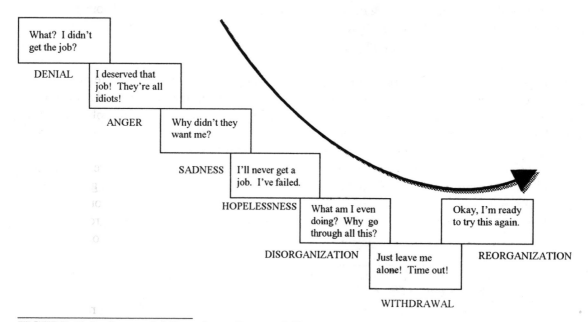

FIGURE 10-1   Sequential Reaction to Loss and Change

Denial. This is the "It can never happen to me" phase, and it's completely normal. It hasn't quite sunk in yet that you didn't get the job. Denial helps by keeping you from getting too hurt from rejection(s). It can be harmful, however, if you don't move on or get too hung up on that rejection (possibly thinking that this is the only job in the world for you). Accepting the loss is a necessary step on the journey to being able to continue on with life.

Anger. Once you have accepted the rejection, the understandable response is anger. "I wanted that job! I deserved that job! They won't get away with this! The process is unfair!" These things may be true, but the fact is you did not get the job. Staying angry too long will, at best, depress you and, at worst, drive you to do something you may later regret, like writing a nasty letter, making a nasty phone call or paying a hostile visit to the employer. It's in your best interest not to burn bridges, should another opportunity arise there in the future. The anger must be dealt with. The challenge is to find an appropriate outlet.

Sadness. After the anger subsides, you may feel sad. Sadness can run from a mild case of the blues to a bout with deep depression. It depends on many factors and reflects the absolute need of a strong support system as you seek work. Don't beat up on yourself too much if you feel down. Who doesn't after rejection? Many people tend to ignore it because being "sad" is not their style. However, rather than fight it, accept it, draw some energy from it, and move on. If it becomes overwhelming to the point of your being unable to continue the job search, or if it begins to seriously affect other areas of your life, get help. You need to work through the sadness, but not let it consume you and keep you from moving on.

Hopelessness. Hopelessness may occur as the feelings of anger and depression subside. The hopelessness may seem overwhelming, but it is a normal part of adapting to rejection. The natural assumption after one or more employers reject you is that you are unemployable. No one wants you. This is not true. It simply means those jobs did not work out. You have to keep going, which isn't always easy because of the natural progression of feelings.

Disorganization. At this point you may want to continue on, but nothing seems to fit anymore. You find it hard to organize your time or your thoughts. You spend time haphazardly reading help-wanted ads and making futile attempts to schedule a productive day. Frustration may set in, and you may simply give up.

Withdrawal. Wanting to give up or withdraw is also natural. It is understandable that you are frustrated, uncomfortable and wanting to simply quit. This is how your psyche lets you rest, regroup and get ready to jump into the battle again. Rather than fight the desire to withdraw, help it along. Get away from job hunting for a while. Go to a movie, take a long walk or even go on a vacation. Retreat and regroup. Do not, however, withdraw by skipping scheduled interviews or by showing up and not putting forth your best effort. If you need a break, take it.

Reorganization. At last! You have worked through the normal feelings associated with being rejected. Here is where you are getting closer to the pot of gold at the end of the rainbow. Having worked through the previous emotional stages, you're now ready to get back out there and get that job.

> The progression of feelings involved in the sequential reaction to loss and change are denial, anger, sadness, hopelessness, disorganization, withdrawal and, finally, reorganization.

According to Nathan and Hill (1992, p.30), many other people go through a somewhat different set of feelings, a pattern they refer to as *the transition curve,* which is characterized by the following chain of reactions:

Shock, denial: Unable to believe that it has happened. 'You're joking!' A feeling of emptiness, perhaps numbness.

Euphoria: Making the best of it, and minimizing the reality of the change. 'Now I've got time to . . . paint the house, take a holiday . . .—I didn't like the job anyway.'

Pining: Hoping that the job will come back—an unrealistic expectation that the next job will be exactly the same.

Anger: Blaming someone—'I never could work with him (my boss) anyway.' 'They should have . . .'

Guilt: Self-blame—'They chose me because I wasn't up to it/did something wrong.'

Apathy: A sense of powerlessness and hopelessness as the reality sinks in.

Acceptance: Letting go of the past, and the emergence of a new energy.

Nathan and Hill's transition curve is illustrated in Figure 10-2.

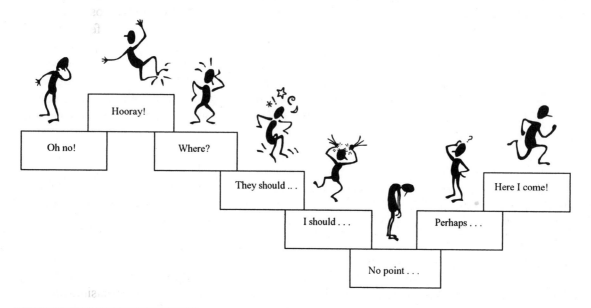

FIGURE 10-2   The Transition Curve

SOURCE: Robert Nathan and Linda Hill. *Career Counseling,* p. 30, © 1992 by Sage Publications, Inc. Reprinted by permission of Sage Publications, Inc.

> Another common progression of feelings following rejection are those of the transition curve, namely, shock or denial, euphoria, pining, anger, guilt, apathy and acceptance.

Regardless of the intensity of the feelings you experience following rejection, how long it takes you to work through the negative feelings depends on how serious the rejection is. The first rejection is not as bad as the second. The more rejections, or the more important a job is to you, the more extreme your reactions may be. Remember: Accept the inevitable and understand that this is how it is going to feel. There is strength in self-awareness. As George Bernard Shaw says: "Better keep yourself clean and bright; you are the window through which you must see the world."

Mullins (1994, p.13) offers this good advice:

> **Don't give up.** Job hunting is psychologically challenging. You will face obstacles, setbacks, and rejections. Some people you encounter in your search will be unfeeling; a few will be cruel. You will get discouraged and you will be tempted to quit looking. However, the economy is creating hundreds of thousands of new jobs every month. . . . Many jobs being created are challenging and pay well. One can be yours, but only if you didn't give up wanting it.

CONCLUSION

The knowledgeable, prepared applicant understands and accepts that *everybody* experiences these negative feelings when they lose something they want. To prepare for and effectively handle rejection in your job search, be aware that it does happen to just about everyone and that the only ones who fail are the ones who stop trying. Avoid negative self-talk and never lose faith in yourself. Each "no" brings you closer to a "yes." But whatever setbacks you may experience, "nos" you may hear or rejection you may feel, DO NOT GIVE UP!

You may be disappointed if you fail, but you are doomed if you don't try.

—*Beverly Sills*

 MIND STRETCHES

1.   What benefits can come from *not* getting a job?

2.   Why is it helpful to understand the sequential reaction to loss and change and the transition curve?

3.   Why is it harmful to ignore negative feelings arising from a rejection to an application?

4.   Why would someone ignore these feelings?

5.   Do you think applicants for criminal justice or security jobs are less likely to deal with their feelings? Why?

6.   Why do you think unsuccessful candidates might lash out at an employer who didn't hire them? Could this ever be successful?

7.   Is there ever one perfect job?

8.   Is there danger in believing there *is* one perfect job?

9.   Who is included in your support system? How can you best use them?

10.   Can you think of "failures" or "losses" in your life that actually benefited you?

INSIDERS' VIEWS

For this chapter, read the *Insiders' Views* by Timothy J. Thompson ("Each Failure Is One Step Closer to Success") and Penny A. Parrish ("Life's Greatest Rewards Can't Be Measured in Dollars and Cents"), found on the Web site: http://www.wadsworth.com/criminaljustice_d/.

REFERENCES

Goulston, Mark and Goldberg, Phillip. *Get Out of Your Own Way*. Perigree, 1998.

Mullins, Terry. "Search Skills: How to Land a Job." *Psychology Today,* September/October 1994, pp.12–13.

Nathan, Robert and Hill, Linda. *Career Counseling*. Newbury Park, CA: Sage Publications, 1992.

SECTION THREE

JOB-SEEKING STRATEGIES

A wise man will make more opportunities than he finds.

—Francis Bacon

You've decided what you're looking for in a career. You've also closely examined your personal characteristics and have found a fit. You've created an impressive resume to demonstrate that fit to potential employers. And you're prepared to handle rejections. You're ready. Where to find jobs and how to get them is the focus of this section. Chapter 11 looks at the application process. It takes you through various strategies for locating job openings and making your availability and interest known. It discusses the importance of the application form and the role of your resume, and it reviews the testing process.

If all goes well to this point, you will be invited for a personal interview. The basics of presenting yourself for an interview are the focus of Chapter 12—how to dress, communicate and follow up. Chapter 13 takes a closer look at the all-important interview process and what to expect from it. Figure S3 illustrates the steps you've already completed and what lies ahead.

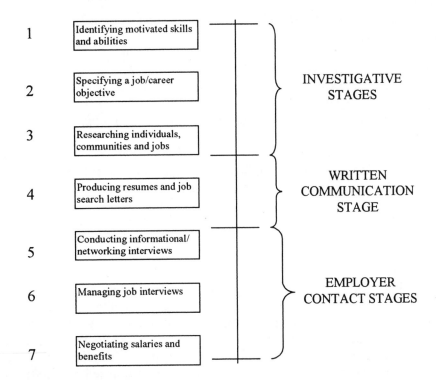

FIGURE S3   Job-Search Steps

SOURCE: Ronald L. Krannich. *Change Your Job, Change Your Life*, 5th ed. Manassas Park, VA: Impact Publications, 1995, p.101. Reprinted by permission.

CHAPTER 11

THE APPLICATION PROCESS:
FINDING AND APPLYING FOR JOBS

(1) Regard job hunting as a real job—and expect that it, like any other job, demands time, persistence, and discipline. (2) Recognize that while you can get a good job through ads or employment agencies, competition for jobs that are advertised tends to be fierce. (3) Apply directly to an employer even without any hint there is a job opening. Positions constantly become available and it's wise to be on a good list. (4) Try to get as many job interviews as you can and concentrate on smaller firms. (5) If you can see a layoff coming, start looking for a job while you are still working. (6) Expect to be discouraged. Guard against anger, apathy, or feeling defeated.

—Sylvia Porter

Do You Know:

➢ What you must identify before beginning your job search and how many hours you should spend each week looking for work?
➢ Which ads to read in the classified section of the paper and which papers to look in?
➢ What specialized periodicals to review?
➢ How the Internet can help?
➢ The variety of other places to check for leads on job openings in your field?
➢ The importance of looking and acting your best during any contact with a potential employer?
➢ How to make contact with a prospective employer by mail?
➢ What networking is and how important it is to your job search? Who you should talk to?
➢ Why it is important to never "burn your bridges"?
➢ What the entire application process usually involves?
➢ What information the application form usually asks for and what impact the Equal Employment Opportunity (EEO) guidelines have had on these application forms?
➢ The importance of follow-up?

INTRODUCTION

Although waiting to hear about a job opening may work once in a great while, you usually must *look* for work. More accurately, you have to *work at finding work*. Serious job searchers find that pursuing employment requires as much, if not more, effort than a full-time job and that a thought-out strategy is essential. A well-developed search demands action. No one who creeps or shuffles along a career path can expect success in this competitive world. They will be trampled over by people who really want to work and to advance. Unmotivated, unenthusiastic, undirected individuals are easily identified and weeded out by employers. Employers are looking for that *special* applicant who exudes drive, energy and genuine enthusiasm. Develop your strategy so you not only maintain the energy necessary to pursue your career goals, but so your energy *shines brightly* to employers.

Don't just plan to look for work. Chase it! Hustle! Scramble! Be creative! Have fun! Turn what can be a frustrating experience into a personal challenge. Each disappointment, each new challenge, is part of the training that will let you succeed. *Get what you want!* Let the process feed you, not defeat you.

If this all sounds a bit too "rah! rah!"—the opposite of the stoic, macho attitude police officers, corrections officers, security personnel and those in related fields are "supposed" to exhibit—think again. Employers are looking for *real* people who truly want the job and will, in turn, do a great job for them. Job hunting is frustrating at times, so you *need* to keep yourself charged up for the process.

DEVELOPING YOUR JOB-SEARCH STRATEGY

To keep on track—physically, emotionally and intellectually—you have to develop a strategy. The first step is to determine *what* you are looking for. Even the smaller newspapers have an incredible number of employment want ads. The unemployed are frequently asked, "How can you not have a job? Hundreds (thousands) are advertised for!" True, but take a closer look. You are not going to apply for every job advertised. Somewhere between *actuarial* and *zookeeper* are the jobs you will consider.

Begin with the questions: "What do I want? How do I get it?" If nothing short of police officer will satisfy you, do not apply for private security positions. On the other hand, might a position as an armored-truck driver, for instance, be a good stepping-stone to lead to your end goal? Unless you are desperate for money, taking a full-time position of no interest or value to your career goals could result in several problems. For example, say you start applying randomly, get a job in an unrelated field and eventually quit for a job you probably should have waited for in the first place. This could make you look like a "job jumper," create hard feelings with that employer when you leave and maybe result in a negative reference.

This doesn't mean you should sit at home unemployed until you get your "dream" job. For a variety of reasons, including financial and emotional, it is frequently much easier to get a job when you have a job. What is important is to identify what you want before going after it.

Mullins (1994, p.12) notes: "Most job seekers suffer more from poor job-hunting skills than from lack of opportunity." Among his suggestions for improving your chances of finding a job quickly is: "Make job hunting a full-time commitment. . . . If you are unemployed, you should spend a minimum of 40 hours a week actively searching for work. As a full-time job seeker, your goal should be at least one interview a day with someone who has the power to hire you."

Don't overlook federal jobs. According to Krannich and Krannich (1995, p.23): "Government agencies always hire, even during the worst of times. They have an average annual turnover rate of 10–14 percent. Furthermore, federal agencies hire nearly 1,000 people each day, or 300,000 to 400,000 each year."

> It is important to identify what you want before going after it. Then you must make job hunting a full-time commitment, spending a minimum of 40 hours a week actively searching for work if you are currently unemployed.

WHERE TO LOOK

Begin with the most obvious place to look for employment—newspaper want ads. After watching the local papers daily for several weeks, you will identify the generally accepted procedure employers in various fields use to advertise for employees. Ads for law enforcement positions, for instance, are usually placed in the Sunday paper, under the heading of "police." Private security positions generally appear under the heading of "security." Is this how it is always done? Of course not.

Think creatively. Ads for police officers could appear under such headings as "law enforcement," "public safety" or "officer." Corrections positions may appear under "prisons," "jails," "guards" and the like. Security jobs may appear under the title of "risk management" or "loss control." Take time to familiarize yourself with all the possible headings your job could fall under and continue to scan the entire listing.

Perhaps a clerk or a secretary placed the ad without knowing anything about the actual job and thought "safety officer" or even "city employee" or "state employee" would be the best spot. Maybe the ad will appear, accidentally or purposely, on a Tuesday only. Do not let yourself get lazy just because such ads are usually in the Sunday paper under a specific section.

 Under what other headings might a police position appear? List them in your journal.

 Under what other headings might a private security position appear? List them in your journal.

 If considering a related field, under what headings might it appear? Note these in your journal.

Job openings are usually placed in the classified ads that appear in columns, row after row. Take time, however, to also check the display (box) ads used most frequently by corporations. These bigger ads are more expensive, but occasionally a city or private employer that wants to state specific needs or is particularly in need of people will use this approach. Scan ALL the newspaper want ads.

Also consider the possibility of ads appearing in papers other than those published in your particular city. A Minneapolis job seeker, for instance, should check the St. Paul newspaper. The Oakland job seeker should check a San Francisco paper. The Seattle job seeker should be looking in a Tacoma paper. Read the local and neighborhood papers as well as those of surrounding cities.

> Begin your job search with the most obvious place to look for employment—newspaper want ads. Think creatively and scan ALL the ads. In addition to your local and neighborhood papers, check the papers of surrounding cities.

Specialty Periodicals

Every field has trade publications. Law enforcement, corrections and private security have many journals, often containing ads. Such periodicals as *The Police Chief, Law and Order, Corrections Today, The Prison Journal, Corrections Compendium* and *Security Management* may not only contain position openings at the higher levels, they also contain current information beneficial to individuals applying in these fields.

Other publications deal with more general topics and could contain an ad for your job. For example, magazines that deal with municipal government could contain such ads. Become familiar with a variety of specialty periodicals. Also become familiar with periodicals that list only jobs. One such publication of particular interest to those seeking employment in law enforcement and private security is the *National Employment Listing Service*, which contains only related employment opportunities.

Other specific publications address only city, county, state or federal jobs. If not contained in such specialized publications, they will usually be posted. If you are interested in a federal job, the *Federal Jobs Register* is a valuable resource. Another source for federal positions or for positions out of the country is the U.S. Civil Service Commission (the address is given at the end of the chapter).

Every field has trade publications. Check the specialty periodicals associated with your chosen field, whether it's police work, corrections, private security or a related criminal justice field.

Using the Internet

Newspapers from across the country can be accessed over the Internet, making it much easier to search for job openings in a variety of locations. Furthermore, you may access the ever-increasing number of Web sites available on the Internet to learn more about a specific company, organization, agency or even community. Go online and search for the agencies, companies or general locations you might be interested in.

Computer bulletin boards are becoming a popular means of interacting with others having similar interests and for finding information about a particular topic. A computerized job network system—*America's Job Bank*—is run by the U.S. Department of Labor and lists approximately 50,000 job openings a week. Frerkes (1998, p.129) notes: "The vast amount of information that is available on the world wide web has opened the doors for job seekers to monitor daily those agencies that are in the process of hiring." Several relevant and potentially helpful Internet addresses are listed at the end of the chapter.

The Internet has become an increasingly valuable resource, not only for job listings but also for information about specific agencies and communities where career opportunities are available.

Other Places to Look

The serious job hunter routinely stops at the federal, state, county and municipal offices every week or two to check job postings and to ask what job openings are available or anticipated. For law enforcement employment, one of the best information sources at the local level is the city or county personnel office. You may be able to subscribe to job listings used by government agencies as well as the privately published services. These are often quite expensive, so become familiar with what your local libraries have. Regularly review these sources.

Another place to look is in your local telephone directory. Check listings under government agencies (local, state and federal) for personnel departments. Employment services and organizations can also help you find jobs.

Placement offices of educational institutions that offer programs in law enforcement, corrections, criminal justice or private security often post job notices and have excellent employment listing services. Contact the career services office on campus for a list of current openings. These offices also coordinate interviews with agencies looking to hire, and have reference libraries or agencies throughout the world. Know where to look and what to look for, and regularly watch postings and other resources. A list of such resources is provided at the following Web site: http://www.wadsworth.com/criminaljustice_d/.

Several helpful publications also exist. *Tips for Finding the Right Job* is a U.S. Department of Labor pamphlet offering advice on determining job skills, organizing the job search, writing a resume and interviewing. *Job Search Guide: Strategies for Professionals* is a U.S. Department of Labor publication that discusses specific steps job seekers should follow to identify employment opportunities.

Many Jobs Aren't Advertised

It is essential to know that many jobs are either not advertised or are actually filled before an ad is placed. How could that be? Probably because an aggressive job seeker with an effective strategy found a way in (long before you ever became aware of the job opening), either by having established a relationship with the employer (perhaps as an intern) or by making the employer aware of their interest before the job opening existed. Frequently, in such cases, an ad is run because of department policy or to meet a legal obligation. Your strategy, then, is to learn about these jobs before these probabilities occur. Just because an employer doesn't yet know a job will open up doesn't mean you should not be trying for it.

Telephone Inquiries

Active job seekers put considerably more effort into their pursuit than just browsing through newspaper ads. You've got to get out there and investigate. An easy, quick, relatively nonthreatening way is to telephone and ask if a certain department, agency or company has, or expects, any openings. Ask if they send out a mailer for job openings or if you could get on a specific list to be notified for a particular job. With a little polite interaction, you may be able to get an individual notice from the contact person you impressed while inquiring. Even if the contact you made proves fruitless, never hang up without asking if they know of anyone *else* who is hiring.

Kenning (1998, p.1) suggests: "Warm up to the idea of cold calling by remembering: You are skilled in the art of information gathering and problem solving. It's just a matter of assigning your skills to a new set of challenges: The Job Search!" When making such calls, begin by asking whoever answers who you should talk with about possible job openings. Then ask if you should contact anyone else at that particular place or elsewhere. Your goal is to develop an ever-expanding list of resources and contacts.

Personal Inquiries

Another approach to inquiring about a position is to stop in. This can be *risky*. First, most employers are extremely busy and usually do not have or take time to visit with someone who has no appointment. This could result in closed doors or in aggravating a potential employer. On the other hand, it shows real interest on your part, as well as a willingness to take risks. If you use this approach, don't take up too much of their time. Get in, deliver your message, and get out in a few minutes.

Never go empty-handed. Have a resume to leave even if you are not able to see anyone. Follow up with a letter, especially if someone took time to talk with you.

Other places to check during your job search include the federal, state, county and municipal personnel offices; your local library for job listing mailers used by government agencies and privately published services; placement offices and employment information resources at local educational institutions and universities; your local telephone directory; employment services and organizations; computer bulletin boards; and government pamphlets and publications. You might also consider making telephone or personal inquiries at companies or agencies that interest you, requesting information about current or anticipated job openings.

ON BEING YOUR BEST

An absolutely essential part of your strategy is to be your best at *every* phase of the job-search process. Because of the natural frustrations of the process, this is sometimes difficult. Yet it is vital that you relate positively, courteously and respectfully to everyone with whom you come in contact. You may not think the receptionist, secretary or person who casually strolls up and asks if they can help you is important. They are. You never know who you are talking with.

If you are making phone inquiries, be away from crying babies, barking dogs and other noises that could be distractions for both you and the person you're calling. Consider dressing as you would for a personal interview. If you look sharp, you will feel sharp, and will then act sharp, making a better impression than if you were calling while lounging in your bathrobe at 11 o'clock in the morning. Besides, you never know if the prospective employer might say something like, "Can you come down right now?" It happens. Also, don't assume your call will be answered by "just a secretary." The phone may be answered by the boss when the receptionist is away from the desk. Furthermore, many employers come in early and stay later than their administrative staff—phone calls at these times may reap unexpected benefits.

When making personal contacts, coming across well is equally important. Applicants who drop off resumes while wearing extremely casual attire or something bizarre, take a possibly fatal risk. There is always a chance you could meet with someone, even if you meant to only leave your resume and ask about possible openings. Perhaps the person responsible for hiring will walk by or has told the person at the front desk to send any applicants to see him/her. Maybe a new receptionist or a temporary employee will mistakenly send you into the employer's office. If you are wearing cut-up jeans and lizard-skin cowboy boots, you have damaged what should have been a spectacular opportunity. The prepared job seeker is always ready for the unexpected.

If not the boss themselves, the first contact person may deliver your message or resume to the boss *with* an editorial comment. It had better be something like:

➢   This applicant sure was polite.
➢   This person dressed well.
➢   This one seemed like she would fit in.
➢   This is the one who called and was so courteous.

You don't want something like:

➢   Wait till you see this slob.
➢   This guy was really rude just now.
➢   This is the gal who hung up on me last week.

You will likely be talked about after you leave, so make sure the talk is positive. You may also get something more from being polite—the person taking your call or greeting you at the front desk may be willing to give you advice or a tip on future openings. It is also possible they may go tell the boss, "There is someone here you should meet," or even call you with information about a new opening. Because you never know, always be prepared. Even if you feel frustrated, frazzled and tired, look like this is *the* most important contact you are making.

An essential part of your strategy is to be your best at *every* phase of the job-search process. During phone contacts and especially during personal contacts, dress and act professionally. Expect the unexpected. You may be talking to the boss and not know it.

CONTACTS BY MAIL

The importance of appearance in making a good impression also applies to written material because it is a direct reflection of you. While you may not actually see the person doing the hiring, if you supply a resume, chances are it will at least get looked at. Provide that person with something that interests them, not something that gives them a reason to throw it away.

Contacting prospective employers by mail is perfectly acceptable. Like telephoning, it is quick, easy and even more nonthreatening. It may, however, be less effective. While it may be hard to say "no" to someone in person, it is easier over the phone, and easiest with a letter (usually by dumping it in the circular file). But letter writing is a viable strategy. Note here the recommendation is *not* "resume mailing," but "letter writing." It makes little sense to send an agency or company only a resume. The receiver will have little idea why it was sent, and even if a position is open, a bare resume shows lack of common sense by the applicant. A cover letter makes the process more personal and sincere by introducing you and telling why you are writing. Whether responding to an ad or merely inquiring about what might be available, include both a cover letter *and* resume.

Writing skills are exceptionally important, and here is a chance to shine. To make a favorable impression when you write, consider the following:

➢   Don't provide a letter without a resume or a resume without a letter.
➢   Don't submit anything in pencil (and write neatly in ink only if you are absolutely unable to locate anyone within the free world who can type it for you).
➢   Don't use sheets torn out of a spiral notebook or lined, three-hole notebook paper.
➢   Don't use the back of a used piece of paper or an old invoice or receipt.
➢   Don't send form letters, especially when they were designed for another job area.
➢   Don't send copies of letters or resumes that have been copied so many times they are faded and hard to read.
➢   Don't fold your material into strange shapes. Enclose it unfolded in a 9 x 12 white envelope.

As difficult as it may be to believe, all of the preceding have been submitted, and all have been thrown away without ever allowing the applicant to recover from the negative impression he or she made.

Employers are busy, especially if they are shorthanded and need to hire more personnel. They will not have time to go through all the applications, so they will look for reasons to throw out most of them. Foolish applicants provide plenty of justifiable reasons to jettison their letters and resumes. When providing a prospective employer with *anything* in writing:

➢   Make sure it is neat.
➢   Make sure it is typed.
➢   Make sure it is personalized for *that* contact. Call to find out who to address it to and the proper spelling and title.
➢   Proofread it; proofread it again; and proofread it some more. Have another person proofread it. Then proofread it one last time. Improper grammar and typos provide an excellent reason to pitch a resume.

When providing a prospective employer with *anything* in writing, make sure it is neatly typed on good-quality paper, personalized and free of errors. Never send a resume without a cover letter or a letter without a resume.

E-MAIL

The Internet has affected all aspects of life, including job seeking. Many departments across the country now have Web sites. Not only is it possible to find job postings on the Web, but often initial applications or requests for applications can be made via e-mail. If you aren't sure whether it's appropriate, or even possible, ask. Don't assume every office is connected to the Internet or that every operator knows how to access e-mail and attachments. While attachments will look as good as the original, you want to make sure someone on the other end knows how to retrieve it. Traditional institutions might expect application materials in traditional ways. On the other hand, submitting your application electronically could be an excellent way to demonstrate your computer literacy.

FAX

While fax machines are popular, the jury is still out on how effective they are in a job search. You should view a fax machine as a tool to work with in some situations. You may make yourself stand out from the crowd of applicants by faxing a letter and resume. If you don't own a fax machine, you can pay for this service at major hotels, large secretarial services or many office supply stores.

For many employers, faxes are a perfectly acceptable means of sending in your resume. While many ads will state that application by fax is acceptable, if you don't know this for sure, ask first. Even then, it may be advisable to mail or hand deliver a hard copy of the material because most faxed documents lose quality. In addition, a fax has the transmission identification material at the top, as required by law, making the received document look more cluttered. Compared to e-mail attachments, faxes do not look as good. If you fax, consider noting in your cover letter, *submitted by fax and mail* or *e-mail*. Faxing provides the information to the employer quickly, with a clean, mailed original to soon follow.

NETWORKING

Because the vast majority of job seekers make several applications, you will want to constantly seek new contacts and new possibilities. After being hired, you may eventually change jobs (maybe several times), so you will need to continue to expand your contacts. This process, called *networking*, is THE most important component of the job search.

"Networking 101" (1997, p.10) reports: "Approximately 70 percent of job openings are filled by people who heard about the job through word of mouth. The more contacts you have . . . , the greater your odds are to be considered for a position." Mullins (p.12) suggests: "Create a network of friendly contacts who can hire you or recommend you to others who can. Developing a network of contacts is the single most important task of a job seeker." Indeed, it's not *what* you know but *who* you know.

Salespeople have effectively used this networking concept for years, only they call it "developing leads." You are a salesperson, selling yourself. The process involves setting up a network of resources who you will not forget and who will not forget you. It begins with making whatever contacts you already have and taking every opportunity to add to this list. You then use each contact to make more contacts, and more contacts, etc., etc., etc. For instance, you make a contact at a particular company or city. You then ask if you should check with anyone or anywhere else. Imagine if each contact gave you two or three other employers' names. You could quickly develop literally hundreds of possible contacts.

What becomes difficult and complex is *how* you develop your networking strategy and to what extreme you should take it. Because networking can, and in fact should, mushroom into many contacts, proceed in an orderly way. This is best done in writing, with a plan in mind. Here's how:

1.   Make an initial contact.
2.   Document that step.
3.   Acquire additional contacts.
4.   Document them.
5.   Take action.
6.   Follow up.

It's easy until you start to develop more than about five contacts. Then you will want to record your efforts on something more workable than scraps of paper. You can buy networking workbooks, but it may benefit you to make up your own networking book. You can design it for your own particular needs, making the entire process more personal, not to mention more gratifying by accomplishing something concrete.

 In your journal, or in a separate networking notebook, list the important information you need to keep track of and organize it so it is workable. Data to be maintained should include:

- ➢   Company, agency, department name, address, phone, e-mail.
- ➢   Names and titles of contacts (spelled correctly).
- ➢   What you did.
- ➢   What you will do.

Also have a separate calendar to set up dates you will contact or recontact sources. The first recontact should be a week or two after the initial contact. Follow up every month thereafter, but be sure to recognize the fine line between an assertive applicant sure to be remembered and a pest they want to forget. Strive for a balance.

Pursue your job search positively and energetically. Develop every opportunity to show yourself off in your best light. Be creative and learn from each experience. Even the contacts that appear to be unproductive give you a chance to learn more about the market and yourself. If nothing else, you come away from the experience knowing you are tough enough to accept a setback and survive. As noted by Bolles (2001): "You only need one YES—and the more NOs you get out of the way, the closer you are to that YES."

Networking is the process of connecting and interacting with the individuals who can be helpful to you in your job search and is a crucial element in an effective job search. Place no limits on your network—talk to anyone and everyone.

ON BURNING BRIDGES

No matter what approach to contacting prospective employers you take, be it responding to an ad, phoning, sending a letter with a resume, sending a fax, e-mailing or stopping in, *never* leave a door permanently closed behind you. Don't burn any bridges that may eventually lead to a great job.

Some people can be insensitive, unfeeling and downright rude. You are bound to get tense yourself because job seeking is difficult. But never show any negative feelings to anyone who may affect your future professional life. Don't be rude or vent your frustrations on anyone where you are applying for work, no matter how they treat you. If they treat you badly, it's probably not *you* they are upset with. They are likely just having a bad day. You may well return, *if* you have kept the door open. If you have sworn at someone, had a temper tantrum or otherwise behaved unprofessionally, you might as well cross that resource out of your networking notebook.

Never burn any bridges. Doing so only removes any opportunities the future may have held for you.

YOU'VE FOUND AN OPENING AND THEY'VE ASKED YOU TO APPLY

Once you've found an opening and have been asked to apply for the position, you can expect to go through several steps, illustrated in Figure 11-1. The order in which these steps occur may vary, but in almost all instances, the first step will be to complete an application form.

The application process usually involves completing an application form, taking a series of written tests, having a preliminary interview, undergoing a background check, having a final interview and taking a medical exam.

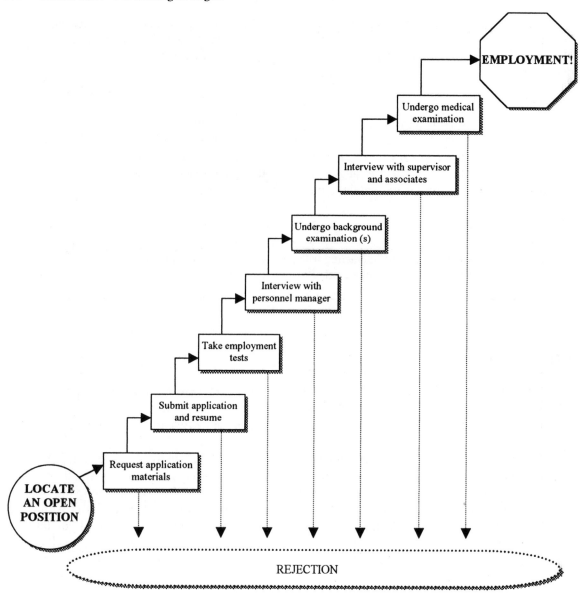

FIGURE 11-1 Typical Employment Process

The Application

Some application forms are very simple. Others are extremely complex. If you have done a thorough job on your resume and have a copy along, you should have all the information you need at your fingertips.

If you are asked to complete the form on the spot, do so neatly using *black ink*—it copies better. Write legibly using your best *printing*. Write on the correct lines on a form. Sloppiness and inaccuracy on a job application may lead the employer to question your attention to detail and ability to follow instructions. Think before you write so you do not have to erase or cross out information. A high-quality erasable pen is a good investment. Be complete. If you do not understand something on the form, ask.

If they will allow you to take the application home, do so. We suggest you type your responses on the form. However, many applicants do not have access to typewriters these days. And trying to format your responses using a computer and running the application form through the printer, hoping everything falls in the right spaces, can be an exercise in futility. Consequently, many forms must be filled out by hand. It is wise to make several copies of the form to practice on, saving the original for your final draft.

Application forms vary greatly in their complexity and depth, but they usually ask for the same information you gathered in preparing your resume, so always have a copy of it with you. Although the Equal Employment Opportunity (EEO) guidelines make mandatory responses to questions about ethnic background, religious preference and marital status illegal, it is usually in your best interest to complete these optional sections.

The Web site (http://www.wadsworth.com/criminaljustice_d/) contains a sample application form as well as Equal Employment Opportunity guidelines.

Armstrong and Schmalleger (1994, pp.23–27) present helpful hints for completing and submitting an application for federal employment:

> - Make your [application] nice to look at and easy to follow. Make sure entries in each block are in the block, not crowding over the lines, . . . Vertically align repetitive data in sequential blocks.
> - Consider hiring professionals to do your form.
> - Say you'll accept a job anywhere. If you don't want to take an offered job, you can always decline.
> - DO NOT LEAVE <u>ANY</u> BLOCK ON THE SF-171 BLANK! . . . No matter what the block asks for, give 'em an answer, even if it's just "N/A."
> - Collect everything you'll need to complete the form. . . . past work descriptions, high school diploma, GED certificate, college transcripts, certificates [and] any special licenses or qualifications.
> - If your work history includes managerial experience, tell them how well you <u>managed</u>, not how you did the work yourself!
> - Do not spend your time and money hand-carrying your [application] to the servicing Federal Office of Personnel Management or the personnel department of the agency to which you are applying.
> - Mail [it] via Certified Mail and get a return receipt, or send it via Federal Express. Why? Because bureaucracies tend to swallow things whole.
> - Do not leave gaps in documentation of employment dates.
> - Do not give up! T-E-N-A-C-I-T-Y is the name of this game. Don't get discouraged because you send in lots of applications but get no calls. Be patient. Try to understand that there's not a lot of "hurry" in the hiring end of the government.

Many departments and agencies are including a written essay as part of the application process, requesting candidates to write two or three pages on a specific topic, such as "Why are you interested in this field?" or "Why are you interested in being hired by this particular agency?"

 Take time *before* you apply for a job to write two- to three-page answers to the following questions:

1. Why have you selected this particular field?
2. Why have you selected this particular agency?
3. Who are YOU? (Write a brief autobiography.)

REMEMBER THE MAGIC WORDS—THANK YOU

Your parents were right. One absolute: *never* leave a contact without following up with a thank you. Not only is this good manners in a world sorely lacking them, but it is also another chance to present yourself positively. The more you can get your name in front of employers, the more they will remember you at hiring time.

You can phone or write your thank you for the opportunity to interview or to submit your resume. If you can't decide which way is better, do both. Don't express your thanks to *only* the chief of police or the president of the security company who took time to see you. Also thank the secretary who took time to set up the meeting or greeted you for your appointment. Show them you are thoughtful and courteous, the kind of person they would like working with them.

Always follow up a contact with a thank you. It demonstrates your good manners and gets your name in front of the employer one more time.

WARNING

If you think job hunting sounds like a lot of work, you are absolutely correct. Every aspect of the process is emotionally and physically taxing and time consuming. You will be approaching other people trying to sell yourself, knowing the chances of immediate success are slim.

None of us likes to hear the word *no*. It becomes increasingly difficult to dial the phone, knock on the door or send the next letter. It is risk-taking at the most critical level. You are setting yourself up for a certain number of rejections. It is difficult, if not impossible, to keep from taking the entire process too personally. A rejection does not have to be a failure. Indeed, it can merely be the elimination of another job on your quest to find the job you are looking for.

Rejection can come for a number of reasons. Primarily, there needs to be a match between the candidate and the department. What may be inappropriate for one agency will be a gold mine for another. Rejection may simply mean it wasn't the best match for the department or for *you*.

Take care of yourself. If the whole thing starts to get the best of you, treat it like you would any other job. Set hours, including breaks. Plan your days. Take an occasional vacation. Finally, recognize the very real need for a support system. Plan time with people who accept you. You can do this informally with family or friends, or more formally by organizing a support group with others in the same position. Such groups work extremely well for sharing support, ideas and helpful hints. Most important, be sure your strategy allows you to keep at it. The next contact could have your job for you.

TESTING YOUR CAREERING COMPETENCIES[*]

INSTRUCTIONS: Respond to each statement by circling the number at the right that best represents your situation.

SCALE: 1 = strongly agree
           2 = agree
           3 = maybe, not certain
           4 = disagree
           5 = strongly disagree

1. I know what motivates me to excel at work.   1 2 3 4 5

2. I can identify my strongest abilities and skills.   1 2 3 4 5

3. I have seven major achievements that clarify a pattern of interests and
    abilities that are relevant to my job and career.   1 2 3 4 5

4. I know what both I like and dislike in work.   1 2 3 4 5

5. I know what I want to do during the next 10 years.   1 2 3 4 5

6. I have a well-defined career objective that focuses my job search on
    particular organizations and employers.   1 2 3 4 5

7. I know what skills I can offer employers in different occupations.   1 2 3 4 5

8. I know what skills employers most seek in candidates.   1 2 3 4 5

9. I can clearly explain to employers what I do well and enjoy doing.   1 2 3 4 5

10. I can specify why employers should hire me.   1 2 3 4 5

11. I can gain the support of family and friends for making a job or career change. 1 2 3 4 5

12. I can find 10 to 20 hours a week to conduct a part-time job search.   1 2 3 4 5

13. I have financial ability to sustain a three-month job search.   1 2 3 4 5

14. I can conduct library and interview research on different occupations,
    employers, organizations, and communities.   1 2 3 4 5

15. I can write different types of effective resumes and job search/thank you letters. 1 2 3 4 5

16. I can produce and distribute resumes and letters to the right people.   1 2 3 4 5

17. I can list my major accomplishments in action terms.   1 2 3 4 5

18. I can identify and target employers I want to interview.   1 2 3 4 5

19. I can develop a job referral network.   1 2 3 4 5

---

[*] SOURCE: Ronald L. Krannich. *Re-Careering in Turbulent Times: Skills and Strategies for Success in Today's Job Market.* Manassas, VA: Impact Publications, 1995, pp.103–105. Reprinted by permission.

20.   I can persuade others to join in forming a job search support group.   1 2 3 4 5

21.   I can prospect for job leads.   1 2 3 4 5

22.   I can use the telephone to develop prospects and get referrals and interviews.   1 2 3 4 5

23.   I can plan and implement an effective direct-mail job-search campaign.   1 2 3 4 5

24.   I can generate one job interview for every 10 job search contacts I make.   1 2 3 4 5

25.   I can follow up on job interviews.   1 2 3 4 5

26.   I can negotiate a salary 10–20% above what an employer initially offers.   1 2 3 4 5

27.   I can persuade an employer to renegotiate my salary after six months on the job.   1 2 3 4 5

28.   I can create a position for myself in an organization.   1 2 3 4 5

You can calculate your overall careering competencies by adding the numbers you circled for a composite score. If your score is more than 75 points, you need to work on developing your careering skills. How you scored each item will indicate to what degree you need to work on improving specific job-search skills. If your score is under 50 points, you are well on your way toward job-search success.

CONCLUSION

Although waiting to hear about a job opening may work once in a great while, you usually must w*ork at finding work*. It is important to identify what you want before going after it. Then you must make job hunting a full-time commitment, spending a minimum of 40 hours a week actively searching for work if you are currently unemployed. An essential part of your strategy is to be your best at *every* phase of the job-search process. *Always* follow up a contact with a thank you.

ADDITIONAL CONTACTS AND SOURCES OF INFORMATION

Career Paths: A Guide to Jobs in Federal Law Enforcement
    by Gordon M. Armstrong and Frank Schmalleger,
    Regents/Prentice Hall Publishers, 1994.
        Lists all major federal agencies, criminal justice positions
        available, addresses and phone numbers

U.S. Civil Service Commission
1900 East Street, NW
Washington, DC 20006

Career Path—a leading site on the Web for job seekers. After selecting a geographical location, the applicant can peruse the major newspapers' classified ads for current openings in that area. http://www.careerpath.com

The Police Officer's Internet Directory—over 1,500 individual home pages of information on law enforcement agencies across the country. Included is a state-by-state breakdown of agencies with current openings. http://www.officer.com

On Patrol—includes free postings of law enforcement opportunities on a state-by-state basis. http://www.onpatrol.com

* Many other links are included on these three Web sites.

MIND STRETCHES

1.   List as many sources as you can in which employment ads might appear.

2.   Why are many jobs filled without being advertised or filled before the ad appears?

3.   List 10 contacts you have available right now through which you could begin networking.

4.   If you were an employer deluged with applications, how would you eliminate 50% of them right away?

5.   What errors could applicants make when contacting a prospective employer by mail?

6.   Whether you contact an employer by phone, mail or in person, what three things would you want that person to remember about you?

7.   What creative things can you do to get the attention of an employer? What possible benefits and detriments can you think of for each?

8.   What strategies will you use to locate employment opportunities?

INSIDERS' VIEWS

For this chapter, read the *Insiders' Views* by Brian Beniek ("From Both Sides of the Process") and John Lombardi, PhD ("Law Enforcement Jobs: Learning How to Get Them Takes the Same Skills Required to Do Them"), found on the Web site: http://www.wadsworth.com/criminaljustice_d/.

REFERENCES

Armstrong, Gordon M. and Schmalleger, Frank. *Career Paths: A Guide to Jobs in Federal Law Enforcement.* Englewood Cliffs, NJ: Regents/Prentice Hall, 1994.

Bolles, Richard Nelson. *What Color Is Your Parachute?* Berkeley, CA: Ten Speed Press, 2001.

Frerkes, Larry R. *Becoming a Police Officer: A Guide to Successful Entry Level Testing.* Incline Village, NV: Copperhouse Publishing Company, 1998.

Kenning, Linda. "Making Contact." In *Jobs,* a weekly publication of the (St. Paul) *Pioneer Press,* March 1, 1998, p.1.

Krannich, Ronald L. and Krannich, Caryl Rae. *Find a Federal Job Fast! How to Cut the Red Tape and Get Hired,* 3rd ed. Manassas Park, VA: Impact Publications, 1995.

Mullins, Terry. "Search Skills: How to Land a Job." *Psychology Today,* September/October 1994, pp.12–13.

"Networking 101." *Career Path Coach,* Vol. 1, 1997, p.10.

CHAPTER 12

YOUR JOB-SEEKING UNIFORM:
PRESENTING YOURSELF AS THE ONE TO HIRE

You never get a second chance to make a good first impression.

—*Will Rogers*

Do You Know

➤ What the employer's investment is in the hiring process?
➤ What the job-seeking uniform is and what elements it consists of?
➤ What the four-minute barrier and primacy effect are?
➤ How you can find out how you come across to others and why this information may be useful?
➤ How what you are wearing influences people's perception of you?
➤ Why it is important to begin your job search in good physical condition?
➤ What the purpose of the interview is and how important knowledge is to this purpose?
➤ What your strategy will be for presenting yourself?
➤ The importance of follow-up?

INTRODUCTION

One critical aspect of how you present yourself is in the written material you submit. The importance of written materials was discussed in Chapter 9. It is emphasized again here because it is a vital part of how you will be viewed. Whatever you do, do it well. Don't submit insufficient, incomplete material or anything that doesn't look perfect. Just as "you are what you wear," so *you are what you write.*

Typos, misspellings, poor grammar, erasures and messy cross-outs tell an employer a lot. You cannot afford to look inept, uneducated, careless or sloppy. The weeding-out process becomes arbitrary at times, particularly with a number of equally qualified applicants. You may find yourself out of the running for something as simple as a misspelled word in your resume. This is not necessarily fair, but it is a fact. How you present yourself begins with your written materials. If you do an effective job, you are likely to get an interview. How should you appear at such an interview? What makes up your job-seeking uniform?

In a sense, we *all* wear uniforms, whether they have badges, patches and whistles, and whether we are actually on the job. A uniform is apparel that makes a statement. The police, corrections or security officer's duty uniform is designed to make a specific statement: *I am in charge!* Clothing worn by undercover officers also makes a statement, although quieter: I fit in (hopefully unobserved). Similarly, nurses have uniforms that meet their professional needs, as do bus drivers, waitresses, letter carriers, custodians, delivery people, orderlies, flight attendants, pilots and military personnel.

When matching clothing to a day's work, consider: What image do I want to project? What encounters will I have today? What does this sport coat say about me? This dress? This tie? This scarf? These shoes?

THE EMPLOYER'S INVESTMENT

Before getting into specifics of *how* to present yourself, look first at the situation from the employer's perspective. When hiring, employers are making a significant financial commitment. The typical medium-sized police agency will spend a few thousand dollars just on the hiring process alone. After an applicant is hired, it is expected they won't be truly productive for at least the first year of employment, so the agency is expending a year's salary just to cover training and administrative costs. Furthermore, that does not include the salaries of those who will be doing the training, guiding, etc. to bring the recruit "up to speed" so that he or she will become a productive team member.

During hiring, employers are also making an extremely important organizational decision. Employers are hiring someone to represent them to the public. In all areas of criminal justice and private security, public perception is critical. Employers can find themselves in serious trouble if they hire the wrong people for these jobs. In fact, employers may face civil lawsuits for "negligent hiring" (holding the employer responsible for hiring unsuitable employees who cause some sort of harm). Combine this with the fact that it is increasingly difficult to fire people, particularly in the public sector, and you can see the importance employers must place on the entire process.

> The employer has a significant investment in hiring the "right" people. In addition to the financial investment, those they hire represent the employer to the public. Also, hiring the wrong people can land an employer in legal trouble via "negligent hiring" lawsuits.

ELEMENTS OF YOUR JOB-SEEKING UNIFORM

Because employers have so much at stake when they hire personnel, and because their decisions are often based on a few pieces of paper and 30 minutes of personal time with you, you *must* make the most of those pieces of paper and 30 minutes. How you present yourself during an interview is an important aspect of the overall getting-a-job process. Your strategy for presenting yourself must encompass the entire spectrum of how the prospective employer views you. Many factors come into play here. Employers will tell you that while someone may appear spectacular on paper, the interview provides an opportunity to eliminate many candidates.

How you appear to the employer is obviously of critical importance. Appearance consists of the "whole person." The physical self, the emotional self and the spiritual/ethical self combine to create the balance that makes up "you." If one aspect outweighs the rest or is significantly lacking, you are out of balance. Something appears wrong. For instance, police officers may work odd schedules and perhaps compound things by attending school on the side. They may not have sufficient time to exercise regularly. Weight gain or a poor nutritional program could affect their health, making them feel run-down, irritable and out of sorts. Officers in this situation should re-examine their lifestyles to restore balance.

Employers will try to view the "whole" applicant during the hiring process. Employers will look for high self-esteem, alertness, intelligence, critical thinking abilities and humanistic traits. They will also consciously watch for indications of sadistic, brutal, obsessive-compulsive personalities as well as those who might become victims of "groupthink" and "deindividualization" in the face of peer pressure. The obvious difficulty is that what employers get to see represents a small portion of your overall identity. After all, how long does it take for you to get to know another person, even yourself, before acquiring an accurate perception? Certainly more than the 30 minutes spent during the average interview.

> Your job-seeking uniform is how you present yourself during an interview. It consists of more than just the clothes you put on—your uniform includes how you come off during the initial contact, your grooming, physical condition, grammar and speech, manners, personality, enthusiasm, knowledge and follow-up. It's your total package.

This is a lot of data to present to an employer, particularly in the short time you have. You must develop a strategy to maximize the opportunities to sell yourself in each area. Properly pursued, you will have more than enough time to provide employers with an accurate picture of you. To best understand this, consider the dynamics of the interview process, that is, the mechanics of the system and the importance of the first few minutes.

THE PRIMACY EFFECT AND THE FOUR-MINUTE BARRIER

In *Effective Human Relations in Organizations*, Reece and Brandt (1987, p.268) discuss the criticality of the first moments of any interaction among people: "When two people meet, their potential for building a relationship can be affected by many factors. Within a few moments, one person or the other may feel threatened, offended, or bored." This tendency to form impressions quickly is called the *primacy effect*, otherwise known as the first impression. According to Reece and Brandt (p.267): "The general principle is that first impressions establish the mental framework within which a person is viewed, and later evidence is either ignored or reinterpreted."

> The four-minute barrier refers to the length of time it typically takes for the primacy effect to occur. According to this concept, the first four minutes of a social interaction are crucial to the continuance of the interaction.

Reece and Brandt (p.268) also suggest: "The way you are treated in this world depends largely on the way you present yourself—the way you look, the way you speak, the way you behave. Although human contact is a challenge, you can learn to control the first impressions you make on others. The key is to become fully aware of the impression you communicate to other people." You can test the primacy effect theory by asking yourself some questions:

➢   Have you ever sat next to someone on a bus, train or plane and almost immediately wanted to talk with them? Or—decided to quickly get your nose into your book or magazine? Why?
➢   Have you ever had someone come to your door seeking contributions for some worthy cause and known almost immediately that you'd probably contribute? Or cut them short? Why?
➢   Have you ever had a teacher you just knew wasn't approachable to discuss a grade you received? Why?
➢   Have you ever gone into a job interview and known within minutes that you were a strong candidate? Why?

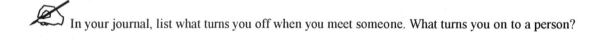 In your journal, list what turns you off when you meet someone. What turns you on to a person?

It is natural to like some people and not others. How do you get to feel that way? How long does it usually take? How do you come across to others? Have you ever considered asking someone how you came across to them when you first met?

DIFFICULT INQUIRIES

It is important to understand *how* you come across to others because you can seldom judge this for yourself. How could you know how others perceive you? Do you dare ask? Most people seldom think of this. It's just too risky. But it may be necessary, particularly if you are experiencing repeated rejections. We can all take constructive criticism. If that is what is needed to identify your weak points, take that risk.

For example, one officer left her initial law enforcement career path to go to law school and then returned to seek employment in the police field. Armed with experience, training and extensive education, she finished number two on almost every interview in which she participated. Why? She had to know. So she called several individuals she had applied to and explained her motives for inquiring—not to criticize, not to take another try at that job, but to understand how she could improve. She was stunned to learn she had not convinced them she did not want to practice law. They were all sure she would stay with them only until a "real" lawyer job was offered to her. Was this *their* fault? Of course not. It was hers for failing to anticipate this reaction and making false assumptions. Her only regret was not taking this step earlier. In this case it worked. She got the next job she applied for.

> Find out how you come across to others by asking. Although it may seem risky, the constructive criticism may help you identify and strengthen some of your weak points, particularly if you've been experiencing repeated rejections.

GETTING TO KNOW EACH OTHER

The goal of the preliminary process is really the same for both the prospective employer and for you: *getting to know each other.* It would be considerably more fair and accurate if time was unlimited. But it is not. For better or worse, you must deal with the brevity of the process and acknowledge the reality of the four-minute barrier. This is not all bad, however. If you recognize the elements of the interview, this is actually an ideal amount of time. Now take a more detailed look at each element of the job-seeking uniform, including what comes before and after the interview.

BEFORE THE INTERVIEW

One critical event before the interview might be a *phone call* to arrange the interview—or even a preliminary telephone interview. Yate (1998) discusses this important aspect of job seeking:

> Whatever circumstance creates this telephone interview, you must be prepared to handle the questioning and use every means at your disposal to win the real thing—the *face-to-face* meeting. The telephone interview is the trial run for the face-to-face, and is an opportunity not to be bumbled; your happiness and prosperity may hinge on it.
>
> Here are some tips:
> > *Take a surprise call in stride.*
> > *Beware of over-familiarity.*
> > *Allow the company representative to do most of the talking, to ask the questions.*
> > *Beware of giving yes/no answers.*
> > *Be factual in your answers.*
> > *Keep up your end of the conversation.*
> > *Speak directly into the telephone.*
> > *Take notes.*

The telephone interview has come to an end when you are asked whether you have any questions. Ask any more questions that will improve your understanding of the job requirements. If you haven't asked before, now is the time to establish what projects you would be working on in the first six months. By discovering them now, you will have time before the face-to-face meeting to package your skills to the needs at hand . . . .

And if you have not already asked or been invited to meet the interviewer, now is the time. Take the initiative. "It sounds like a very interesting opportunity, Ms./Mr. Smith, and a situation where I could definitely make a contribution. The most pressing question I have now is, when can we get together?"

INITIAL CONTACT

The interview itself is the brass ring you strive to get. When you get it, you *must* be on time. Before your interview date, it's important to know exactly where you're going so you can get there on time. Making excuses for a late arrival as an opener for your interview gets you off to a rocky start. So, when you are called for an interview, get clear directions on how to get to the interview. Make a trial run of the actual trip so you know how to get there and how long it takes. Plan to arrive 10 minutes early to allow for traffic delays or parking problems.

CLOTHING AND GROOMING

Clothes make the person—and get (or lose) the job. Like so many other things, the "experts" have made a science of dressing for success. John T. Malloy, who coined the term *wardrobe engineering,* was among the first to stress publicly the link between professional accomplishments and wardrobe in his well-known book *Dress for Success.* His research indicates that your credibility and likeability are immediately established by what you are wearing.

It cannot be overemphasized that those doing the hiring for criminal justice and security jobs are likely to be older, conservative *men.* When a male applicant comes in with long hair, an earring and a tattoo, those doing the hiring will have already made up their minds before the first question has been asked. It isn't fair, and it probably isn't right, but employers are looking for people who will not cause problems by deviating from the norm all the time. Wharton (1997, pp.59–60) asserts the path to a successful career begins with a great first impression:

> A job interview is a lot like a screen test: If you want to get hired, you'd better look the part. That means putting forth your sharpest image while avoiding small but potentially deadly gaffes, like a defiant clump of hair jutting from the back of your head. . . . When it comes to clothes, a little research goes a long way. Stroll through the lobby of your would-be workplace, or watch the parking lot at quitting time to see what employees are wearing. . . . Dark-blue and gray suits almost always work.

Wallach (1986, pp.21–22), suggests: "Clothes talk. They say volumes about how we feel, how we want to be perceived, how we see others. We communicate through our appearance. The way we package ourselves sends out a particular message." Wallach (p.20) explains that the wrong clothes can make you feel awkward and out of place. Conversely, the right kind of clothing can make you feel confident and competent: "Most of us have also had the pleasure of wearing something that we feel makes us look attractive. That gives us confidence, and the confidence helps us to do a good job. All of these positive feelings become self-fulfilling. The better we feel about ourselves, the better the job we do."

> Research indicates that your credibility and likeability are immediately established by what you are wearing.

Few would argue with the research that tells us that people's appearance has a direct impact on how they come across to others and how they will be treated. Since clothing is extremely important, how should you dress for a job interview to make a favorable impression? You have dressed effectively if your interviewers do not even remember what you were wearing. You want them paying attention to you, not your clothing.

In planning an "appearance strategy," begin by identifying exactly what job is being interviewed for. An applicant for an executive position would dress differently than an applicant for a manual labor position. An interview for an officer position falls somewhere in between. Start with several givens:

➤ The jobs themselves are conservative.
➤ Extremists are generally not well received.
➤ The fields are regarded as important and seek to be viewed as professions.
➤ You've got to look the part.

Begin by deciding on clothes that fall between the extremes, that is, *conservative*. A spangled three-piece suit and lots of gold jewelry is obviously inappropriate. So is a hopsack loincloth or a low-cut dress. Most agree that a smart looking, fresh, low-key appearance is called for.

Comfort is a factor. You will not perform up to your potential if you are dressed uncomfortably. If you do not feel good, it will show. Therefore, pick clothing you feel comfortable wearing. You can build on your interview outfit from this point.

A suit is traditional for an interview—for men and women. A suit conveys a statement: the person wearing it is businesslike, is capable of creating a positive image and is taking the interview and the interviewers seriously. The same can be said for a sharp sport coat with a nice pair of slacks, or a good-looking skirt with a neat blouse or sweater. The final decision is yours, but consider the following:

➤ Is your outfit conservative? Is it comfortable?
➤ Could a suit work to your advantage or disadvantage? (Might a rural jurisdiction view a suit as "too much"? Might another jurisdiction view a tweed sport coat as "too little"?)
➤ What do you own now? Chances are you feel comfortable in clothing you own.
➤ Can you afford to buy new clothes for your interviews? Can you afford *not* to?
➤ How do you think you look?

A frequently overlooked area is that of accessories: socks, belt, tie, jewelry, shoes, etc. In addition to being conservative, you should use *common sense*. To review a few basics you probably already know:

➤ No hats worn indoors.
➤ White socks? Absolutely NOT.
➤ Socks that are too short, or droop, or have runs or holes in them? Ridiculous.
➤ Hosiery that's more appropriate for evening or holidays? Hold off for the office party.
➤ An old, cracked, mismatched leather belt? Absurd.
➤ Too much jewelry? Leave it at home.
➤ Still using your father's old clip-on tie? Spend a few dollars for a new one.
➤ Worn-out heels or scuffs on the back of the heels from driving? Replace them.
➤ And don't forget to shine your shoes.

Avoid wearing pins or other jewelry identified with a particular fraternal, religious, athletic or other group or club, as you risk offending someone participating in the interview and give them something other than your face to focus on. Do not give them excuses to avoid eye contact. Also avoid loud colors, wild patterns or any unusual apparel. Seek help from clothing store clerks, who are generally fashion conscious and can offer advice regarding your clothing needs. Consider other resources when setting up your dressing strategy, such as books and magazines. Such an approach may give you a slight advantage. Finally, since your perception of yourself is too subjective, solicit feedback from someone you trust. Ask them how you look. Hear the answer—good or bad—and make any necessary improvements.

Another consideration is personal grooming. Although these things may seem obvious, before an interview evaluate such things as hair and nail care, makeup, antiperspirants, fragrance and breath freshness. Some things can be fixed relatively quickly; others may take more time.

Make sure your fingernails are clean and trimmed. Women should use discretion in how long they allow their nails to grow. You don't want a prospective employer wondering if you can type a report or even pick a pen up without difficulty. If you choose to wear nail polish, select something subtle.

Women who wear makeup should choose a natural or professional look, not a dramatic look. Avoid heavy applications of eye shadow or cheek color, and select a lipstick that is flattering but doesn't scream "Read my lips!" Before the interview, make sure there is no lipstick on your teeth. If you're uncertain about how to achieve a professional look with makeup, consult a local department store cosmetics clerk.

Know if your antiperspirant works well in anxiety-producing situations. If it doesn't, find a new one! You'll be nervous enough without the added worry of body odor. However, don't overdo it on the fragrance. Go easy on the strong aftershave or perfume. While most people find body odor offensive, many people are just as offended by strong fragrances. Some people suffer allergic reactions to such smells, and it will do you no good if your interviewer has a sneezing fit throughout your entire interview.

Pay particular attention to your breath and oral hygiene. There is no bigger turn off than *bad breath,* and many people don't even know when they have it. But your interviewer will know. Be sure to brush and floss your teeth before an interview, and avoid drinking liquor or eating exotic foods. These things can stay on your breath long after you've ingested them. Furthermore, never smoke or chew gum during an interview. Put out the cigarette or spit out the gum before you even enter the building. Check yourself in a mirror one final time before entering the interview room. And *smile*. A friendly smile can be key to the impression you make during those critical first four minutes. Make them feel good when they look at you.

The bottom line is: you are selling something—*you!* You need the tools to make that sale. If you do not have the proper clothing to make a good impression, buy some, even if it means borrowing money. You can pay back the loan once you get the job. You *must* appear like someone the interviewers would want representing their city, county, department, agency, institution or company.

PHYSICAL CONDITION

Closely related to clothing and grooming is your physical condition. Chapter 6 was devoted entirely to physical fitness and its importance. The fact is simple: Few other professions require you to be more physically fit than those of criminal justice and private security. You are not expected to be at your peak for only a few seasons or to compete in a once-in-a-lifetime event like the Olympics. You need to be in top physical condition every day you report for duty. The public depends on it. Your partners depend on it. *Your* life may depend on it. The very nature of the job is stressful. Many officers die not at the hands of criminals but as victims of their own clogged arteries and unhealthy hearts.

Employers in these fields *will* notice your physical condition. Every police, corrections and security administrator knows it's hard to keep their officers in peak shape as the years go by. They certainly don't want to start out with out-of-shape officers. It's not good for the employee, and it's not good for the department. Every organization is concerned about its public image. So much of criminal justice and security work is accomplished by easily identified officers. They are often uniformed and drive marked cars. No department wants overweight, unfit officers representing them.

> Your job-search strategy should include being in good physical shape, not only because employers expect it, but because you will feel more confident about yourself. And confidence shows.

Finally, don't smoke. If you do—quit. An increasing number of police departments and private employers are including "nonsmoker" in their initial requirements. Public buildings are also quickly becoming totally smokefree. Besides the obvious health-related problems, smokers today look out of place, and many feel smokers present a bad image. Further, most smokers don't realize just how obvious the odor they have clinging to them is. An interview panel of nonsmokers will almost certainly be overwhelmed by the offensive odor of an applicant who smokes. It sends a message you don't want to send.

GRAMMAR AND SPEECH

Individuals employed in criminal justice and security are expected to present themselves like any other professional. As educational requirements for applicants increase, so do standards about communication skills. Use of slang, obviously mispronounced words or limited vocabulary can embarrass an applicant. Furthermore, people who speak nonstandard English rarely recognize the handicap they carry. Ask someone who speaks "good" (standard) English to listen to you and see if your speech needs improving.

Like physical fitness, communication skills take time to develop. Some people are better than others, and some simply need to brush up in this area. If you need to improve the way you speak, take some speech classes. Join Toastmasters. Volunteer in ways that require you to interact with the public. Feeling confident in how you sound will make you feel better because you will know you will be perceived better.

Be yourself. Trying to come off too intellectually or too much like a seasoned professional will be perceived as phony. Don't address your interview panel as though you were giving a grand performance at Radio City Music Hall. Present yourself as you are.

MANNERS

Good manners make a great impression. They start with being on time for your appointment. If circumstances you cannot control dictate that you will be late, call to explain your delay. Shake hands with people at the beginning and end of each contact. Make your handshake an extension of yourself. It can communicate warmth, strength and confidence. Use a firm, full, deep grip and maintain eye contact. You might want to ask some friends how they feel about your handshake and, if need be, work to improve it. Reece and Brandt (pp.281–282) offer seven "rules of etiquette" important in a business setting:

1. *When establishing new relationships, avoid calling people by their first names too soon* . . . . Informality should develop by invitation [call me Bob] rather than by presumption.
2. *Avoid obscenities and offensive comments or stories* . . . . Never assume that another person's value system is the same as your own.
3. *Do not express strong personal views regarding issues that may be quite controversial* . . . . There is seldom a "safe" position to take in the area of politics or religion.
4. *Never smoke in the presence of a fellow employee, customer, or client unless you are sure he or she will not be offended.*
5. *Avoid making business or professional visits unless you have an appointment* . . . . A good rule of thumb is always make an appointment in advance and arrive promptly.
6. *Express appreciation at appropriate times.* A simple thank you can mean a lot. Failure to express appreciation can be a serious human relations blunder.
7. *Be aware of personal habits that may be offensive to others* . . . . Chewing gum is a habit that bothers many people, particularly if you chew gum vigorously or "crack" it. Biting fingernails, cracking knuckles, scratching your head, and combing your hair in public are additional habits to be avoided.

Never let any contact with a prospective employer end without thanking the individual(s). Good manners go a long way toward impressing people.

PERSONALITY

The stress associated with the job-search process makes it hard to appear as well as you need to. Stress and anxiety can intimidate you to the point that you sit rigidly upright during the interview, responding with short, one-word responses—the only goal being to live through the interview. Relax. Be real. Let them see *you*. You wouldn't buy a car or house based solely on how it looked from the outside. The same goes for hiring someone.

ENTHUSIASM

Do you want the job, or do you *WANT* the job? Employers aren't interested in hiring someone who will pursue their work halfheartedly. They want people who greet each day as a unique challenge, make the most of every opportunity and do a *great job*. If you meander into the interview and respond casually to questions, why should they hire you? You must show them that you don't just want *a* job, you want *this job* with *this organization*. Let them know why. If you don't, someone else will. It is amazing how so few applicants, when asked *why* they want the job, exclaim it is because they really want to work here, for *this* organization. When the interviewer asks if you have anything else you'd like to ask or say, you should make it absolutely clear that you really *do* want this particular job and that you will do a great job for them . . . and be enthusiastic about it!

KNOWLEDGE

The biggest error applicants make when presenting themselves to prospective employers is misunderstanding what the employer is looking for. In the hiring process, this can be fatal. The purpose of the hiring process is for applicants to present themselves—the only thing the employer is interested in learning about is *you*. But most applicants go into the process thinking the employer wants to learn how much the applicant knows. If you were applying for a position as a brain surgeon or scientist, *what* you knew might be of primary importance. But for criminal justice and security jobs, particularly at an entry-level position or at the initial promotional stages, employers recognize that the right kind of person will be able to learn and grow with the job. If you get "hung up" thinking knowledge is all-important and concentrate entirely on memorizing facts, data, laws, rules and procedures, you have missed the point. Interviewers want to get to know *you*, not your capacity for memorizing. In fact, this is why the application process is so frightening for most applicants. They worry that they do not know enough. This is *not* what employers are looking for. Frerkes (1998, p.63) states:

> The primary focus of the oral board process is to establish the applicant's command presence, integrity, initiative, interests, communication skills, tolerance for stress and judgement/decisiveness. It is their opportunity to assess the applicant's desire for professional growth, commitment to the community, whether he or she is people-oriented and has the potential to be a professional law enforcement officer.

The purpose of the interview is for the employer to have a chance to get to know *you,* not your capacity for memorizing or how much you know.

In reviewing the elements of your job-seeking uniform, you can see where an overemphasis on what you *know* could effectively prevent you from concentrating on the important factors—showing good manners, being enthusiastic about the job you're applying for and letting your true personality shine through. The incorrect assumption is that you will be hired for what you know instead of for who you are.

Nonetheless, knowledge *is* important. That is why it is included as part of your job-seeking uniform. Part of what the employer must know about you is what you know, but it is only one part, and a fairly small one. Depending on what field and position you are being interviewed for, you will need to know certain things. For example, in Minnesota, a person applying for any law enforcement position must know elementary law such as the use of deadly force applicable and some fundamental Fourth Amendment search and seizure concepts. Such an applicant should be ready to answer questions about basic procedures, for instance, situations dealing with Miranda, citizen safety or officer safety. You might want to take some criminal justice classes to help prepare. Ask people who have applied for similar jobs what questions they were asked.

You should be able demonstrate how you would solve more complex legal issues. For example, if asked about fifth-degree assault, be able to tell the interviewer where you would go for that information. Or, given a hypothetical situation and asked how you would respond, be able to explain the process you would use to analyze the situation rather than just saying what you would do.

It is also important to know about the organization you're applying to. *Never* enter an interview without having first checked out the Web site of the hiring authority. Not only does this make a statement about your interest in the position and agency, but it also speaks to your computer ability. If the hiring agency has a Web presence, it is here you will likely find their mission statement and other valuable information. Frerkes suggests (p.64): "Be prepared to show a hiring authority that you care enough to know the particulars of that community. Educate yourself." For example, you should research and learn details about the follow specifics of a community:

- Population
- Racial climate
- "High profile" issues
- Unemployment rate
- Type of government system in place

- Size of the police force
- If community policing has been implemented
- Chief's name and how long he/she has held the position
- Recent increases or decreases in crime statistics

If no Web site exists, or you're unable to locate a computer with Internet access, the local chamber of commerce may be able to provide up-to-date data.

Take advantage of what you now know about what to expect during the interview and *plan your strategy* as to how you will present yourself.

Mullins (1994, p.12) offers some advice on what to expect during an interview and how you should prepare for it. He refers to it as an "interview story" which typically consists of three scenes:

> Scene One: Lasting about three minutes, this scene consists of small talk and is really a compatibility contest. . . .
> Scene Two: Lasting about 15 minutes to an hour or more, this scene is mainly you telling your story. . . .
> Scene Three: Lasting only a minute or two, this scene closes the interview and sets up the next steps.

 In your journal, write down your plan for these three scenes.

1. Scene One: What things will you do when you first enter the interview room? How can you show that you are polite, friendly and comfortable with yourself and the situation? Remember, this scene takes up most of the four-minute barrier time. What impression are you going to make and how? Write down your plan.

2. Scene Two: This is your sales pitch scene—you must sell the interviewer on *you.* According to Mullins (p.12), during this scene:

    > You need to explain your skills, abilities, accomplishments, and ambitions. Emphasize your ability to add value to the employer. If you can claim credit for increasing sales, reducing costs, or improving quality, now is the time to do so. If you have any holes in your experience or blemishes on your record, handle them now. As you conclude this scene, stress your ability and willingness to perform at a high level.

    Write your script for what you will say during this scene. Practice it. Get comfortable with it. Many people are uneasy talking about themselves or "tooting their own horn." That's what Scene Two is all about. Write down enough to keep you talking for at least 10 minutes (although realize it won't be 10 minutes *straight*—just have enough to say). Don't expect the interviewer to carry the conversation here—chances are you'll hear little from them during this scene.

3. Scene Three: How will you end the interview? Mullins (p.12) says:

    > Do not allow the interviewer to close with the usual, "We'll be in touch with you when we decide something." This statement leaves you powerless to influence the decision. Instead, you should end the interview by saying, "I'll keep you posted about developments in my job search." This comment keeps you in control, allowing you to follow up with additional information that may improve your chance of being hired."

    Write in your journal a closing comment or a positive question that might be asked at the end of an interview. A comment regarding the time frame of your job search sends the message that you are enthusiastic to get going. Make your statement something you'd feel comfortable saying. Practice saying it. When the interview comes to a close, don't be caught off guard. You want your comment ready to roll off your tongue for the strongest possible conclusion to your interview story.

FOLLOW-UP

Follow-up refers to the extra steps taken after the interview, the time when most applicants sit and wait to hear from the employer. Just as you must never leave a contact with an employer without saying "thank you," you must not walk out of an interview never to be heard from again. A single follow-up thank you letter can give you another chance to show off how well you wear your job-seeking uniform by reviewing such elements as:

- Grammar
- Manners
- Personality
- Enthusiasm
- Ability to follow up
- Knowledge

Six of the nine elements in your job-seeking uniform can be reinforced *after the interview*. You can also demonstrate again your proficiency with written material, and you provide the employer with one more reason to remember your name positively. Imagine the employer sitting with half a dozen or fewer resumes that all look good, pondering a decision. Suddenly you call to say thank you for the interview. This simple thank you can tip the scales in your favor.

How you follow up is up to you. Some employers prefer not to be called while they are making a decision. While a phone call may not be a bad idea, it should not replace a letter. A letter is a necessity. Write to everyone who participated in your interview. Get their names, proper spellings and titles from the secretary on your way out or call the secretary later to get this information. Remember a thank you for the secretary too.

> Always follow up after the interview with a thank-you letter and possibly even a phone call. However, recognize the fine line between being remembered positively and becoming nothing more than a pest. Don't lay it on too thick.

CONCLUSION

Your job-seeking uniform is just that—how you present yourself during an interview. It consists of more than the clothes you put on, however. Your uniform includes how you come off during the initial contact, your grooming, physical condition, grammar and speech, manners, personality, enthusiasm, knowledge and follow-up. Take advantage of what you now know about what to expect during the interview and *plan your strategy* as to how you will present yourself. Pick out your job-seeking uniform and put it on *before* your interview, just to make sure it fits and that you're comfortable in it. The more you wear it, the more natural it will feel. But you must practice putting it on and wearing it for it to be most effective. Plan how you will present yourself as *THE* one to hire.

MIND STRETCHES

1.   What three things have made you feel accepted by another person while you attempt to break the four-minute barrier? What three things have made you feel unaccepted by another person while you attempt to break the four-minute barrier?

2.   How would you work your responses to Question #1 into the job application process?

3.   List opportunities you could create to sell yourself besides the traditional resume and interview.

4.   Why is it important to approach the elements of the interview as a whole rather than looking at the pieces separately?

5.   Why is it important to develop a *strategy* rather than just jumping into the interview process?

6.   Who could you ask for constructive feedback on how you come across to others by your clothing? Your handshake? Your cover letter and resume? Their initial reaction to you?

7.   Which elements of the interview do you think you need to work on? How will you do so for each?

8.   How might videotaping yourself be beneficial in preparing for an interview?

INSIDERS' VIEWS

For this chapter, read the *Insiders' Views* by Trooper Robert P. Meyerson ("Be Prepared") and Lt. Brenda P. Maples ("Presenting Yourself as *THE* One to Hire"), found on the Web site: http://www.wadsworth.com/criminaljustice_d/.

REFERENCES

Frerkes, Larry R. *Becoming a Police Officer: A Guide to Successful Entry Level Testing.* Incline Village, NV: Copperhouse Publishing Company, 1998.

Mullins, Terry. "Search Skills: How to Land a Job." *Psychology Today,* September/October 1994, pp.12–13.

Reece, Barry L. and Brandt, Rhonda. *Effective Human Relations in Organizations,* 3rd ed. Boston, MA: Houghton Mifflin Company, 1987.

Wallach, Janet. *Looks that Work.* New York: Viking Penguin, Inc., 1986.

Wharton, David. "Fit to Be Hired." *Men's Fitness,* November 1997, pp.58–60.

Yate, Martin John. *Knock 'em Dead with Great Answers to Tough Interview Questions.* Boston: Bob Adams, 1998.

CHAPTER 13

THE INTERVIEW: A CLOSER LOOK

Whenever you are asked if you can do a job, tell 'em, "Certainly I can"—and get busy and find out how to do it.

—*Theodore Roosevelt*

Do You Know

➢ What the definition of *interview* is?
➢ What purposes the interview serves?
➢ What five types of interviews you may encounter and how they differ?
➢ How likely you'll be able to negotiate your salary?
➢ How you should close an interview?
➢ What the importance of follow-up is?

INTRODUCTION

The interview. It even sounds ominous. Fear of the unknown can be paralyzing. So take a good look at what you might expect because the interview *is* what it's all about in the job-hunting game.

Webster's defines *interview* as: "A formal consultation usually to evaluate qualifications (of a prospective student or employee). A meeting at which information is obtained." Here are some facts about job interviews:

- Interviews are anxiety provoking.
- Interviews are necessary.
- Everyone has to have them.
- Everyone working has had them.

An interview is a meeting between someone who has a job opening and someone who needs a job, at which information is obtained and exchanged.

PURPOSES OF THE JOB INTERVIEW

As discussed in Chapter 12, for you, the purposes of the interview are to show the panel the "real" you and to find out who the "real" employer is. For employers, the purpose of an interview is to get to know you. Ask any employer, and they will have stories of applicants who looked nothing short of spectacular on their resumes but were absolutely unacceptable in person. A good resume, in addition to the other preparatory material and contacts, is just your ticket *into* the interview. An advantage of the preliminary phases of the job-seeking process is that you can get outside help, for example, proofreading your resume. But once you are led into the interview room, you are on your own. It is completely up to you—as it should be. Simple? Your entire future based on a brief interview?

195

Bolles (2001) likens the interview to the "dating game." He notes: "*Both* of you have to like the other, before you can get on to the question of 'going steady.'" According to Bolles, employers have four key questions:

➤   Why are you here? (Why did you pick us?)
➤   What can you do for me?
➤   What kind of person are you?
➤   How much are you going to cost me?

The main thrust of any interview is to see how you interact on a personal level. This is extremely important. The process of getting a job and developing a strategy to meet this challenge boils down to two critical aspects:

➤   Having a resume that can withstand the "weeding out" process.
➤   Developing a strategy to not only withstand the interview process, but to emerge victoriously.

The Purposes—Up Close

The personal interview can fulfill several purposes.

The primary purposes of the personal interview are for the employer to:	
• Get a look at you.	• Observe how you analyze problems.
• Listen to you.	• Test your people skills.
• See how you perform under stress.	• Test your knowledge.

Looking at You. Employers would no more hire an unknown person than they would purchase a home or a car they had never seen. They want to see what they are getting. Particularly for a job in criminal justice or private security, you do not want to make a negative impression by presenting yourself in an extreme manner. If hired, you will represent the agency. To most future clients you will *be* the agency. Think about it! Rest assured the interviewers will be thinking about it.

Remember the importance of grooming. Find the restroom on your way into the building to make that final check: comb your hair, straighten your tie, adjust your slip, zip up your zipper. *Look sharp. Be sharp.* Also get a drink of water.

Listening to You. No matter how great your resume looks or how sharp you look, employers want to know that you also speak English well. There will probably never be a better test of this than during the job interview. In addition to testing your general grammatical skills, employers want to hear how you sound. They want their employees to sound *normal*. If you get uptight during an interview (and understand that everyone does), just be yourself. Do not try to cover up your anxiety by being cute, funny, smart-alecky or a host of other facades you've probably seen people try when uptight.

What if you *sound* nervous? Your voice may crack, you may say something you did not intend to, or you may just plain forget where you were or what the question was. Don't panic. It is reassuring to employers to see you as capable of recognizing a mistake and being able to reorganize and continue. Do not fake it. If a major goof occurs, simply proceed as follows:

1. Take a deep breath.
2. Admit to the interviewer(s): "This job is really important to me, and I guess I'm more nervous than I thought."
3. Continue with your answer.

There is nothing wrong with being honest. If you're really nervous, admit it; 99.99% of the time interviewers are sympathetic. Your honesty will make a positive impression. Also, take a moment before you answer a question, especially if the question is *not* one you "practiced." What may seem like an eternity to you will likely be only a few seconds. Never answer without thinking through your response.

Seeing How You Perform Under Stress. Some employers use a "stress interview." The rationale is that the job you are seeking is stressful, so they want to see what you do under stress. Such interviews often involve "rapid-fire" questions during which you have little or no time to think about your response. The interviewers may appear hostile or demanding to you. They may ask questions you just can't answer—either because you lack the expertise or because there *is* no answer.

Because the purpose of stress interviews is to see how you will act, do your best to keep your wits about you. Brainstorm all the possible weird things that could be set up in an interview. Ask others what they have undergone in interviews, and you will be as well prepared as you can be for this experience. Fortunately, these interviews are not too common. Stress interviews are discussed further on page 200.

Observing How You Analyze Problems. You may be asked to solve problems but, particularly at an entry-level position, you are *not* expected to know every answer. For example, an interview for a police dispatcher might include such questions as, "What would you do if 25 747s crashed in various parts of the city at once?" A potential corrections officer might be asked, "What would you do if you were the only guard in your pod and, during a power outage, 21 inmates became embroiled in a massive knife fight?" Or a potential security officer might be asked, "What if you were accosted by 17 chapters of Hell's Angels demanding a solution to world hunger?" Remember that even if there is an answer, in all probability you are not expected to know it.

Prospective employers want to know if and how you think. A good strategy is to begin your answers with your own variation of the "policy/will learn" statement. That is, you understand that every company or department is likely to have its own policy on how to handle most situations and that you are also eager to learn. For example, if asked, "How would you handle a situation in which you find an open door to an office after hours, and the boss is inside with his partner's wife?" A reasonable answer could be: "Because I have had no previous security experience, that situation is certainly a difficult one. Based on the information you have given me, I would follow the applicable company policy; for instance, filling out an incident report if required, as well as immediately advising my supervisor. In addition, I would anticipate learning how the company would want me to handle such sensitive situations during my training period. If it is not brought up, I will bring it up now that you've asked me about it." During such analytical interviews, rather than looking for a right answer, the interviewers are interested in the *process* you use in coming to some conclusions.

Testing Your People Skills. Your resume may look spectacular, but if you don't come across as friendly, sincere and respectful, you will not get the job. No matter how nervous you get, no matter how frustrating the interview is, do not forget your manners. Let the interview board know you appreciate their time and the challenging questions raised. Shake hands with each interviewer, smile, say "yes" not "yeah," and use *common sense.*

This is all more easily said than done. Whether or not the interview is specifically designed to create stress, it will! The "little things" are so easily forgotten. Before the interview, make a list of what you want to do. For example:

➢   Shake hands with everyone when introduced.
➢   Look at everyone personally during your responses.
➢   Thank the group at the end of the interview and again shake each interviewer's hand.

Thinking about it all ahead of time will put it in your head, making it easier to remember during the pressure of the interview.

Testing Your Knowledge. You may also be asked questions to check your knowledge in specific areas, depending on the state in which you are applying. For police officers, you could be asked about very basic statutes, for example, the deadly force law. You should be prepared to answer as many of these questions as possible, but do not panic if you cannot. In such a situation admit that you do not know, but that you would look it up in the state statute book, or the traffic code or wherever it is likely to be found. *Do NOT guess.* If you draw a blank, admit it. In such a case, you may want to follow up with a letter providing the answer to show you can find needed information. According to Mounts (1997, p.65):

> What is the reason for an oral interview? Is it to test your technical knowledge? Generally speaking, the answer is no. In most cases, your technical knowledge will be, or has already been, addressed in the written examination and through various performance evaluations. However, some interviews do test part of your technical knowledge coupled with your conceptual skills, such as: quality of work experience and training, stability, ambition, ability to work with others, communication skills, manner, speech, decision making, and interpersonal skills.

Most of the important purposes of an interview can be addressed during one question posed by the panel. A common question for police officer applicants is: "What would you do if you stopped an off-duty officer for drunk driving?" Try the "policy/will learn" approach to come up with an answer. For example, "If the department had a policy, I would follow it. I would certainly advise my supervisor. Recognizing that DWI is a serious offense and that police officers are not above the law, I would. . . ." You get the idea. Such a question gives you a great chance to appear at your best—or worst.

A final word regarding preparation: Never go into an interview (personal, phone or otherwise) without checking the prospective employer's Web site and reviewing their mission statement—this knowledge will set you apart from the competition.

Imagine you are an employer seeking to fill the position of either police, corrections or security officer. An applicant has just walked into the room. List in your journal five things that would turn you off immediately.

Next, list five things that would strike you positively.

A San Francisco financial recruiting firm surveyed 100 large corporations to find out how some job applicants performed during the interview. Among the responses were the following:

➢   Said he was so well qualified, if he didn't get the job it would prove that the company's management was incompetent.
➢   Asked to see the *interviewer's* resume to see if the personnel executive was qualified to judge the candidate.
➢   Announced she hadn't had lunch and proceeded to eat a hamburger and french fries in the interviewer's office.
➢   Wore a Walkman and said she could listen to me and the music at the same time.
➢   Dozed off and started snoring during the interview.

Unbelievable, but true. What should you do during the interview? Bolles suggests paying attention to not only *what* you say but also *how* you say it. He notes various studies have shown that the people who get hired are typically those who speak half the time in the interview and let the employer speak the other half of the time. Bolles also advises that when it is your turn to speak in the interview, you should talk no shorter than twenty seconds and no longer than two minutes at any one time.

TYPES OF INTERVIEWS

Interviews provide employers with a chance to observe you from a variety of perspectives. The majority of interviews can be classified as:

- Informational
- Mass
- Stress
- "Unnecessary"
- Courtesy

Informational Interviews

This is the "classical" interview, where you are asked to come in so employers have a chance to check you out in the areas previously outlined. These interviews are straightforward. Presumably you enter this interview in a relatively equal position with the other applicants. You have no say about what format your interview will take, so "go with the flow." The interview may be formal, relaxed or somewhere in between. You may have only one interviewer, or there may be several.

The formal interview is rather rigid, with questions being asked one after another and the interviewers giving little or no response to tip you off as to how you are doing. They purposely do not respond so that you will not have any advantage over other applicants. This can be rather disconcerting since everyone likes feedback, but just continue on. On the other extreme, you may find yourself caught off guard by the informality of your interview. Your interviewers may be so laid-back, it may seem they don't even care. While possible, don't let a group that likes to have fun throw you off. In either case, provide your interviewer with as accurate a picture of yourself as you can. Just because you find yourself in a formal setting doesn't mean you must perform as rigidly as a stick, nor should informality lull you into a false sense of security and make you lose your edge.

The informational interview is the classical interview. These interviews are straightforward and are typically one-on-one, although there may be more than one interviewer present.

Mass Interviews

The number of individuals that employers like to interview varies. One or two applicants may be invited to be interviewed if they are exceptionally strong candidates, or many people may be asked in. Many applicants present themselves so poorly that a general informational meeting can serve to weed out a number of them. "Assembly line" interviews are hard on everyone, including those conducting the interviews. Applicants seem to melt together, making it difficult to remember who was who. This is when it is critical to not only provide a very strong interview, but to also pay particular attention to follow-up.

Mass interviews involve several candidates being interviewed in rapid succession, or in "assembly line" fashion. In these situations, candidates may blur together in the interviewers' minds, and you must pay particular attention to your follow-up to stand out from the crowd.

Stress Interviews

Here you have good news and bad news. The good news first: True "stress interviews" are seldom conducted. The bad news is that criminal justice and private security do lend themselves to this type of interview. These jobs involve a great deal of stress, so the approach is justified to see how applicants respond under stress. Don't expect these to be comfortable. They are designed not to be. You cannot do anything about it. Go into the interview with the commitment that, regardless of the type of interview you are confronted with, you will do your best.

During stress interviews rapid-fire questions give you little time to think about your answers or to regroup before the next question. The interviewer may seem harsh, if not downright mean. Furniture may be placed in unusual configurations; for instance, your chair may be put in a corner—or maybe you won't even have a chair.

Recognize what the game is here—to get you uptight. You *should* feel tension. In fact, you have much more reason to be concerned if you *don't* respond nervously to this setup. Draw energy from a stress interview and maintain your cool. Use the strength that brought you this far. When you get the job, you'll find yourself confronted with similar stress. The interviewers want to be sure you won't become overly defensive, hostile or panicky. While many interviewees would tell you that *every* interview is a stress interview, in fact, few are set up to purposely get you uptight.

The stress interview's purpose is to get you uptight so the interviewers can evaluate how you handle stress. Rapid-fire questioning, interviewer hostility and unusual furniture configurations may all be parts of the stress interview.

"Unnecessary" Interviews

Many jobs are filled before they are even advertised, but do not let this fact influence you too greatly. What if the job is offered to someone else? Who's to say that person will accept it? If they do, who's to say it will work out? What if the job isn't what the new hire expected? What if someone even higher up at that agency doesn't like that person? Most important, what if they like *you* better?

No interview is unnecessary. It's just that some seem more necessary than others. Yes, it is frustrating to be called to an interview merely so the employer can prove he or she has done a search before hiring the pre-determined first choice. However, employers are also uncomfortable with this process. If you do well in the interview, the employer may keep you in mind for the next opening. At the very least, it is a chance to practice your interview skills and find out you can survive rejection. Both opportunities are valuable. Because you are unique, you may be the perfect candidate. Never let an opportunity pass by. You have no way of knowing if this job will be *the one*. A lot can be said for the person who tries, even in the face of adversity.

> "Unnecessary" interviews may be conducted when the position is already filled but policy demands the position still be advertised or that a certain number of people be interviewed. Make the most of this opportunity—no interview is truly needless.

Courtesy Interviews

Never dismiss an opportunity by saying, "Ah, I only got this interview because the chief knows my dad. He did it as a favor to him." So what? It doesn't matter *how* you got into an interview, just that you did. Once you're there, it's all up to you. Some opportunities to interview do result because the applicant knew someone or was related to someone in the agency. And that's just fine. You've heard the saying, "It's not *what* you know but *who* you know." All that matters is that *now* you have the chance to impress the interview panel. Worrying about how you got there consumes valuable energy. Go for it!

> Courtesy interviews are done as favors or because of "connections," but they are still legitimate interviewing opportunities. Again, make the most of them.

Teleconferencing—A New Twist

Technology is changing the way jobs are pursued and found. While face-to-face meetings between job seekers and prospective employers are still most common, videoconference interviews are growing in popularity. Two primary reasons for the increasing use of this method are that others beyond the formal process can view the interview and that applicants a long distance away from a potential employer can effectively compete for a position without having to travel extensively.

Such "interviews" may consist simply of a candidate's videotaped responses to questions or it may be a "live" interview via video hookups, such as is done routinely on the national evening news. Internet technology makes it equally convenient for prospective employees or employers to communicate, interview and negotiate long-distance.

Some strategies to optimize this opportunity include applicants presenting themselves in different modes to set off their personality. For example, some questions could be answered in a dress uniform, others in a suit, and yet others more casually in a sweater. A fire service applicant might answer questions with a fireplace or fire truck behind him. This is a chance to plan how to present yourself in your best light and to be far more in control of the situation than in most conventional interviews.

TYPICAL QUESTIONS

Countless lists have been compiled of questions you should anticipate and be prepared for during job interviews. Some of these questions are construed as quite "self-incriminating," as noted by Weiss and Dresser (1998, p.48):

> Kill questions relate to being fired, arrested, experiencing discontent with an employer, problems with a supervisor, being too slow and so on. Red flag questions are those that can place the interviewee on the defensive, or in a negative light. These go on forever and can include:
>
> > "My worst characteristic is . . ."
> > "If I could change one trait about myself . . ."
> > "People criticize me because . . ."
>
> And
>
> > "My weakest point is . . . ."
>
> An applicant must be honest and answer the questions. Many people are not shrewd enough to provide a positive illustration of a success in dealing with a shortcoming.

To tackle the common interview question of "What is your biggest weakness?" Nelson and Dauten (1996, p.D3) recommend: "Just name your best attribute, then put the word 'too' in front of it." Kinsman (1996, p.D4) offers tips on how to respond to some "chilling" questions:

Why should I hire you? . . .
> Start by talking about your work experience that has prepared you for this job and then talk about your educational background that will lend an understanding on the job.

Why have you been out of work for so long? . . .
> Say that you were trying to approach your period of unemployment as a career opportunity and that you were looking for a position that truly matched your talents.

What are your future plans? . . .
> A potential employer usually wants to find out if you have a commitment to this job . . . .
> Employers want to hire individuals who have a vision of their future.

Why were you fired from your last job? . . .
> Prepare an honest, thoughtful description of the reasons behind your firing. Make certain, however, that you don't begin to weave together a detailed defense of your position or bad-mouth your former employer . . . . Most employers are less concerned about why you were fired than in how you respond to questions about it.

Pearson (1998, p.57) suggests some other questions that might be asked during an interview:

- How can your skills and abilities meet the needs of this position?
- What was the most enjoyable part of your previous position?
- Why did you leave your last position?
- What are your career goals?
- What are some of the things you look for in a job?
- If you could have an ideal job, what would it be?

Following are some typical questions. As you read through them, consider this particularly relevant comment from Yate (1998): "To some of the toughest questions, there is never a 'right' answer—that's what makes them the toughest—but there is always a right approach."

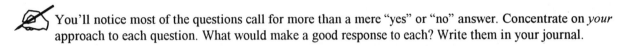 You'll notice most of the questions call for more than a mere "yes" or "no" answer. Concentrate on *your* approach to each question. What would make a good response to each? Write them in your journal.

1. What makes you think you would be an asset to this agency?

2. When did you first consider joining the police/corrections/security field?

3. What public service organizations or clubs do you belong to?

4. Do you realize that your previous training will be of little value in the job you are applying for?

5. Do you have applications in at other agencies?

6. Are you married? If so, what does your spouse think of your career choice and the odd hours you'll be working?

7. Are any of your friends members of this agency?

8. Do you have any relatives who are members of this agency?

9. When did you first think about becoming a police/corrections/security officer?

10. Have you ever taken any tests for law enforcement/corrections/security positions?

11. Have you ever considered the hazardous nature of the work that you may have to perform?

12. Have you talked over the conditions, opportunities and attitudes of members of this agency with the agency?

13. What are your hobbies?

14. Have you trained for this position by going to any coaching schools, taken any courses or the like?

15. If you are chosen for the job, would you make it your lifetime career?

16. Has the security of the job or the desire for service been your main reason for applying for this position?

17. What is your attitude about unions in police/corrections/security fields?

18. You are a member of this agency and a fellow officer has been injured along with civilians. To whom would you give your first attention?

19. You are a member of this agency and you suspect that a fellow officer is committing thefts in the district/office/business while off duty. What action would you take?

20. You are patrolling on the midnight-to-morning watch and have been walking hours without seeing anyone. Would you find an unoccupied auto and rest?

21. You receive an order you believe to be in error from your superior. What action would you take?

22. Who would you rather please in your work, your superior officer or the public?

23. What kind of job do you feel this agency is doing?

24. How would you improve the quality of work in this agency after you have been trained?

25. What is your present occupation? Do you feel the training you have received will benefit you if selected to join this agency?

26. What do your friends think of you joining this agency?

27. Have you ever had difficulty with any law enforcement agency either as a juvenile or as an adult?

28. Give us a brief idea of what a good law enforcement/corrections/security officer should be in the way of character, knowledge and physical condition.

29. What are your greatest strengths? Your greatest weaknesses?

30. Where do you expect to be 10 or 20 years from now?

31. Why should you be hired?

32. What are your strongest attributes?

33. Are there things the agency should be concerned about?

34. Is there anything else you would like to say or ask?

The following questions should be anticipated by those seeking positions in law enforcement.

35. Why did you choose the police department instead of the fire department?

36. Have you ever stood around when you saw a crowd gathered about a serious accident or when a police officer was investigating a crime or making an arrest?

37. Do you listen to police calls on shortwave radio? If yes, and you hear a call that sounds serious, do you go to where the officers were sent?

ou are off duty and a purse-snatcher runs past you with the victim in pursuit. What action would you take?

39. You find that your superior drinks to excess and is drunk on the job. The place your superior drinks is on your beat. What action would you take? Would you say anything to the bartender who serves your superior?

40. Should the police and fire departments be integrated into a single unit known as a public safety department?

41. Should this agency perform such tasks as letting locked-out people into their homes, escorting single women home at late hours, removing debris from the street that has accidentally fallen from moving vehicles?

42. What is this agency's responsibility in respect to juvenile delinquents?

43. Under the authority of government you would represent, could you use deadly force against a citizen where your life or the life of someone else was threatened? Could you take another person's life under any other circumstances?

Guidelines for Replies to Commonly Asked Interview Questions

Having studied these questions and prepared answers, see how close you come to the following guidelines.

1. Indicate such items as interest in working with people, interest in serving the public and having completed so many hours of related course work.

2. Frequently the oral board gives great weight to someone who has considered law enforcement, corrections or security as a career for a long time.

3. You might mention Rotary, Lions, Kiwanis, various veterans' organizations, as well as such high school organizations as Key Club or anything similar.

4. This is a "loaded" question. Politely take exception. All training you have received in citizenship, first aid, governmental organizations and the like is important. Rifle club memberships are also important. The value lies in understanding the functions of departments, etc.

5. Answer frankly, but indicate that the agency in question is your first choice.

6. It is hoped that your "significant other" enthusiastically backs your decision.

7. Be able to recall the names of police/corrections/security officers you know.

8. Answer truthfully, even if the relationship is extremely remote.

9. The oral board may give great weight to someone who has been considering that particular career over time.

10. Answer frankly. It might be best to indicate that this agency is your first choice.

11. Indicate that you are aware of the hazards in dealing with the criminal element, such as handling aggressive prisoners or driving at pursuit speeds, but that you do not consider law enforcement, corrections or security any more hazardous than other occupations. You might indicate that some training you have received and some experience you've had in observing procedures have helped alleviate this hazard.

12. Talk to members of the agency before the interview. Know the agency's salary range and something about the agency itself and the city/industry, such as its approximate size, its type of government/management and so on.

13. Organize your thinking so your answer stresses activities related to law enforcement/corrections/security. Among these may be target shooting, skeet shooting, hunting, youth activities such as scouting, or sports, particularly wrestling, boxing and the martial arts.

14. This is a good chance to list the related courses you have successfully completed.

15. Answer this question affirmatively.

16. Job security and service to the public are two factors in your decision. Other factors might be the chance for advancement, growth in a professional organization and the satisfaction of doing a worthwhile job.

17. Generally officers do not feel that police unions contribute to professionalization. Be careful, however, a member of the oral board may also be the primary union representative.

18. The most seriously injured person should get first attention.

19. Recommended action depends on the basis for the suspicion. If you have sufficient evidence to be considered reasonable cause, you have no alternative but to report your facts to a superior. This is for your own sake and the good of law enforcement/private security. Without sufficient facts, severe damage could be done, and the reporting officer could be open to civil damages.

20. Officers are not paid to "rest" on duty. Alternatives might be to stop in at a restaurant for a cup of coffee where you would still be considered on duty and available for assignment.

21. Follow the order if not seriously in error. An alternative is to call the error to the superior's attention and, after doing so, abide by that decision. Officers who refuse to obey orders do so at their own peril. Officers should refuse any order that involves an illegal act. Short of an illegal act, it would be the superior's responsibility if he/she gave an erroneous order.

22. This question is similar to "have you stopped beating your wife yet?" Chances are the superior's objectives are the same as yours in public service. If pleasing the public means overlooking offenses and violations, this is wrong.

23. You feel the agency is a good one or you would not be applying. Have some basis for this belief, however, such as conversations with officers, articles in the paper or conversations with citizens, particularly people who have had some dealing with the agency.

24. Such things as continued education, home study and in-service training would help improve the quality of your work after being hired.

25. In addition to specialized knowledge, law enforcement/corrections/security officers should know something about a great many things. Therefore, most experiences and training you have had will be of some benefit.

26. Generally, your friends would approve of your joining the agency.

27. Answer frankly.

28. Because of the nature of the work, criminal justice and security officers in effect "live in a fishbowl." Therefore, they must make sure their character and activities are beyond reproach. They must maintain excellent physical condition and continue to search for knowledge throughout their careers.

29. Strengths should be very apparent from your resume. Employers are especially interested in such characteristics as leadership, ability to communicate, compassion, loyalty and the like. And since you may be asked to list as many weaknesses as you did strengths, don't get too carried away on your strengths. Stick to around three. Make the weaknesses portion of this question work to your advantage. Do not be negative, but be honest, and pick a strength that you have perhaps carried to extremes, for example, "I sometimes pay too much attention to details." Or "I am a perfectionist."

30. Take your time on this one. You should indicate that you expect to grow and develop professionally and be promoted accordingly.

31. Be prepared to explain what you can contribute to the agency. This is a favorite interview question.

32. Blow your own horn. List some positives like "enthusiastic," "professional," etc. Know what the word *attribute* means! See the response for #29, discussing strengths.

33. If there is a problem in your background, be honest about it. But there is not a need to list every issue you may wish you had handled differently.

34. See the upcoming "Closing the Interview" section.

35. Law enforcement is a challenging, interesting, diversified career with great opportunity for service and working with people.

36. Be sure your answer does not indicate you have interfered with any police/security activities. Confine your answer to incidents in which you helped by furnishing license numbers, relating the direction of flight a suspect took, pointing out witnesses, identifying participants and the like.

37. Such activity is usually frowned on by law enforcement officers and might indicate the person is overzealous.

38. In such instances, an officer is never off duty. Appropriate action should be taken depending on if you and/or the probable purse-snatcher is armed. Officers in plain clothes should identify themselves, probably by pinning their badges on their lapels, etc. At least, get an accurate description of the suspect.

39. The answer depends on the circumstances and how obviously drunk the superior would appear to others and if he or she is known as a police officer. Know department policy. If any police officer, regardless of rank, indulges in activity that might discredit the agency, it is the officer's responsibility to report the matter to a superior. Be careful to state only facts. Record the time, date and to whom such a report is made.

40. Traditionally, both fire and police service oppose integration. While the concept has some merit in financial savings, frequently the objectives of the two agencies are so different that it makes the idea impractical.

41. Opinions differ considerably as to the responsibility of law enforcement relative to this area. Generally, this kind of public service is good public relations and may have some crime prevention value as well. The public expects help in emergencies.

42. Since juvenile delinquency is a serious problem in our society, it is a major responsibility of law enforcement officers. There is disagreement as to the amount of rehabilitative activity in which a law enforcement agency should engage. Generally, authorities agree that law enforcement personnel should handle the law and leave rehabilitation to other agencies whose personnel are better qualified.

43. Answer in the affirmative to the first question. The answer to the second question would depend on the law, department policy and procedures and circumstances.

Rigdon (1995, pp.132–136) asked some of America's toughest interviewers to share their most frequent questions, as well as their suggestions on how to respond. Here is some of what they said:

> ➤ *What exactly do you want from us? Describe your ideal job.*
> Many people dodge these types of questions by giving a generic, safe answer. To make a better impression . . . prepare by writing an "employment ad" that describes your dream job. . . . [forcing] you to focus on exactly what you want and what you have to offer.

> ➤ *Where do you want to be five years from now?*
> The best way to botch this one is to not have an answer . . . make long-term goals a part of [your] answer but . . . focus on the short term.

> ➤ *What's your greatest accomplishment?*
> Many candidates flub this question. . . . [by] responding with responsibilities rather than *results*. . . . "[Describe] the big picture, not just the activities."

> ➤ *What are your weaknesses?*
> Many candidates try to highlight vague weaknesses that can be viewed as assets. They say "I'm impatient," . . . or, "I work such long hours that my family life is out of balance." Don't try it. Interviewers are sick of hearing these stock answers. Instead, be honest, but emphasize the actions you've taken to deal with a weakness. . . . [Try] this type of answer: "Sometimes I would push back deadlines to turn in higher quality work. However, I've learned to delegate more, and I've only slipped once in the past year."

What all the interviewers' suggestions have in common is taking a good, hard look at yourself and what you want *before* going to the interview and preparing to handle tough questions such as these. Think about them and decide how you will answer, and don't worry about making a mistake:

> It *is* possible to recover from an honest faux pas. When Fred Benson of Weyerhaeuser applied for a White House fellowship . . . , he took a red-eye flight from overseas to make his interview on time. Walking bleary-eyed into the room, he was blinded by the sun glinting off a glass table and could make out only the silhouettes of the panelists. Extending his hand to the chairman, he knocked a pitcher of water into the man's lap.

> In that instant he gave up all hope of getting the position. "I have a feeling that I have nowhere to go but up from here, so I'm going to be very relaxed in this interview," he told the panel. He was—and got the job. Now he helps interview finalists for the fellowships (Rigdon, p.136).

NEGOTIATING

Negotiating is sometimes not possible. The majority of criminal justice jobs are union jobs, or at least are positions that bargain collectively. Therefore, you will have little room to negotiate, particularly at entry-level positions.

Likewise, security positions generally permit little room for you to make demands. As you work your way upward in either the public or private sector, you may find room to negotiate. At almost all entry-level, and even mid-level lateral movements, you could easily appear too demanding if you want too much. Be realistic. Recognize the limitations of these careers. If you have specific needs, however, pursue them as far as you can.

The opportunity to negotiate a salary in these fields, particularly in entry-level jobs, is very limited.

CLOSING THE INTERVIEW

The final impression you make on your way out is also important. Here is an opportunity to shine as the ideal, enthusiastic candidate. The interview is likely to close with the interviewer asking, "Is there anything you would like to ask?" Every other candidate will say something like, "Well, no, not really." Boring. Unmemorable. Your strategy should include having several closing questions, not about how many vacation days you'll get but rather questions about the starting date or a likely assignment.

Always leave on an assertive, upbeat, energetic note. Regardless of the words you choose, make sure the message comes across loud and clear: *I want this job, and I'll be spectacular at it!* One of the strongest conclusions an applicant ever gave me was to simply say, "You'll never regret hiring me!" Don't be too brash or boastful. Make your closing statement brief and to the point. Any last minute chance you have will be ruined if you drag it out with question after question or statement after statement. As is true throughout your overall strategy, seek a balance.

In summary, let the interviewer know that you *want* the job. You would be astonished by how few applicants ever communicate that they've applied for the job because they *want* the job!

> Close the interview on an upbeat note by asking about a starting date or what a typical assignment might be. Never close by asking about salary or benefits. Finally, let the interviewer know that you really *want* the job.

FOLLOW UP

Punctuate your interest with a follow-up. A follow-up is an easy way to score points during the hiring process because few applicants have developed a strategy that includes plain old courtesy. At the least, send a letter telling the interviewer(s) you appreciate the time and opportunity to meet. Such a letter not only demonstrates politeness but also offers one more chance to impress the employer with your strong points. Anything in addition, within reason, will probably benefit you.

> *Do not* forget to follow up. As stressed in previous chapters, following up helps you score points in the hiring process by demonstrating your courtesy and getting your name in front of the interviewer one more time.

MAKING A DECISION

Making a decision is something you probably can't imagine would be a problem. Selecting from several jobs would be a great problem, right? If this does become your "problem," take your time before deciding. Usually employers are happy to give you a reasonable time to make a decision.

If you are a final contender in another agency, you now have a card to play. There is nothing wrong with contacting these other employers to let them know you would like to work for them, but you have been offered another job elsewhere. Suddenly you have increased your desirability, because someone else wants you too.

At some point you need to decide. Weigh as many factors as you are aware of. Seek input from others, and then take that risk and make your final decision. The workplace culture is a major consideration:

> One of the greatest determinants of job satisfaction is also the most difficult to pin down during interviews. A good fit comes from first looking inside yourself, then into an organization's culture. Workplace culture is like the air you breathe: essential to the operation of all systems yet nearly invisible to the eye.
>
> Having accepted a position, an organization's values and expectations will define your days. But beforehand, when all parties are on good interview behavior, the truth of what working there is like can get lost amid their smiling descriptions and your hopeful ears. . . .
>
> An environment is neither good nor bad. One individual's dream is another's disaster, which makes understanding yourself the first piece to the puzzle ("How to Get a Read . . .," 1998, p.J33).

The *Occupational Outlook Handbook* recommends: "If possible, speak to current or former employees of the organization." This will provide invaluable insight into the workplace culture and help you determine if it's a good fit for you. If you are the kind of person who prefers a more relaxed environment, accepting a position in a very formal agency where socializing is frowned upon and little after-hours camaraderie exists can feel very unfulfilling. If, on the other hand, you prefer a very "buttoned-down," more impersonal type of work climate, where little mixing of professional and private life exists, taking a job in an agency where coworkers openly share and discuss their families and like to hang out together after hours can leave you feeling alienated when you choose not to participate.

Even if you are not going to accept a position with an agency, let them know you appreciate them. Who knows, maybe you'll join them in the future.

A QUICK REVIEW

Review these job interview tips given in the *Occupational Outlook Handbook* and review them again when you have an interview lined up:

Preparation:
- Learn about the organization.
- Have a specific job or jobs in mind.
- Review your qualifications for the job.
- Prepare answers to broad questions about yourself.
- Review your resume.
- Practice an interview with a friend or relative.
- Arrive before the scheduled time of your interview.

Personal Appearance:
- Be well groomed.
- Dress appropriately.
- Do not chew gum or smoke.

The Interview:
- Answer each question concisely.
- Respond promptly.
- Use good manners. Learn the name of your interviewer and shake hands as you meet.
- Use proper English and avoid slang.
- Be cooperative and enthusiastic.
- Ask questions about the position and the organization.
- Thank the interviewer, and follow up with a letter.

Test (if employer gives one):
- Listen closely to instructions.
- Read each question carefully.
- Write legibly and clearly.
- Budget your time wisely and don't dwell on one question.

Information to Bring to an Interview:
- Social Security number.
- Driver's license number.
- Resume. Although not all employers require applicants to bring a resume, you should be able to furnish the interviewer with information about your education, training and previous employment.
- Usually an employer requires three references. Get permission from people before using their names, and make sure they will give you a good reference. Try to avoid using relatives. For each reference, provide the following information: Name, address, telephone number and job title.

CONCLUSION

The interview is what the job-hunting game is all about. Prepare by anticipating commonly asked questions and practicing your responses to these questions. Also prepare a few questions of your own to ask the interviewers. Close the interview on an upbeat note by asking about a starting date or what a typical assignment might be. Never close by asking about salary or benefits, and realize that the opportunity to negotiate a salary in these fields, particularly in entry-level jobs, is very limited. Finally, let the interviewer know that you really *want* the job. And *do not* forget to follow up.

ADDITIONAL CONTACTS AND SOURCES OF INFORMATION

Brush up on your interview skills at http://www.careerbuilder.com/gh_int_htg.html. You'll find tips on "making a good impression," what not to do during an interview and more.

 MIND STRETCHES

1.   Why would a mass interview put you at a disadvantage? An advantage?

2.   How could you make the interview process more enjoyable and memorable for an employer?

3.   At what point during any phase of the hiring process can you become a pest rather than an impressive, aggressive candidate? How can you maintain an awareness of this and prevent it?

4.   What could you do to remain cool during a "stress" interview?

5.   What could you do if you really blew an interview?

6.   What techniques could you use to deal with the understandable stress and anxiety everyone experiences during interviews?

7.   Why should you follow up with an employer you've applied to, even if you take a different job?

8.   List your three greatest concerns about being interviewed. How can you reduce these concerns?

INSIDERS' VIEWS

For this chapter, read the *Insiders' Views* by Jim Chaffee ("Your Turn to Star") and Capt. Albert J. Sweeney ("Promotion Interviews"), found on the Web site: http://www.wadsworth.com/criminaljustice_d/.

REFERENCES

Bolles, Richard Nelson. *What Color Is Your Parachute? A Practical Manual for Job-Hunters and Career Changers.* Berkeley, CA: Ten Speed Press, 2001.

"How to Get a Read on Corporate Culture." (Minneapolis/St. Paul) *Star Tribune*, January 11, 1998, p.J33.

Kinsman, Michael. "Even When Expected, Questions at Job Interview Can Be Chilling." (Minneapolis/St. Paul) *Star Tribune*, April 14, 1996, p.D4.

Mounts, Harry C. "The Oral Interview." *Law Enforcement Technology*, July 1997, pp 65–71.

Nelson, Mark and Dauten, Dale. "Your Biggest Weakness? Try Your Greatest Strength." (Minneapolis/St. Paul) *Star Tribune*, May 5, 1996, p.D3.

Occupational Outlook Handbook. 2000–2001 Edition. U.S. Department of Labor. Bureau of Labor Statistics. Washington, DC: U.S. Government Printing Office, April 2000.

Pearson, Robert. "Effective Interviewing." *Security Technology and Design*, November 1998, pp.56–58.

Rigdon, Joan E. "Ace That Job Interview: What You Say Is Important, But How You Say It Is Crucial." *Reader's Digest,* July 1995, pp.132–136. [condensed from *The Wall Street Journal*]

Weiss, Jim and Dresser, Mary. "Job Hunt Karate." *Law and Order*, May 1998, pp.47–52.

Yate, Martin John. *Knock 'em Dead with Great Answers to Tough Interview Questions.* Boston: Bob Adams, 1998.

SECTION FOUR

YOUR FUTURE IN YOUR CHOSEN PROFESSION

The future comes one day at a time.

—Dean Acheson

Destiny is not a matter of chance, it is a matter of choice; it is not a thing to be waited for, it is a thing to be achieved.

—William Jennings Bryan

What is the recipe for successful achievement? To my mind there are just four essential ingredients: Choose a career you love . . . . Give it the best there is in you . . . . Seize your opportunities . . . . And be a member of the team.

—Benjamin F. Fairless

The road to happiness lies in two simple principles: find what it is that interests you and that you can do well, and when you find it, put your whole soul into it—every bit of energy and ambition and natural ability you have.

—John D. Rockefeller, III

There are no secrets to success. It is the result of preparation, hard work, and learning from failure.

—General Colin L. Powell

Once you've landed your "dream job," another challenge begins. How do you not only make certain you keep the job, but also make certain you excel? Chapter 14 addresses this major challenge. Chapter 15 discusses how you can enhance your chances for promotion, and Chapter 16 looks at job loss and starting the job-seeking process all over.

Preparation for the future is critical because that's where you'll be spending the rest of your life!

CHAPTER 14

AT LAST! YOU'VE GOT THE JOB!
CONGRATULATIONS!!!

When you are making a success of something, it's not work. It's a way of life. You enjoy yourself because you are making your contribution to the world.

—Andy Granatelli

Do You Know

➢ What needs to be done once you get the job?
➢ As you keep trying to do well, what is important?
➢ How to be "appropriate" on the job?
➢ What the likely effects of "knowing it all" will be?
➢ How to approach politics on the job?
➢ How to respond to criticism?
➢ Why being yourself is critically important?
➢ How to maintain yourself?

INTRODUCTION

By the time you get to this chapter, you will have covered an exceptional amount of material that should give you a genuine edge during your job search. You have taken a look at where to find jobs, how to write a resume, how to best present yourself, how to interview, how to follow up and even how to deal with those inevitable rejections. Hopefully you were able to assimilate all this information and emerge victorious.

Hold everything! The race is not over yet. In a sense, it is just beginning. The only thing expected of the unsuccessful candidate is to be a good loser. But for the successful candidate, the ultimate challenge is just ahead. Getting a job brings a whole new set of challenges, especially in fields where you usually face a six-month to one-year probationary period. Kaminsky (2001, p.32) states: "The avowed purpose of the probationary period is to provide some protection to an organization while it determines whether or not the new employee is all that the organization hoped they would be when hired."

Entry-level employees, in particular, are subject to a multitude of unwritten rules. Because criminal justice and private security are fields traditionally closed to outsiders, you have no basis to understand the expectations. You'll learn all too soon that the expectations are extremely high.

Starting a new job is like going to court. It doesn't happen all that often, but when it does, officers are expected to know what to do without having to be told ahead of time. To make an error could be very serious. The same with getting the job. Do you act like the old-timers? Do you act like the rookies? It is imperative that you have at least some idea of what to expect. Call it learning from others' mistakes.

What a bitter disappointment it must be to be successful in the pursuit of your dream job—only to lose it because you don't know what the circumstances demand. While many job applicants who could probably do the job just fine never get the chance because they cannot interview adequately, the opposite is true as well. Many people who cannot perform adequately get the job because they came across very well during the interview. Being successful in an interview does not guarantee success on the job. You must have some idea of what to expect and what the circumstances demand if you want to hold on to the job.

Here's what needs to be done once you get the job:

▪ Keep trying.	▪ Wait until you are asked.	▪ Be yourself.
▪ Be appropriate.	▪ Understand politics.	▪ Maintain yourself.
▪ Know nothing.	▪ Accept criticism maturely.	

KEEP TRYING

Do not stop putting forth your best effort just because you have the job. If anything, make even greater attempts to fit into the new job than you did to get it. As Abraham Lincoln was fond of saying: "Things may come to those who wait, but only the things left by those who hustle." This is particularly true for those who have not had a professional-type job before. Criminal justice and security jobs are demanding, both in expectations and workload. You will be expected to perform as a professional, even at an entry-level position. Most employers expect you to know the basics. They seldom take time to ask if you do.

It is far better to ask a "dumb" question than to make a dumb mistake. No one likes to appear unintelligent, but employers know that no one knows it all. Employers want to have employees who are intelligent enough to direct themselves while knowing enough to stop and ask for help when needed. In effect, there are no dumb questions.

Keeping a job takes constant effort. You must not be afraid to ask questions, for not doing so may lead to mistakes that may cost you your job.

BE APPROPRIATE

This aspect of easing into your new job may seem terribly simplistic, but it's not. The job you have landed is a far cry from most other entry-level jobs such as working at a fast-food restaurant, washing cars or bagging groceries. The usual horseplay and immature attitudes frequently found at such jobs are simply not tolerated in any criminal justice or security job. Anything short of professional behavior is not good enough. These fields are constantly seeking to prove their professional image and demand employees who will help in this mission.

It is hard for new employees to know just what *is* appropriate behavior, unless they have been police explorers, reserve officers, interns or have had some other association with the criminal justice or security fields. Few outsiders know what goes on "inside." For a newly hired individual, a conservative, low-key, quiet approach is not only appropriate, it's key to survival.

The best way to discover what behavior is appropriate is to simply assume a wait-and-see approach and take the necessary time to observe what is happening around you. You will see what behavior is approved of and disapproved of. A quiet approach for a new employee is always appreciated, while giving you a chance to ease into an admittedly uncomfortable new role. As Fought (1998, p.36) explains: "New officers are trying so hard to fit in that this very effort causes them to stand out. . . . If the neophyte officer observes two senior officers in conversation with their forearms resting on their sidearm, you will be sure he or she will practice this salty stance in the mirror at home."

Particularly younger people who have had little experience in the job world are susceptible to starting out with some rather "extreme" behavior. An overconfident, "cocky" attitude is often a cover-up for some very natural feelings of discomfort, self-doubt and personal reservations. Coming on too strong, however, can be very abrasive to fellow workers. Such an attitude tends to keep people at a distance when you really need them to reassuringly welcome you to your new job.

> Learn appropriate behavior by assuming a conservative, low-key, wait-and-see approach, taking the necessary time to observe what is happening around you and observing what behavior is approved of and disapproved of.

KNOW NOTHING

It is frequently easy to tell who the new kids on the block are. They are often overbearing and brash, seeming to go out of their way to show the world they know it all—or at least *think* they know it all. Actually, the more experienced officers become, the more those officers acknowledge that there is always more to learn.

Fact: a hierarchy exists in every police department, correctional facility and security corporation. Entry-level employees, especially *new* entry-level employees, are at the bottom of the ladder. You may never recover from the damage unintentionally done by telling anyone above you how *they* should be doing something. Many rookies destroy relationships with senior officers (maybe senior by only a year) by advising them on a better holster to carry, or a safer way to make a traffic stop, or which lights to use on the squad car during a motorist assist.

Maybe the rookie is correct, as rookies have usually received up-to-date training that reflects better ways of doing things and have not had time to develop bad habits. *This is not the point.* You will have plenty of time to do it your own way. Irritate anyone early on and word will spread that you are a "know it all."

This is not advice to "play stupid." If you are asked for an opinion, give it. If you have to make a decision, make it. Show interest and a desire to learn. It may be difficult to admit to yourself and others that you *are* new and really do *not* know it all. But if you pretend that you do, you will have shot yourself in the foot. Not only will others not think you are dumb if you ask questions, they will appreciate the fact that you really want to learn.

> Being a "know it all" will likely earn you a negative reputation and delay your being accepted by others in the department, institution or agency.

WAIT UNTIL YOU ARE ASKED

This is a continuation of "know nothing." Officers in law enforcement, corrections or private security are in positions of respect. They tend to expect it and generally receive it. Particularly as a new employee, you will get more respect from other employees if you show respect for them. They deserve it. They have passed those difficult early stages of the job. They are now "regulars" and have a great deal to offer you as a newcomer. Give them the opportunity to share their wisdom with you.

Make it clear you know you have much to learn, and take advantage of this opportunity to ask questions. Do not, however, ask questions that are personally or professionally challenging to the individual (for example, "Why would you wear a holster everyone *knows* is dangerous *and* ugly?"). A better way might be to ask what equipment the officer suggests you consider when you purchase your gear.

It will not make a positive impression to say to an officer you are riding with, "My instructor told us to tag such a violator for speeding. Why didn't you?" Rather, you might ask what other violations could have been written or how the officer decided what to write on that particular stop. Many officers feel their own department or agency does not adequately recognize them for their knowledge and ability. To have someone new ride with them and ask well-thought-out, inquisitive questions is flattering to that officer. Your presence can be a positive experience for both of you *if* you take full advantage of it.

Keep in mind that people working in criminal justice and security make their living getting lied to by the best. Do not pretend to be interested or ask questions to "set up" the officer to tell you something for an alternative purpose. You will be spotted before you get the question completed, and you will be off to a terrible start.

Is it possible to ask *too many* questions? This is difficult to answer. Determine this on your own. Teachers *want* students to ask appropriate questions, but also come to cringe at those always-present students who chronically ask questions for the sake of hearing themselves talk.

UNDERSTAND POLITICS

Every organization has its own politics. Webster's defines *politics* as: "competition between interest groups or individuals for power and leadership in a government or other group." That is a fitting definition, but the complexities are so deep you can be caught in the political web before ever being aware of its existence.

To understand politics, recognize that politics are impossible to understand. This is an area to be particularly careful of. Even seasoned veterans can easily fall prey to internal politics. Politics can be a deadly game and should be avoided.

The biggest problem is that newcomers do not know where the political lines are drawn. While certain people tend to be more than willing to give advice, such advice may not turn out to be at all sound. Eventually you will learn who you can talk to openly. Some people are willing to share helpful insights; others may well set you up for a fall. Some things you might innocently say may offend someone. *You just do not know*, so don't take a chance. For example, if someone talks negatively about another employee, don't get involved. You may want to nod or grunt appropriately, but if you also start making comments about others, you will quickly expose yourself as a gossip.

Experienced officers learn that it is best to never write anything they do not want to show up because it inevitably will surface. Similarly, it is a good practice to never say things you don't want heard because statements always seem to get repeated. People will tell you things in confidence. An eight-hour shift in a squad car, working a cell block or on security duty lends itself to sharing a lot of thoughts and ideas. Should you make the mistake of telling others what was told to you, you may cause some serious relationship problems for yourself and others. Never say anything you do not want repeated, and never repeat what is told to you in confidence.

> Do not play politics. Do not try to understand politics. Do not get yourself drawn into politics. This is important advice for anyone on the job, but absolutely crucial for a newly hired individual.

Dauten and Nelson (1997, p.D5) observe: "Performing well and playing politics may not be enough when [the] time comes for reducing [the] work force." They advise that the best way to keep a job is to cultivate relationships by developing skills involving rapport and getting people to like you.

ACCEPT CRITICISM MATURELY

A natural aspect of getting into any new job is learning. Considering that most people learn from their mistakes, you, too, should want to learn from *your* mistakes—they present great opportunities. Everyone (yes, *everyone*) makes mistakes at work. Naturally, the newer you are, the more mistakes are likely to occur. Employers expect this and would probably feel you weren't trying if mistakes weren't made.

So what's the big deal about making mistakes? The problem is that many people can't deal with thinking they are capable of making mistakes. Whether ego or just plain embarrassment, many individuals react inappropriately to being told they did something wrong. Failure to respond appropriately to criticism received at work can negatively affect a critical phase of the new job.

Frequently, part of field training or the probationary period is seeing how recruits or new employees handle constructive criticism. Assuming you learn from your mistakes and are able to prevent them from reoccurring too often, what is really critical is that you can maturely accept critical comments and process them, hopefully improving as a result. To argue with a trainer or superior is a poor choice for those who have been at the job for a only a short while. It could prove fatal for someone on probation. Take advantage of the occasional times someone offers criticism to not only improve the particular skill at issue, but to make sure the person leaves thinking about how professionally you handled the situation.

One aspect of this process that people often fail to recognize is that offering criticism is frequently as difficult to do, or more so, than receiving it. If you accept the comments in a positive way, even thanking the person for offering the comments, you may well end up scoring far more points than you will ever realize. It would be a serious mistake to get angry, challenge the superior, have a temper tantrum or go shooting your mouth off to others, even if you felt wronged. In the unlikely event that you genuinely do feel you are being harassed or ill-treated, discuss this with the person first, and only then proceed up the proper chain of command to deal with it. In some situations, new employees have, for whatever reason, not hit it off with a trainer. Personality conflicts do occur, as do outright illegal discrimination and harassment. But the real issue will be how you choose to handle it.

For example, a newly hired individual had extremely offensive body odor. When the supervisor suggested that perhaps a change in deodorant might be in order, the new employee became incensed and stormed out of the building. When she returned to work the next day, she was told that she no longer had a job there. It was *not* the body odor that caused her to lose the job—that was correctable. It was her immature, hostile reaction to the suggestion that cost her the job.

> Accept criticism maturely for such instances provide great opportunities for you to learn from your mistakes. Recognize also that offering criticism is frequently as difficult as receiving it, and if you accept the comments in a positive way, you may score far more points than you will ever realize.

BE YOURSELF

You managed to get the job by being yourself, and you will succeed by being yourself. Don't get down on yourself because you're nervous, afraid or feel inadequate—we all feel this way when we start new jobs. The first few weeks *are* going to be rough. Draw energy from it rather than allowing it to exhaust you.

> It is important for you to be yourself. Starting a new job, particularly in a field you are not used to, is uncomfortable and requires an adjustment. You will become exhausted if you spend energy putting on an act. Save your energy for learning the job.

Police, corrections and security officers make their livings dealing with people who are trying to run scams on them. Many of these individuals are very good and may be able to fool the professionals at first. You will not be able to. Trying to do so will only result in your being labeled as someone trying to be someone you are not. Officers must be honest!

Peer pressure is always hard to cope with. As a rookie, you will be expected to do as you are told. If you are unfortunate enough to get drawn into a bad group of fellow employees, you will face some tough decisions. Do not engage in brutality. Use the minimum force necessary under the circumstances to accomplish the objective. Do not let peer pressure lead you to violate this important principle. Recognize that to stand by and watch unethical, possibly illegal, behavior is only slightly less devious than actually participating. If you don't think you can resist the temptations from within or without, get out now.

If you are not happy, do something about it. These jobs are *not* for everyone. If you are unhappy, or if you can foresee problems, admit this to yourself as soon as you become aware of it. It is sad to see people suffer for years at jobs they dislike—especially those in jobs that provide the individual with a great deal of power and authority. Perhaps some officers "go bad" by becoming terribly abusive or sarcastic because the job is just no longer right for them . . . and it shows. Further, consider that professionals who dislike their work do not have the necessary concentration to be safe. Many horrible things can result from remaining in an unfulfilling job for too long.

MAINTAIN YOURSELF

Burnout. We've all heard about it. Maybe you've been there. Most of us have at one time or another. When starting a new job, consider ways of balancing it to keep it as attractive as it was when you first heard about it. Don't overdo it. Keep up your other friendships, activities and interests. Take care of your physical self: eat right, exercise and get enough sleep.

It is also important to keep your guard up, to stay on your toes and be mentally sharp. This also means not getting too lazy, comfortable or complacent in your position. Messmer (1995, p.31) advises: "Without getting too paranoid, keep yourself mentally prepared for the possibility that the job may not work out. Stay in touch with recruiters. Maintain your networking activities. Keep current. Be visible. And be alert to signs that your company is in trouble or that your job may be in jeopardy."

Maintain yourself physically and mentally. Stay current not only with things related to the job but also with things that interest you outside of work. This helps prevent burnout.

Do not become cynical because of the nature of the work, the clientele or opinions expressed by fellow officers. Watch out for "burnout," and use R&R time effectively to relieve stress. Do not become a "mooch," sponging off cooperative retailers, which usually begins with free coffee. Remember the concept of *quid pro quo*, that is *those who give usually expect something in return*.

The longer you remain in a job, any job, the harder it is to let go of the benefits. You will be much further ahead if you are honest with yourself and leave if the work does not suit you. Similarly, the work may suit you just fine, but the job may not. For a variety of reasons, not every employment opportunity will fit everyone. If you know you want to be a police, corrections or security officer, but personalities or any other factors make this particular job less than satisfying, do *not* stay around. It is unlikely that things will improve. There *is* a job out there for you. Your job is to find it.

CONCLUSION

Congratulations! You've got the job! These words will, and should, be a deserved conclusion to a significant amount of work. Relish them. You are well on your way to professional career fulfillment. Don't let your guard down, and don't give up pursuing excellence. Set exceptional goals for yourself and you will be exceptional.

Bear in mind, your success during the interviews will not guarantee you success on the job. You must have at least some idea of what to expect and what the circumstances demand if you want to hold on to the job. Remember, keeping a job takes constant effort. You must not be afraid to ask questions, for not doing so may lead to mistakes that may cost you your job. Work in criminal justice, security and related fields is important. It is satisfying. It says something about you that people working in other fields cannot boast. Congratulations on choosing these fields to pursue employment in and for making the effort to do it well.

YOUR GAME PLAN FOR EXCELLING ON THE JOB

Take time *now* to write out, on a *separate* piece of paper, three goals to help you excel in your new position. Put the paper someplace you will see it often. Let these goals guide you as you embark on your exciting new career. And again, congratulations!

MIND STRETCHES

1. Have you ever been "too enthusiastic" at a new job? Why do you think you were? Did it hurt you?

2. What behaviors have you observed in people in uncomfortable situations (like in a new job)?

3. Why do you think important people often seem so "down to earth"? Conversely, why do you think many "not-so-important" people act so brash?

4. How long does it take to fit in at a new job? What helps you fit in?

5. Have you ever felt pressured at a job to behave in a way you did not feel comfortable? How did you handle this situation?

6. Why do you think people, particularly officers, seem to like to complain or be negative? What traps can this create for new employees?

7. What dangers are there in "taking sides" in an office dispute? How can you avoid becoming involved?

8. Can people who work together get along "too well"? Are "office romances" good or bad? Can they be avoided, or do they "just happen"?

9. How would you handle a situation in which you knew a co-worker was doing something illegal, immoral or unethical? Would you respond differently if the person was a peer or your supervisor?

10. At what point do you think people stop growing and developing professionally? What opportunities exist to help you maintain your own personal and professional vitality?

INSIDERS' VIEWS

For this chapter, read the *Insiders' Views* by Linda S. Miller ("Surviving Probation") and Sgt. Lawrence J. Fennelly ("Let's Be Honest"), found on the Web site: http://www.wadsworth.com/criminaljustice_d/.

REFERENCES

Dauten, Dale and Nelson, Mark. "Best Way to Keep a Job Is to Cultivate Relationships." (Minneapolis/St. Paul) *Star Tribune*, March 2, 1997, p.D5.

Fought, Richard. "Growing Pains: Career Development Follows Predictable Path for Most." *Police*, October 1998, pp.34–40.

Kaminsky, Glenn F. "Effective Utilization of the Probationary Period." *The Law Enforcement Trainer*, March/April 2001, pp.32–33.

Messmer, Max. *Job Hunting for Dummies*. Foster City, CA: IDG Books Worldwide, Inc., 1995.

CHAPTER 15

THE CAREER LADDER:
INSIGHTS INTO PROMOTIONS AND JOB CHANGE

If you can dream it, you can do it.

—*Walt Disney*

Do You Know

➤ Whether the promotional process differs from initial job seeking?
➤ What changes, besides promotions, may lead to personal and professional growth?
➤ What factors motivate people to seek change in their professional lives?
➤ Which basic job-seeking skills apply?
➤ Whether changing jobs can help or hurt future job-seeking efforts?
➤ If you can ever have "too much" education or education in the wrong area?
➤ How important "off duty" activities are?
➤ When networking is important (other than during the job search)?
➤ How important the oral interview is to the promotional process?

INTRODUCTION

While this book began as a guide to help individuals find employment in criminal justice or security, it has also introduced you to information regarding the employment process as well. This chapter provides suggestions on how to prepare for the promotional process and what to expect. For the new job seeker, just *getting* that first job is the dream. But eventually everyone seeks change. For some it is seeking promotions on the way to "the top." For others it is changing within their present agency or looking for opportunities with others. And some want to change professions altogether.

Make no mistake about it—the world of work has changed dramatically over the decades. It is no longer the norm to remain in one career with one employer until retirement. While there is nothing wrong with that, if a person finds a niche and enjoys doing the same thing daily, the fact is that more and more people are changing jobs, either because they want to . . . or have to.

The final chapter discusses the impact of job loss and change. But what about the *desire* to change? This hasn't been considered the "norm" in a field of work that has traditionally involved staying with one agency, possibly seeking internal transfers or promotions. This chapter examines both. It also addresses the seemingly increasing desire people have to switch to entirely different careers. Whether seeking a promotion or other job change, developing a strategy will make the transition more successful.

You must keep in mind several important aspects of the promotional process. First and foremost, the basic job-seeking skills and strategies you are developing will also serve you well throughout your promotional ventures. Regardless of the level of employment you aspire to, you will still need to provide information about yourself that presents you as THE one to promote. Promotional interviews are similar to initial job interviews. Almost all of what you learned about getting your first job will continue to be important throughout your working life, which is why it is important to develop a job-seeking strategy that works well for you.

Second, it is important to create a plan for yourself. Life itself presents numerous opportunities, as does work. By thinking ahead, you not only develop some ideas of where you want to go in life (and work), but how to recognize the many opportunities that present themselves. Recall how many careers people normally have during their lives. When you consider all the promotions or job changes people experience, it is easy to see how important it is to know how to prepare for opportunities. Arnold (2000, p.63) states:

> Few police officers plan their careers. Most do not focus on promotion possibilities early enough, and have not prepared enough—either through formal education or assignment selection—to equip themselves for leadership roles. Strategic career planning can be a kind of road map to professional success.

Third, recognize that in criminal justice and security positions seniority and "paying your dues" also play important roles in promotions.

Promotion-seeking skills are very similar to the basic job-seeking skills and strategies you are developing. Both scenarios demand you present yourself as THE one to hire/promote.

PROMOTIONS: WHAT THEY ARE AND WHERE THEY ARE

Traditionally, promotions are considered to be upward moves, usually within the same organization where one is presently employed. This is a valid concept for many promotions, but try thinking of promotions in a much broader way. Any promotion is a change, but is every change a promotion? Take it one step further. Obviously, every promotion provides new challenges, but so does every change. . . even those that don't initially appear to be upward. Consider *any* job change as an employment opportunity. This includes promotions, transfers and, yes, even demotions or dismissals.

Think about it for a moment. Many people who have confronted what appeared to be overwhelming adversity end up saying it was the best thing that ever happened to them. Why? Because they grew from the experience. Any change, even one that appears negative, presents an opportunity. The bigger the challenge, the greater the opportunity for personal and professional growth.

Promotions are but one type of change that provides new professional challenges and allows for growth. Often the most adversarial changes, such as demotions or dismissals, lead to the greatest amount of personal and professional growth.

MOTIVATIONS FOR SEEKING CHANGE

The chapter on rejection addresses how you should strive to obtain energy from the process, and how you should control the process rather than let it control you. It *can*, *should* and (eventually) *will* result in growth for you. Richard Obershaw, founder of the Burnsville (Minnesota) Counseling Center of Grief, is fond of saying "a rut is a grave with the ends knocked out." And it is this feeling that frequently compels people to set their sights on bigger, better, or at least different, careers. While previous generations felt a stronger desire to remain at one job, it has become more common for people to follow their desire to find whatever feeds their souls.

Of course, considerations like better pay, more benefits or a desire to move to another community motivate people to change jobs. Other reasons may not present themselves as "positive" reasons for the change—downsizings, reorganizations, closings and even involuntary terminations force people to change. The work world is seeing upheaval the recent generations have not experienced. Layoffs are occurring by the tens of thousands. No job is guaranteed secure forever, even in government and union work, which previously had been considered untouchable.

Motivations for seeking change include better pay, better benefits, the desire to live and work in another community, downsizing, reorganizations, closings and involuntary terminations. Some of these reasons originate in the individual; some are forced upon the individuals—all lead the individual to change.

Whether change results from unanticipated factors or your desire to better yourself professionally, seek a bigger paycheck with improved benefits or move to a different place, your job-seeking skills will serve you a lifetime.

SIMILAR SKILLS

Take time to reflect on the entry-level job search and the promotional process, and you can see the similarities. In fact, both are going to result in different jobs. . . new jobs, and the skills you will need are the same:

➢   Cover letters (sometimes called "letters of interest" in the promotional process).
➢   Resumes (now providing more specific training and experience records).
➢   Test-taking skills.
➢   Interview skills.
➢   An overall positive appearance as THE one to hire.

The job-seeking skills needed during the promotional process include writing effective cover letters and resumes, taking tests, interviewing and presenting yourself positively as THE one to hire or promote.

The changes you will notice as you work on your promotional strategies are simply a fine-tuning of the skills you developed earlier. It is through explaining how you have developed professionally and why you want the change that makes this job-seeking process different from an entry-level job search.

INCREASING YOUR CHANCES FOR PROMOTION

As Bernstein (1998, p.67) succinctly states: "The road to promotion is one of hard work and personal commitment." Fulton (2000, p.118), asserting that "preparation is the key to getting promoted," suggests a 10-step plan:

1. Start early.
2. Learn from others (e.g., When fellow officers make a solid arrest, ask how they did it.).
3. Avoid problems (e.g., When officers around you make mistakes, learn from their mistakes.).
4. Be committed.
5. Prepare, prepare, prepare.
6. Make your intentions known—Let the "higher-ups" know you are willing to accept the responsibility of a promotion.
7. Get a mentor.
8. Learn the rules—Is the department's emphasis on academics, the written exam or the oral interview?
9. Get the resources you need.
10. Do your best.

Fulton's final word of advice: "Your best chance for getting promoted is to be a professional at every rank you hold, prepare for the next rank, and always do the best you can." Rachlin[1] also suggests several ways to increase your chances for promotion:

Broaden your experience. Take advantage of opportunities as they present themselves, and avoid spending your entire career in one area. While running the bicycle safety rodeos may not be the most exhilarating police experience, it provides the opportunity to develop administrative experience and learn more about another area of the business. And, perhaps most importantly, it shows you are a contributor to your agency, and that says a lot about your level of professionalism. Obtain experience in as many areas of the agency as possible, including operations, administrative services and budget planning. If rotational opportunities are available, take them!

Grow in your job. You can always learn more about a position, but to do so often requires applying innovative ideas and a fresh perspective. Never stop trying to expand your horizons.

Take on challenging assignments. This might include implementing new programs (safety, training, etc.), acquiring new equipment or technology, or undertaking a variety of other special projects. Think about ways to improve the agency and how to go about making the improvements. Let supervisors know you want challenging responsibilities that will benefit the entire agency. Recognize that most people do only what is expected of them—what is asked of them. I frequently advise newly hired people that it truly is not difficult to be a star! First, do that which is, indeed, expected of you. Many don't. Second, take the occasional opportunity to do something beyond what is expected of you. It will get you noticed.

Accomplish things. Finish what you start and do the task well. Develop a reputation for follow-through, dependability and quality—these are things you'll be evaluated on. Keep in mind it is far better to be selective in taking on tasks than to take on so many you end up failing to complete them.

Move on to other agencies. While not always possible, it may present a great opportunity to expand your range and depth of experience. Again, be discriminating and don't hop frivolously from one agency to another. Seek out ones that present wise career steps and will further your managerial experience. There is a challenge in knowing how, what and where to move to. While in the corporate world it is almost expected that the really good people will seek for and be sought by other organizations, this is not

---

[1]   Adapted from Harvey Rachlin. "How to Improve Your Chances of Getting Hired." Part of "The Hiring of a Police Chief." *Law and Order,* March 1995, pp.25–27. Reprinted by permission.

necessarily the case in traditional criminal justice and security positions. In fact, it may be viewed as a detriment by some agencies that an applicant has been a "job jumper." Be selective!

This is not a big problem for people employed in larger agencies. Employment in federal, state and large municipal agencies permit many opportunities for change, new challenges and promotional advancement. Smaller agencies may demand that the motivated employee take new jobs outside their agency. These changes should be pursued as a part of your plan for achieving your employment goals, just like all other areas of developing your strategy. Change merely for the sake of change may become self-defeating. If you don't stay at a new job or a new assignment long enough to really benefit from it (or be of benefit to your employer), this may cause understandable concern to those doing the hiring. It's a tough call, and an individual one, to pursue another opportunity "too soon." Take the time necessary to think through frequent changes.

Take opportunities that further your planned career path, but do not get carried away, jumping from one job to another. Be selective in your moves, or such job jumping may damage your future options in your profession.

Further your education. Obtain as much education as you can. With standards rising all the time, and more and more qualified people acquiring advanced education, you must keep up to stay competitive. Take courses that will help you in your profession. The possibilities are almost endless!

Education is akin to experience—you cannot acquire "too much" education or education in the wrong area.

It is difficult to understand how anyone's education could be viewed negatively, but it may. The two reasons that surface most frequently are a fear the applicant will soon move on to a "bigger and better" job and the fear of intimidating those "above." It is difficult to view this as anything more than jealousy, but some supervisors don't want their subordinates to have more education than they have. Do not fail to acquire advanced education because of what others might think, but be prepared to defend the choice, as well as to assure others that such education will benefit the department. Never stop learning.

Obtain special training. Take advantage of special training programs to demonstrate your commitment to staying current on topics related to your field, a desirable attribute in those seeking promotions. Once you obtain a degree, do not rest on your laurels. Take every opportunity to add to your knowledge. This makes you attractive to a promoter. So many training opportunities are available that to merely list every class becomes overwhelming. Don't let your really important message get lost in reams of photocopied course certificates. Pick and choose both the classes you take and the course documentation you present during the promotional process. Develop an overall strategy to get you where you want to go. Rather than taking every class you can get into, determine which will serve you best.

Be active in associations. Promoters look favorably upon those actively involved in fraternal, federal, state or other types of associations. Such participation demonstrates a commitment to the profession. Even officers serving at the entry level have many opportunities to join professional organizations. Membership in these groups not only provides a superb opportunity to keep on the cutting edge of your profession, but it shows you are willing to make the extra commitment to develop your professionalism. Again, "too many" may not be as helpful as selecting several organizations that speak to your commitment to better yourself.

> Being actively involved in such "off duty" activities as professional organizations and associations demonstrates a commitment to your profession, which is looked upon favorably by promoters.

Develop a network of contacts. As with the job search, networking for a promotion is very important. The more people you know, and the more people who know you, the better off you'll be. Again, becoming involved in professional organizations and associations is a great way to learn more and to get your name out there.

> Networking is as essential to promotion efforts as it is to job-seeking efforts.

Collect letters of commendation. These tools reflect positive actions in which a candidate was involved. For promotional purposes, letters that highlight leadership abilities or management skills are particularly valuable. Don't be shy about asking for letters. Many people will tell you they appreciate your work but may need some encouragement to document it. You have a responsibility to yourself to do everything you can do to best convey your excellence. A good supply of such personal recommendations will put you in a great position to include the best and most applicable for your next effort.

Be a spokesperson. "Enhance your reputation (and resume) by delivering speeches at conferences and writing articles. Have something important to relate, and be selective where you relate it. Speak at professional and civic conferences, and write for general publications and professional journals" (Rachlin, p.26). Give careful consideration to the issues facing your profession and how you or your agency have addressed such issues. Use your knowledge and experience to offer solutions to problems facing your industry.

Develop a public appearance image. Take every opportunity to improve your public speaking skills. When you are associating with those you work with, or with people who could be called on to comment on you as a candidate, NEVER let your guard down. All the effort you have made to develop a positive reputation can be destroyed with one error in judgment. More often than not, alcohol is involved. Even at a social gathering, eyes are on you. Innocent comments, too, can come back to haunt you. Recall that the job-seeking process is a job in and of itself. So is grooming yourself for promotion. Keep this in mind when associating with others who may, in any way, influence your career development. If you are engaging in any activities away from work that could be construed as unprofessional—reevaluate it.

Research your interview. As with the initial job-seeking interview, research your potential future path by gathering as much information about the interviewing department or agency and the surrounding community. Know how the agency is organized, what the various divisions are and what they do, and any special circumstances or programs the agency is involved in.

Promote yourself. Keep track of your accomplishments and add them to your resume. These achievements are what promoters are looking for, so you must be certain to provide documentation.

Be a leader. Leadership may be demonstrated in many ways, including developing and implementing new programs, taking charge in an emergency situation or supervising assignments and projects within your agency. Showing leadership shows you care. Employers, your co-workers and the community—all want to know you care. So step out and be a leader.

Seek Feedback

Feedback is always beneficial, particularly for those who have not gotten the promotions they sought. Face it, most people are either too polite or too intimidated to tell an applicant why they didn't succeed. It takes guts to ask for honest feedback, but once you ask for it, you must be willing to accept it.

Seek A Mentor

Along with feedback, it is helpful to develop a relationship with someone you respect who can provide support and advice and lend an ear during the frequently stressful, sometimes discouraging, process of seeking employment goals. Support is considerably more important than many think, and the friendships that develop as a result of these mentoring relationships are a great benefit as well.

PREPARE FOR PROMOTION

Garner (1998, p.28) notes: "Years ago, there were very few programs or products for helping you get promoted. Today, there are books, videos and courses to help you pass promotional exams, oral boards and assessment centers. The officers who take advantage of such resources are more likely to get promoted than those who rely on their own perceptions of what it takes to be promoted." Fulton (1999, p.82) adds:

> The serious candidate for promotion will have given a great deal of careful thought to the pending career milestone before he elects to take the plunge. . . . He will have conducted an honest self-assessment and determined that he's making the right choice for the right reasons. . . . He will have looked carefully at what his agency expects of its first-line supervisors and reached the determination that he is both willing and able to measure up. . . . He will have examined his former peers who have preceded him into supervisory ranks and concluded that he would fit in well as a contributing member of the work group.

IMPROVING PROMOTIONAL EXAM PERFORMANCE

DiVasto (1990, p.24) notes: "There may be nothing in the work life of an experienced police officer that can generate as much anxiety as a promotional exam. Officers who face armed hoodlums without so much as a blink will lose sleep for weeks worrying about a promotional exam." DiVasto[2] suggests some strategies to help reduce text anxiety. These strategies are to be implemented before and during the exam as follows:

Part I—Before the Exam

1. Have a clear idea of what material the exam will cover. Some departments publish reading lists, some circulate written materials, others just rely on word of mouth. . . .
2. Commit yourself to buy, borrow or share the books you'll need. Many of these, such as state codes and S.O.P. manuals, you might already have. Other materials, such as textbooks, you might have to buy or borrow. . . .
3. Determine what the test format will be. Find out, for example, if you'll be required to answer essay questions, true-false questions, multiple-choice questions, or a combination of these. . . .

---

[2] Adapted from Peter V. DiVasto. "Improving Promotional Exam Performance." *Law and Order*, May 1990, pp.24, 29. Reprinted by permission.

4. "Train" for the exam. . . . Set out . . . a training plan . . . [including these] elements . . .:
   a. Commit yourself to study a minimum of 100 hours for your exam. . . . only eight hours a week for the three months prior to the exam. . . .
   b. Begin studying not less than three months before the exam date.
   c. Set out your study plan on a calendar. . . .
   d. Find the time that is best for you to study. . . .
   e. Don't take on any major responsibilities, projects, or other energy-consuming activities while you're studying. . . .
   f. Give yourself time to relax a few days prior to test day. . . .
5. Before the test day arrives, be sure you know the time, place and what you're expected to bring. . . .
6. On the day of the exam, allow for extra time to drive to the test site, and plan on being there early. . . .

Part II—Taking the Exam

The most common type of written promotional examination is multiple-choice. . . .

1. Divide the test into hour-long segments. If there are one hundred questions and two hours in which to do them, plan on spending an hour on each fifty questions. If there's no time limit, allow yourself about a minute and a half per question or forty questions an hour.
2. Read each question very carefully and restate it to yourself in its most basic terms. If there are "distracters" in the question, eliminate them as you read. . . .
3. Answer each question by supplying the correct answer before you look at the choices. Your answer should match up with one of the choices listed.
4. Answer every question in your one-hour block before you go on to the next block. . . .
5. If you can't come up with the correct answer, eliminate the obvious wrong answers. . . .
6. Once you've eliminated the wrong answers, your choices will generally be down to two. Reread the question, restate it to yourself and take your best guess.
7. If you're taking a test made up from standard textbooks, forget the "real world" answer. . . . the test maker doesn't ride in your patrol car. He is going by what the text writer said is correct, not how you would do it on the street.
8. Beware of the right answer to the wrong question. . . .
9. Take a few minutes of break time between each of your one-hour segments.

IMPROVING PROMOTIONAL INTERVIEW PERFORMANCE

Narramore[3] (1991, pp.161–162) has devised a comprehensive review on how to prepare for a promotional interview:

> The people involved in an interview to evaluate your qualifications try to ascertain three basic facts about you. These are the most important traits you will need to convey to the panel:
>
> ➤ You can handle the job.
> ➤ You will do the job to the best of your ability.
> ➤ You are a manageable team player.
>
> Candidates who communicate to the evaluators "yes" to the above questions will score the highest. You must be able to demonstrate willingness and ability during the interview process.
>
> The first time I competed for the position of police sergeant was a disappointment I will always remember. I felt very comfortable after taking the written examination. I had scored high and was in an excellent position. Because I felt so confident, I did nothing to prepare for the oral interview. I felt showing up in all my glory

---

[3] Adapted from Randy E. Narramore. "Preparing for a Promotional Interview." *Law and Order*, September 1991, pp.161–162. Reprinted by permission.

and answering the questions to the best of my ability would be enough. That was a very big mistake. I finished in the top five overall, but I was not in the winner's circle. I looked back and learned from my mistake. That experience taught me to take that extra step of preparedness for every phase of the testing process.

The interview is the most important part of the promotional process. A successful candidate will make the "question and answer period" an exchange of ideas between law enforcement professionals. Accomplishing this means you are qualified and prepared. . . .

Law enforcement agencies look for specific traits in individual profiles to help determine the type of supervisor a candidate may become. Being more skilled and more qualified does not prove they will be a team player. Education and experience alone does not guarantee they will fit into the scheme of the organization. Several traits are reviewed during an interview: ambition, motivation, communication skills, devotion, conviction and confidence. . . .

Narramore also addresses the basic "traps" so many well-qualified candidates fall prey to, some of which are so damaging, recovery is next to impossible:

Failure to listen to the question. Every question asked by an interviewer demands a specific answer. Do not ramble on with superfluous responses. Be brief, yet concise. For example: if asked how many years you have been in law enforcement, provide a specific number. However, if you are asked to relate your feelings about illegal drugs, provide a more general answer.

Not taking enough time before answering questions. Do not answer a question immediately. Think about what you are going to say. This gives the impression you consider your responses and do not respond spontaneously.

Answering questions not asked. Answering a question not asked is annoying. When the board wants more information, they will ask for it.

Not being brief and to the point. The board does not want drawn out answers providing little information. If you do not know the answer, don't attempt to deceive the board with flowered responses. Be brief and to the point.

Not turning a negative into a positive. You may be asked a question regarding a negative area of your career, or be asked to discuss a major weakness. Try to turn the atmosphere into something positive. Admit you had a certain weakness, but were able to recognize it and took the steps necessary to correct it.

Being flippant or a joker. Oral boards do not like flippant responses. One improper response could ruin the entire interview.

It is not always the best person who receives the promotion. The ones who receive the promotions are usually those who have qualities of efficiency, hard work and reliability. If you follow the above suggestions, you will have a much better opportunity receiving that promotion you deserve.

Mahoney (1991, p.89) describes a category of applicant known as the "I'm Ready But Don't Understand How to Express It" candidate:

This group is normally comprised of a few candidates who at just about every interview process, initially appear to be front-runners for promotion but who end up falling somewhere in the middle of the pack. This is not because they aren't qualified, but because they made some basic errors in preparation, errors that repeat themselves time and time again.

Mahoney (pp.89–92) notes reasons candidates fail to perform well during the oral interview, including:

Not knowing the questions. It's almost a given that [the candidates] will be asked, "Tell us about yourself and why you are the best candidate," "What have you done to prepare yourself for the promotion?" . . . . Yet, time after time, when asked, candidates look at the panel members as though they've been asked to expound on the Theory of Relativity. . . . Every applicant for promotion should have a 2–3 minute "commercial" prepared . . . .

"Narrow focus" response. Candidates working in specialized assignments tend to see the entire organization from the limited perspective of their own job. . . . Candidates that view their job or department through only a narrow focus are not going to be perceived by an interview panel as being ready for promotion. Successful applicants must be able to perceive their department in broad terms and understand the internal and external forces that affect day-to-day operations.

Interacting with board members. Generally, oral interview board members are conservative, middle-aged law enforcement managers, predominantly male . . . . Board members frown on the use of even the mildest of profane words or phrases during an interview. . . . Avoid interjecting things of a personal nature into opening or closing statements. . . . Don't wear jewelry that proclaims allegiance to a particular college or organization . . . consider the length of your responses . . . [and] pace yourself accordingly.

> The oral interview is the most important part of the promotional process. Prepare for it as enthusiastically as you did for your initial job-seeking interview.

As you prepare for your promotion interview, you may also want to reread the *Insider's View* by Sweeney. This may also help you organize your thoughts.

CONCLUSION

Because work is such a significant part of life, job satisfaction is vital. Not only do satisfactory jobs provide monetary and other employment-related benefits to enable you to live the lifestyle you desire, but your job helps you feel the way you do about yourself.

Promotion-seeking skills are very similar to the basic job-seeking skills and strategies you are developing. Both scenarios demand you present yourself as THE one to hire/promote. Additional job-seeking skills needed during the promotional process include writing effective cover letters and resumes, taking tests and interviewing. Networking and researching the interviewing department or agency are also important elements. Whatever your reasons for seeking a new job or a change in the job you have, your ability to develop successful job-seeking strategies will help you realize your goals. Promotions and professional advancement require a well-thought-out plan that you will implement over time.

 MIND STRETCHES

1.   What promotions do you see as being of interest to you now? In one year? Five years? Ten years?

2.   If you were promoting someone, what characteristics would you look for?

3.   Why would actions "off duty" influence employers?

4.   Name what you are doing now that employers would view favorably.

5.   Name anything they could view unfavorably.

6.   Do you think someone could be "overeducated"? Why or why not?

7.   What schooling do you think could help in your job pursuits?

8.   Consider those around you who have been promoted. What have they done to benefit themselves?

INSIDERS' VIEWS

For this chapter, read the *Insiders' Views* by Capt. Luis Velez ("What Are They Looking For? Tips On the Promotional Process in Law Enforcement Agencies"), Sgt. Richard D. Beckman ("Making the Most of Your Law Enforcement Career") and J. Scott Harr, JD ("Identifying Your Worst Job-Seeking Enemy . . . It Isn't Who You Think It Is!") found on the Web site: http://www.wadsworth.com/criminaljustice_d/.

REFERENCES

Arnold, Jon. "Strategic Planning for Career Development." *The Police Chief,* April 2000, pp.61–63, 196.

Bernstein, Jeff. "Preparing for Promotion." *Law and Order,* February 1998, pp.67–68.

DiVasto, Peter V. "Improving Promotional Exam Performance." *Law and Order,* May 1990, pp.24, 29.

Fulton, Roger. "Moving Up the Ladder." *Law Enforcement Technology,* February 1999, p.82.

Fulton, Roger. "10 Steps to a Promotion." *Law Enforcement Technology,* May 2000, p.118.

Garner, Gerald W. "Are You Ready for Promotion?" *Police,* July 1998, pp.22–24, 28.

Mahoney, Tom. "How (Not) to Fail an Oral Interview." *Law and Order,* March 1991, pp.89–92.

Narramore, Randy E. "Preparing for a Promotional Interview." *Law and Order,* September 1991, pp.161–162.

Rachlin, Harvey. "How to Improve Your Chances of Getting Hired." Part of "The Hiring of a Police Chief." *Law and Order,* March 1995, pp.25–27.

CHAPTER 16

JOB LOSS AND CHANGE: THE ROAD LESS TRAVELED

In the middle of difficulty lies opportunity.

—*Albert Einstein*

Success is how high you bounce when you hit bottom.

—*General George Patton*

Do You Know

➤ What besides death and taxes is inevitable?
➤ How common job-loss grief is?
➤ Why an effective strategy to deal with job loss is needed?
➤ What myths about employment are common?
➤ What basic survival strategies are needed?
➤ What emotions are normally experienced following job loss?
➤ What depression is? What to do if it occurs?
➤ When you should begin your job search after losing your current job?

INTRODUCTION

The cold, hard reality is that *getting* a job cannot be fully and properly addressed without discussing loss of that job. A fact of life is that you will lose every job you get, eventually. It will happen to you. It happens to everyone. It's just one more example of how life is a series of changes accompanied by inevitable losses. Tischler (2001) notes: "In the first five months of [2001], U.S. companies cut 652,410 jobs—38,650 more than in all of 2000." The recent terrorist attacks in the United States and abroad have delivered a further economic blow to the job market, adding hundreds of thousands more to the ranks of the unemployed.

Sometimes leaving a job is unexpected and unwanted. Sometimes it's a desired change. Sometimes it's a promotion or a demotion. Eventually it will be retirement. Maybe it has just happened to you, which is why you are focusing on this chapter. However, this is not as grim as it may sound because, like anything else, a well thought-out strategy will make this ebb-and-flow of life more manageable.

This chapter is titled *Job Loss and Change* because even desired, positive employment changes are challenging. People often are surprised at the sadness accompanying these changes. In fact, the stress and fear of change prevents some people from pursuing promotions or other job opportunities, or to turn them down when offered. This may not make sense now, but it will. As Pulley (1997, p.144) explains:

> Everyone who loses a job goes through a transition. It is impossible to avoid. We go through transitions throughout our life; they accompany the passage of time. Transitions always involve a loss. Something must be left behind in order to usher in something new. This is why endings and beginnings are the two sides of the same coin. You can't have one without the other. An ending is a beginning, and a beginning is an ending.

Transition is inevitable. And job loss is inevitable. It happens to everyone.

"Who are you?" said the caterpillar.

"I—I hardly know, Sir, just at present," Alice replied rather shyly, "at least I know who I *was* when I got up this morning, but I think I must have been changed several times since then."
> —Lewis Carroll, *Alice's Adventures in Wonderland*

Think about this. You, too, have experienced transitions and loss to one degree or another. Maybe not a job loss—yet—but a loss, even if only resulting from change. As noted by Birkel and Miller (1998, p.35):

Job-loss grief is a universal experience.

Analogies sometimes help explain areas of life we have limited experience with, like losing a job. Bridges (1980, p.4) paints a vivid picture of what job loss might feel like: "Being in between . . . careers takes on a particularly painful quality when those things themselves are changing profoundly. It is as if we launched out from a riverside dock to cross to a landing on the opposite shore—only to discover in midstream that the landing was no longer there. (And when we looked back at the other shore, we saw the dock we left from had just broken loose and was heading downstream.) Stuck in transition between relationships and identities that are themselves in transition, many Americans are caught in a semipermanent condition of transitionality."

Another analogy comes from observing skydivers. The shock of the loss of employment is like falling out of an airplane (and may be every bit as terrifying). Lacking experience, you tumble earthward with absolutely no control, fearing for your life. Skydivers, however, have learned to control themselves during a free fall by adjusting themselves so that they *are* in control. They have developed a strategy to manage the descent. They return safely to earth, exhilarated. The key is *control*.

If you are reeling from job loss, you will find—like the skydiver—that when you are ready, the chute will pop open, and you will make a gradual, controlled descent (if you are prepared). The previous weeks or months may be a blur, but it's all part of dealing with job-loss emotions. Once you've slowed down and are more in control, you can reset your sights on where you want to land and get yourself there. But, as with skydiving, you don't just jump out of the plane without thinking. It requires thought and planning. And if, or when, you get shoved out the door, it becomes even more important that you have a plan— quickly. This chapter is intended to help you develop a plan, a strategy. You may not need the strategy now, but you will eventually.

WHY IS HAVING A STRATEGY SO IMPORTANT?

It is as important to develop a strategy to deal with job loss as it was to get the job in the first place. Why? Because it *will* happen, and it can be significant and downright painful.

An effective job-loss strategy will not only enable you to feel more in control of very difficult circumstances, but it will allow you to move on in a healthy manner to the next job.

And there *will be* another job.

THE MYTHS AND HARD TRUTHS ABOUT WORK

Employment has changed drastically in the past several decades. Yet, despite these changes, people continue to believe in several myths about employment when they should, instead, be acknowledging some hard truths about unemployment.

The Myths

Myth #1: My employment is secure—after all, I got the job, didn't I?
Myth #2: If I do a good job, I'll continue to be recognized for it and be assured of a secure future.
Myth #3: Job loss can happen only to someone else—not me.
Myth #4: Even if it does happen to me, I'll be able to handle it without a problem.

Myth #1: My Employment Is Secure—After All, I Got the Job, Didn't I?

What is meant by *secure*? If it means you will always have your current job, this is incorrect. At most you will retire. Or you could be fired. You could be promoted, transferred to another division or even find yourself on long-term disability after being injured on the job. You might move. But you will *not always* have a particular job just because you once got it. Of course, it is everyone's hope that any particular job will end when *we* want it to. After all, it's *our* job. It belongs to us. It's a part of us, and we're a part of it. But unless you are truly self-employed, you do *not* own your job. Even the self-employed do not necessarily have a job that will last a lifetime.

No one is immune from the possibility of losing their job. And those who think they are may well be most at risk. Job loss is becoming an increasingly familiar scenario and one that must at least be acknowledged. To do otherwise will lull you into a complacency that makes you even more susceptible to risk. As Pulley (p.12) notes:

> A recent poll shows that since 1980, three-quarters of American adults have been affected by job loss, either personally or within their own family, and one in ten says that a lost job has precipitated a major crisis at home. Within the country, this growing tide is swelling into a tidal wave that threatens to engulf us with anxiety and insecurity. [A 30-year employee of Xerox] said, "Losing my job was the most shocking experience I've ever had in my life. I almost think it's worse than the death of a loved one, because at least we learn about death as we grow up. No one in my age group ever learned about being laid off."

It doesn't matter if you are union, senior, government employed, or just really, really good at your job. There *are* circumstances that could, and eventually will, cause you to lose your job. The question is: *How will you handle it?*

Myth #2: If I Do a Good Job, I'll Continue to Be Recognized for It and Be Assured of a Secure Future

This is an old paradigm. It's the way things might have been for our parents or grandparents, but it's no longer what employees can expect. In fact, it's just the opposite. A frightening prediction made in 1970 by Alvin Toffler in *Future Shock* anticipated societal change: "In the three short decades between now and the twenty-first century, millions of ordinary, psychologically normal people, will face an abrupt collision with the future. Citizens of the world's richest and most technologically advanced nations will find it increasingly painful to keep up with the incessant demand for change that characterizes our time. For them the future will have arrived too soon."

The future is now. More and more people have had their employment collide with this future, and they *are* in shock. No doubt you know some of these people. And you may well find yourself among them. Cutbacks, downsizing and other synonyms for *job loss* are occurring not only in corporate America. With the national cry for "Lower taxes!" public sector programs, personnel and even entire departments, once the bastion of security, are increasingly finding themselves part of the tax-reduction "solution." No shield can fully protect employees from inevitable change—not unions, not job performance, not popularity.

Myth #3: Job Loss Can Happen Only to Someone Else—Not Me

Wrong. Remember, that "someone else" is a "me." In 1999, *Caregivers Quarterly* (Lindgren, 1999, p.1) reported that for the first time in the publication's history of providing grief and bereavement services, they were focusing on a loss not directly relating to death and dying, but on a loss being experienced by increasingly large numbers of people: job loss. "For a worker who mourns the past, the new relationship with the work world is not one of hope and promise, but of compromise and anxiety." How we deal with job loss is vitally important.

Myth #4: Even if It Does Happen to Me, I'll Be Able to Handle It without a Problem

It is all too easy to judge those experiencing the natural range of emotions resulting from job loss as "weak," self-pitying or otherwise not up to the task. Anyone who has lost a job will tell you it takes considerable courage to address this change. When Birkel and Miller (p.44) note that the typical "white collar" worker will experience at least one involuntary job loss, you cannot ignore the possibility, even the probability, that it will be you . . . someday.

We do not want to paint too bleak of a picture. Loss and change are a part of life, and one that actually builds character for most who experience it. It is just an area all too often ignored until it is on our own front doorstep. Every one of us who has "been there" has a whole new appreciation for the intensity of emotions that surface and a willingness to extend an understanding hand to those who will need it.

The Hard Truths

Instead of buying into the myths about work and hoping the "inevitable" doesn't happen to you, Tischler offers some hard truths to help you "respond to the new era of downsizing without downsizing your dreams":

Truth #1: There are worse things than being laid off—like staying in a bad job for "security."
Truth #2: In fact, losing your job may be the best career move you'll ever make.
Truth #3: But don't be surprised if you are unemployed longer than you expected at first . . .
Truth #4: . . . Even though it often pays off to move fast.
Truth #5: By the way, the Internet won't necessarily solve your job-search problem.
Truth #6: You might have to settle for less money too.
Truth #7: And you might find yourself at a more conservative company.
Truth #8: You may also have to consider a different city.
*Truth #9: For all the turmoil, never forget that your professional life span is longer than that of most
         companies.*
Truth #10: So your real job is to find what you love and then find a way to do it. (Return to Truth #1.)

Tischler cushions these harsh realities with some final, more optimistic, words of advice:

> Don't forget the most important lesson of all. Markets go up, and markets go down. Digital technologies catch fire and then burn out. But through it all, the defining truth of the business world is that people are still front and center. If you're a talented person with a real passion for your work, you are living in the right times—layoffs or not.

Recall from Chapter 1 that service industries, including social services, legal services and protective services, are currently among the most rapidly growing occupations in the United States, with this trend projected to continue through 2008. While this bodes well for those presently seeking employment in criminal justice, security and related fields, it does not guarantee this trend will last indefinitely nor does it give you immunity from future job loss. Things change. Be prepared.

DEVELOPING A STRATEGY

It's always better to have a plan in place before the emergency strikes, so if you happen to be reading this chapter *before* you need it—good for you. But human nature as it is, you'll probably give it a lot more consideration when you find yourself needing it. Even then you can get a plan in place quickly and benefit from it. You'll find yourself needing just a few basics, but they are very important.

Basic job-loss survival strategies include:

➢ Building a support network now—for fun, for closeness and for information.
➢ Building a "survival nest egg" of at least six months' living expenses, maybe longer.
➢ Balancing your life so your job isn't the only important thing to you.

As you build your network, consider volunteering for an organization you are interested in. As Wendleton and Dauten (1999, p.1J) suggest, networking at its best is "not hunting, but helping."

 List in your journal individuals you want to keep in contact with not only for future job networking, but because you enjoy them. Can you help any of them now? Can they help you?

 What volunteer opportunities might interest you and might also benefit you in a job search?

Smith (1993, p.59) recommends the following additional survival strategies:

➢ Set aside a regular time to explore and plan your life.
➢ Get as much information as possible about the new situation.
➢ Know yourself—how you react, how you make decisions, how you relax.
➢ Take care of yourself and your body.
➢ Express your feelings—use anger constructively; keep the best memories, but live in the present and let go of the past.
➢ Set new goals, make decisions, and look for alternatives to replace what is missing.
➢ Practice relaxation and deep breathing; become calm.

Layne (2001) suggests you "learn how to transform a layoff into a savvy sabbatical—a time to recharge your batteries and learn new skills without sabotaging your resume." Once strictly the domain of rabbis and tenured professors, sabbaticals are now benefiting a variety of displaced, downsized professionals wondering "What do I do now?" Loosely defined, a sabbatical is "time off"—a break, a retreat, a rest. It does not mean you can sit in front of the TV all day, eating cold pizza and waiting for the phone to ring with your next job offer. Instead, according to career coach Hope Dlugozima: " 'Sabbatical' holds a certain power and intrigue to it. It denotes a plan of action and a deliberate path" (Layne).

Dlugozima advises people to take advantage of the upheavals in life and use this downtime to "build up rather than keep up, thrive rather than survive, and seek rather than hide." Use this time to ask yourself, "If I could do anything, what would I do?" Travel, volunteer, do new things and grow: "The smartest career move that you can make after a layoff is . . . [to embark] on a sabbatical that will restore self-esteem, independence, and drive" (Layne). Specific strategies are discussed in Dlugozima's *Six Months Off: How to Plan, Negotiate, and Take the Break You Need without Burning Bridges or Going Broke* (Henry Holt Publishing, 1996).

 How much money would you need if you suddenly lost your job?

 What interests or hobbies have you put off due to lack of time or money?

Survival strategies set a foundation for you to proceed. While they may seem elementary, they can be overlooked in the midst of chaos. They address the areas that need to be worked with and worked through: awareness, acceptance, support, putting the past behind you, and finally, moving ahead. You need to progress through all these areas. And that's one of the most challenging parts of the process.

THE SEQUENTIAL REACTION TO JOB LOSS AND CHANGE

You can't go around the emotions of job loss and change; you must go through them. There is no shortcut. Chapter 10, which dealt with *not* getting a job, discussed the predictable process most people experience when they lose something important (Figure 10-1). Whatever begins the sequence of emotional, sometimes physical, responses to job loss, the emotions are so universal that we know they've got to be dealt with. Failure to do so will keep you stuck in that phase (e.g., becoming overly angry or sad), and will affect all other areas of your life.

The normal emotions experienced following job loss are denial, anger, sadness, searching, withdrawal and reorganization. The sequence in which these emotions occur may vary and emotions may repeat themselves.

These emotions were explained more fully in Chapter 10, but we'll briefly recap them here:

- *Denial* is normally experienced as, "I can't believe this happened to me." The ability to *accept* the loss is a necessary step in being able to continue on with life.
- *Anger* is "Why me?" You lost your job—who wouldn't be upset? But don't lash out at those close to you or burn bridges with your former employer. Another opportunity may arise there in the future, or if your former employer may be called for a reference. Deal with the anger by finding an appropriate, constructive outlet.

- *Sadness* is another emotion to expect along the way. Do not ignore it. You need to let yourself feel the sadness so you can work through it and move on.
- *Searching* may involve you going back to your place of employment, even if only to drive by. You might call. You may hold on to the hope that "they" will come to their senses and ask you, beg you, to come back. It's like survivors going back to the disaster scene—it provides a reality check. Give yourself time to check out the old as you prepare to move on to the new.
- *Withdrawal* may be hard for family and friends to understand and may create stress for everyone. Pulling away lets you do your emotional work inside while you step back and assess where you fit into the world now. This takes time, and only you can do it. So when your family and friends see you as more quiet and withdrawn, no one need worry. It's simply another part of the process.
- *Reorganization* is when you've worked through the previous emotional stages and are ready to rebuild. Going through this exhausting set of emotions makes it understandable why people resist change—good or not. Young police officers have difficulty understanding why they keep getting called back to the same address on domestic disturbance calls. "If it's so bad, why doesn't one of them just leave?" The answer is that even as difficult as the situation is, it's known. It's predictable. What's on the other side of that door is unknown. Only when the pain exceeds the risk will change occur.

> All changes, even the most longed for, have their melancholy; for what we leave behind is part of ourselves; we must die to one life before we can enter another.
>
> —Anotole Frarie, writer

Change is hard. To expect anything less is unrealistic. The emotions experienced are normal, natural.

Managing the Responses

It is not enough to know and anticipate the feelings you will experience. You must effectively *manage* them as well. This is *not* easy because of the intensity of the emotions and (fortunately) the relative lack of experience most people have dealing with such significant loss. What you do not want to do is add to your difficulties by letting the emotions overtake you. You will feel anger, but don't make inappropriate, hostile phone calls to or confront a former employer you blame for your job loss. Does this happen? Yes, even to extremes. We've heard about former employees who act their anger out with violence, sometimes even killing former employers and coworkers. It's probably not coincidence that workplace violence is increasing at the same time job loss is increasing across the country.

Nor do you want to take the emotions out on people trying to support you. You're angry. You're sad. The denial factor may keep you from seeing that it's your lost job causing these feelings. But you think you've got problems now, having lost your job? You don't want to lose those close to you, too. It is possible to "grieve other people right out of your life." Here is where you will benefit from objective help, professional or otherwise. Get it!

Understanding, accepting and managing the emotions associated with job loss is a huge step in moving forward. However, you must guard against one emotion that can be devastating: depression.

DEALING WITH DEPRESSION

The numbers of people suffering from depression is far greater than people may realize. It can be a miserable state to be in, and left untreated, can become debilitating and lead to illness and even suicide.

> Depression is not about being sad. It's about being in a cloud that casts a dark shadow over everything. The hopelessness associated with it may become devastating.

Those who experience depression know you can't just "snap out of it" or "tell yourself it will all be O.K." If it were this easy, no one would be depressed. Allow yourself to feel all of what you are going through. You don't have to like it, but you do need to accept it, and to accept help if the feelings become overwhelming. Perhaps no other group as a whole is less willing to reach out for help than criminal justice professionals. After all, they are there to help others, those who can't help themselves. It's surely not the stereotypic macho cop who admits to someone else, much less to themselves, that they need help.

Depression to some degree *will* result from job loss. The associated negativity and hopelessness can cast a bleak shadow over everything. Following are some thoughts from Byron's study of people in transition and their advice to others (1995, pp.171–177) that may help you as you walk a path that may seem unbearably long. It's helpful to know that others have been there and survived.

> ➤ Don't be too hard on yourself, or set too many demands; this, like everything, will be resolved one way or another, sooner or later.
> ➤ Expect rejection. Don't take it personally.
> ➤ Be positive and work hard at the search (a new job won't just happen).
> ➤ Let your pride push you rather than hold you back.
> ➤ You are not simply what you do, and you should realize that the job revolution has resulted in people being out who have done nothing wrong.
> ➤ You are not what you own or your title.
> ➤ Never, ever believe your job is secure.
> ➤ Only a positive attitude will propel you into a good job that is the right job for you.
> ➤ Have your network in place before you ever need it.
> ➤ Nothing is forever. Things change. People change.
> ➤ Hang in there.

Things can get away from you. Don't try to go it alone. If you were a police, corrections or security officer, you'd never respond to a call alone if you knew you'd need additional officer-power and firepower at the scene. You'd never hesitate to call for help on the street, so don't hesitate to call for help now if you need it.

> If you are depressed and need help—get it. It could be a matter of life and death.

Talk to friends, see a counselor or psychologist, join a support group, see a psychiatrist and get on medication if need be. Ask anyone. And if you don't like one answer, keep asking. But whatever you do, GET HELP. It takes a strong, courageous person to reach out in the midst of despair. But you can do it. You can!

Another way to break out of depression is to tackle the job search for your next job.

GOTTA GET WORKING

You know how to get a job. After all, you got the job(s) you no longer have.

As you move through the emotional steps of job loss, keep working at finding new work. As your energy level permits, keep developing the job search.

As you move forward, you'll build momentum and develop increasing energy to be even more creative in this effort. Birkel and Miller, members of Professionals in Transition (PIT), have set forth what they refer to as "PIT's Top Ten Guerrilla Job-Hunting Tactics" (pp.144–147):

1. Remind yourself to be a winner.
2. Conduct a multilevel campaign (work with job-hunting allies, market yourself, and conduct informational interviews).
3. Create a business card (front: name, address, phone and general area of expertise; back: career objective and bulleted list of key strengths/skills).
4. Meet employers' needs (cover letter with left column headed "Your Needs" taken from advertisement and right column headed "My Qualifications").
5. Use large mailing envelopes (to stand out from other mail received).
6. Volunteer (there's always someone worse off than you).
7. Get out and meet people (to find advocates in your job search).
8. Recruit a coach (find a personal advocate to encourage and support you).
9. Keep a journal (to spot trends and learn from them).
10. Stay proactive (control your job search; reemployment possibilities are everywhere).

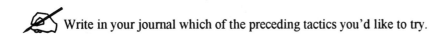 Write in your journal which of the preceding tactics you'd like to try.

One tactic some people who have lost their jobs seriously consider is a lawsuit against the former employer.

TO SUE OR NOT TO SUE

No one who has lost their job thinks it was fair. It may well have not been. But unless it was illegal, no judge will care. Even then, you need to think whether a lawsuit is the way to proceed.

It doesn't hurt to consult with a lawyer. It would help you put this possibility to rest. Employment law is very complex, and a discussion of when a dismissal is illegal is beyond the scope of this book. It depends on your particular circumstances. Do you have a contract? Are you a veteran? What does your employee handbook include? Are you union? And the list goes on. You need legal counsel for answers.

Even if you have a legal cause of action, consider the consequences of suing a previous employer: What is the likelihood of prevailing? What will future prospective employers think of this action? Will a lengthy lawsuit prolong your agony and prevent you from beginning the healing process? How much might it cost? All these questions need to be considered. A competent attorney will be able to help with this, which is why they are also called counselors at law. But know that suing solely out of anger is never a good idea.

CONCLUSION

> The American Dream is a myth that puts us in danger . . . . The irony is that in pursuing. . . the American Dream, we often lose ourselves. We lose touch with our true nature and our real passion. We lose touch with the inner resources that provide us with energy and feed our soul. . . . We become our position, while our spirit quietly bleeds from inattention . . . . The loss of a job can bring forth new questions. We ask fewer questions when things are going well, or when we are too busy to stop. . . . When that busyness stops, things come out of the shadows. . . .

> We are afraid that if we lose our job, we will lose our self. Yet it is when a crack develops that the soul has an opening, a doorway, to get in and be seen. It's when things are falling apart that we look again. When things are coming apart, it feels bad and frightening, and it can be devastating. But therein lies the hope . . . . Recovery from job loss means rediscovering our gifts. It means reclaiming the fragmented parts of ourselves that were ignored while we were working. It means healing the splits. . . [and] putting Humpty Dumpty back together again (Pulley, pp.24–26).

The upside of job loss is examined in the first *Insider's View* for this chapter. In fact, if you are currently in an unfulfilling position, Mr. Driggs' contribution may make you consider losing your job voluntarily. It certainly builds a strong case for making sure you give adequate consideration to the work you choose to do. Job loss can also increase your awareness of the importance of workplace dignity when changes need to occur. Perhaps you'll be the one to explain positive ways to help employees through a period of loss or change. For sure, you'll be better able to walk the path again, as change continues to be a part of our lives.

Remember: All endings lead to new beginnings. It just might not seem like it at the time. But you must believe there will be another side—a brighter side, a new job, new opportunities, new friends, a whole new world.

ADDITIONAL CONTACTS AND SOURCES OF INFORMATION

How to Plan, Negotiate, and Take the Break You Need without Burning Bridges or Going Broke, by Hope Dlugozima. Henry Holt, 1996.

CareerBuilder.com – Provides a Layoff Survival Kit including discussion boards where people can commiserate and share job-hunting tips.

FastCompany.com – Serves people's individual career needs with six custom-built Career Zones. Each Career Zone contains Web-only stories, interactive tools, expert opinions and valuable connections to help Fast Company readers get ahead in the new economy.

JobHuntersBible.com – Richard Bolles, author of *What Color Is Your Parachute?* guides career changers and suggests what to do once they've exhausted Internet job sites.

JobSearching.org – sponsored by the Professionals in Transition (PIT) support group, this site helps the unemployed cope and retool skills.

Monster.com – Has suggestions for stress management and repositioning yourself in a tough market.

 MIND STRETCHES

1.   If you needed them today, who makes up your support network?

2. What losses have you experienced? How did you work through the steps?

3. Why does job loss affect more than just the individual?

4. Why do you think job loss is more common now than in years past?

5. Do you think job loss can be harder to deal with than death? Why or why not?

6. Why do people think job loss can't happen to them?

7. What would you do to help yourself if you lost your job today?

8. Why do people feel bad even if they choose to leave their jobs?

9. If you were to lose your job now, would you say, "That's what I was" or "That's what I did?"

10. Why do you think some people put more emphasis on their jobs than on the rest of their lives?

INSIDERS' VIEWS

For this chapter, read the *Insiders' Views* by John Driggs ("Who's In Control: You or Your Work?"), Richard J. Obershaw ("Job Loss and Grief") and J. Scott Harr ("Removing the Arrow: The Scott Harr Story"), found on the Web site: http://www.wadsworth.com/criminaljustice_d/.

REFERENCES

Birkel, J. Damian with Miller, Stacey J. *Career Bounce-Back! The Professionals in Transition*^{SM} *Guide to Recovery & Reemployment*. New York: AMACOM: American Management Association, 1998.

Bridges, Willliam. *Transitions: Making Sense of Life's Changes*. Reading, MA: Addison-Wesley Publishing Company, 1980.

Byron, William J. *Finding Work without Losing Heart: Bouncing Back from Mid-Career Job Loss*. Holbrook, MA: Adams Publishing, 1995.

Layne, Anni. "How to Move Forward When You're Between Jobs." *Fast Company*. Boston: Gruner and Jahr USA Publishing, June 2001. Online at: http://www.fastcompany.com/invent/invent_feature/sabbatical.html

Lindgren, Amy. "Grief and Loss in the 'New Workplace.'" *Caregivers Quarterly*, Winter 1999, pp.1–2.

Smith, Maggie. *Changing Course: A Positive Approach to a New Job or Lifestyle*. San Diego: Pfeiffer and Company, 1993.

Pulley, Mary Lynn. *Losing Your Job—Reclaiming Your Soul: Stories of Resilience, Renewal, and Hope*. San Francisco: Jossey-Bass Publishers, 1997.

Tischler, Linda. "10 Hard Truths about Layoffs." *Fast Company*. Boston: Gruner and Jahr USA Publishing, June 2001. Online at: http://www.fastcompany.com/invent/invent_feature/10truths.html

Wendleton, Kate and Dauten, Dale. "Networking Isn't Just Stalking a Resume." (Minneapolis/St. Paul) Star Tribune, May 23, 1999, p.1J.

EPILOGUE

In three words I can sum up everything I've learned about life. It goes on.

—Robert Frost

A beginning. An end. A new beginning. This describes life, including your working life.

Work. It's much more complex than most people realize. Work can feed our souls, but it can also destroy them. Striking a balance in life is what "success" may well be. Home, family, education, faith, health, recreation . . . and work. Unfortunately, many people allow, knowingly or otherwise, the work component to overshadow the others, causing an imbalance that can affect every aspect of life. The danger in letting your work define you was encapsulated well by E.L. Sopow, Vancouver, Canada, during a discussion about work, job loss, change and resilience:

> Most people have come to equate what they DO with who they ARE. This means when they lose their job they experience two out of the three forms of death—death of self-image and death of hope. And in some unfortunate cases, the third form of death—clinical—is also a consideration. We might learn from biology rather than business school when it comes to dealing with death. Nature has survived 3.8 billion years by facing a crisis with enhanced communications, increased connectivity, and cooperation leading to evolution. We are not cogs in a machine. We are a network of complex, adaptive systems.

From an evolutionary perspective, the ability to adapt to a changing environment is a prerequisite for survival. Presently, the world of work seems more than ever to be a world of change. Adaptation may be one of the best strategies for success or, at the very least, survival in the work environment. You can't afford to get caught up in "what was," assuming things will always remain the same. They won't. They can't. It's just not the nature of things. In fact, the definition of "security" as it relates to the workplace has changed to such a degree that some argue it's gone altogether. "Employment security" is now best defined as having a well-thought-out strategy to adapt to change, to be secure with change.

Dr. Susan Stanek, training and development consultant, endorses the plan of people developing a *dual* career path to better prepare themselves for job change. Whether people tire of a primary job or find themselves needing another job, having the education and training to fit into another position is a wonderful means by which to adapt. This approach has served many people well, whether they found themselves estranged from their original position, by their own decision, or taking advantage of early retirement, yet not ready to quit contributing to the world around them in some way.

Through reading this book and completing the exercises within, you have had the opportunity to do far more than merely learn to write a resume. You have had the opportunity to develop ideas on where you would like your work life to take you. You've been encouraged to consider the necessity of balancing the many aspects of life, including work. And you've prepared yourself for the changes you will surely face. Some of them will be good. Some won't. All will contribute to make up the person you are . . . and that, unquestionably, is of great value.

Work. It is so much a part of our lives. It deserves careful consideration. But in the end, it's true . . . it's only a job!

APPENDIX A

IACP POLICE CODE OF CONDUCT[*]

All law enforcement officers must be fully aware of the ethical responsibilities of their position and must strive constantly to live up to the highest possible standards of professional policing.

The International Association of Chiefs of Police believes it is important that police officers have clear advice and counsel available to assist them in performing their duties consistent with these standards, and has adopted the following ethical mandates as guidelines to meet these ends.[**]

Primary Responsibilities of a Police Officer

A police officer acts as an official representative of government who is required and trusted to work within the law. The officer's powers and duties are conferred by statute. The fundamental duties of a police officer include serving the community; safeguarding lives and property; protecting the innocent; keeping the peace and ensuring the rights of all to liberty, quality and justice.

Performance of the Duties of a Police Officer

A police officer shall perform all duties impartially, without favor or affection or ill will and without regard to status, sex, race, religion, political belief or aspiration. All citizens will be treated equally with courtesy, consideration and dignity.

Officers will never allow personal feelings, animosities or friendships to influence official conduct. Laws will be enforced appropriately and courteously and, in carrying out their responsibilities, officers will strive to obtain maximum cooperation from the public. They will conduct themselves in appearance and deportment in such a manner as to inspire confidence and respect for the position of public trust they hold.

Discretion

A police officer will use responsibly the discretion vested in the position and exercise it within the law. The principle of reasonableness will guide the officer's determinations and the officer will consider all surrounding circumstances in determining whether any legal action shall be taken.

Consistent and wise use of discretion, based on professional policing competence, will do much to preserve good relationships and retain the confidence of the public. There can be difficulty in choosing between conflicting courses of action. It is important to remember that a timely word of advice rather than arrest—which may be correct in appropriate circumstances—can be a more effective means of achieving a desired end.

---

[*] Adopted by the Executive Committee of the International Association of Chiefs of Police on October 17, 1989, during its 96th Annual Conference in Louisville, Kentucky, to replace the 1957 code of ethics adopted at the 64th Annual IACP Conference.

[**] The IACP gratefully acknowledges the assistance of Sir John C. Hermon, former chief constable of the Royal Ulster Constabulary, who gave full license to the association to freely use the language and concepts presented in the RUC's "Professional Policing Ethics," Appendix 1 of the Chief Constable's Annual Report, 1988, presented to the Police Authority for Northern Ireland, for the preparation of this code.

SOURCE: Reprinted with permission from the International Association of Chiefs of Police, Alexandria, Virginia. Further reproduction without express written permission from IACP is strictly prohibited.

Use of Force

A police officer will never employ unnecessary force or violence and will use only such force in the discharge of duty as is reasonable in all circumstances. Force should be used only with the greatest restraint and only after discussion, negotiation and persuasion have been found to be inappropriate or ineffective. While the use of force is occasionally unavoidable, every police officer will refrain from applying the unnecessary infliction of pain or suffering and will never engage in cruel, degrading or inhuman treatment of any person.

Confidentiality

Whatever a police officer sees, hears or learns of, which is of a confidential nature, will be kept secret unless the performance of duty or legal provision requires otherwise. Members of the public have a right to security and privacy, and information obtained about them must not be improperly divulged.

Integrity

A police officer will not engage in acts of corruption or bribery, nor will an officer condone such acts by other police officers. The public demands that the integrity of police officers be above reproach. Police officers must, therefore, avoid any conduct that might compromise integrity and thus undercut the public confidence in a law enforcement agency. Officers will refuse to accept any gifts, presents, subscriptions, favors, gratuities or promises that could be interpreted as seeking to cause the officer to refrain from performing official responsibilities honestly and within the law. Police officers must not receive private or special advantage from their official status. Respect from the public cannot be bought; it can only be earned and cultivated.

Cooperation with Other Officers and Agencies

Police officers will cooperate with all legally authorized agencies and their representatives in the pursuit of justice. An officer or agency may be among many organizations that may provide law enforcement services to a jurisdiction. It is imperative that a police officer assist colleagues fully and completely with respect and consideration at all times.

Personal/Professional Capabilities

Police officers will be responsible for their own standard of professional performance and will take every reasonable opportunity to enhance and improve their level of knowledge and competence. Through study and experience, a police officer can acquire the high level of knowledge and competence that is essential for the efficient and effective performance of duty. The acquisition of knowledge is a never-ending process of personal and professional development that should be pursued constantly.

Private Life

Police officers will behave in a manner that does not bring discredit to their agencies or themselves. A police officer's character and conduct while off duty must always be exemplary, thus maintaining a position of respect in the community in which he or she lives and serves. The officer's personal behavior must be beyond reproach.

APPENDIX B

ASIS SECURITY CODE OF ETHICS*

PREAMBLE

Aware that the quality of professional security activity ultimately depends upon the willingness of practitioners to observe special standards of conduct and to manifest good faith in professional relationships, the American Society for Industrial Security adopts the following Code of Ethics and mandates its conscientious observance as a binding condition of membership in or affiliation with the Society:

ARTICLE I

A member shall perform professional duties in accordance with the law and the highest moral principles.

Ethical Considerations

I-1   A member shall abide by the law of the land in which the services are rendered and perform all duties in an honorable manner.

I-2   A member shall not knowingly become associated in responsibility for work with colleagues who do not conform to the law and these ethical standards.

I-3   A member shall be just and respect the rights of others in performing professional responsibilities.

ARTICLE II

A member shall observe the precepts of truthfulness, honesty and integrity.

Ethical Considerations

II-1   A member shall disclose all relevant information to those having a right to know.

II-2   A right to know is a legally enforceable claim or demand by a person for disclosure of information by a member. Such a right does not depend upon prior knowledge by the person of the existence of the information to be disclosed.

II-3   A member shall not knowingly release misleading information, nor encourage or otherwise participate in the release of such information.

ARTICLE III

A member shall be faithful and diligent in discharging professional responsibilities.

Ethical Considerations

III-1   A member is faithful when fair and steadfast in adherence to promises and commitments.

III-2   A member is diligent when employing best efforts in an assignment.

---

* Reprinted with permission from the American Society for Industrial Security.

247

III-3   A member shall not act in matters involving conflicts of interest without appropriate disclosure and approval.

III-4   A member shall represent services or products fairly and truthfully.

ARTICLE IV

A member shall be competent in discharging professional responsibilities.

Ethical Considerations

IV-1   A member is competent who possesses and applies the skills and knowledge required for the task.

IV-2   A member shall not accept a task beyond the member's competence nor shall competence be claimed when not possessed.

ARTICLE V

A member shall safeguard confidential information and exercise due care to prevent its improper disclosure.

Ethical Considerations

V-1   Confidential information is nonpublic information the disclosure of which is restricted.

V-2   Due care requires that the professional must not knowingly reveal confidential information or use a confidence to the disadvantage of the principal or to the advantage of the member or a third person unless the principal consents after full disclosure of all the facts. This confidentiality continues after the business relationship between the member and his principal has terminated.

V-3   A member who receives information and has not agreed to be bound by confidentiality is not bound from disclosing it. A member is not bound by confidential disclosures made of acts or omissions which constitute a violation of the law.

V-4   Confidential disclosures made by a principal to a member are not recognized by law as privileged in a legal proceeding. The member may be required to testify in a legal proceeding to information received in confidence from his principal over the objection of his principal's counsel.

V-5   A member shall not disclose confidential information for personal gain without appropriate authorization.

ARTICLE VI

A member shall not maliciously injure the professional reputation or practice of colleagues, clients or employers.

Ethical Considerations

VI-1   A member shall not comment falsely and with malice concerning a colleague's competence, performance or professional capabilities.

VI-2   A member who knows, or has reasonable grounds to believe, that another member has failed to conform to the Society's Code of Ethics shall present such information to the Ethical Standards Committee in accordance with Article XIV of the Society's Bylaws.

APPENDIX C

RESUME WORKSHEETS

Name: _____

Current Address: _____

Permanent Address: _____

Phone Number(s): _____

E-mail: _____

Colleges: _____

_____

Professional Schools: _____

_____

Internships: _____

_____

Certificates Held: _____

_____

_____

Other Educational Experiences: _____

_____

_____

High School: _____

EMPLOYMENT HISTORY
(Note: Make as many copies of this page as you have had jobs so you can complete one page for each job you've had.)

Dates Employed: From _____ to _____

Employer: _____

　　　　　　Address: _____

　　　　　　Phone/E-mail: _____

　　　　　　Supervisor: _____

Position/Title: _____

Responsibilities: _____

_____

_____

_____

_____

Skills Acquired: _____

_____

_____

_____

_____

Achievements/Awards: _____

_____

_____

_____

Salary (NOT included in resume): _____

Reason for Change (NOT included in resume): _____

_____

Position Desired/Employment Objective: _____

_____

_____

Other information that may be put in your resume includes the following:

Birthdate: _____ Height: _____ Weight: _____

Health: _____

Travel (willing to travel?): _____

Location (willing to relocate?): _____

Military (service, dates, rank, honorable discharge): _____

_____

Reserve status: _____

Professional Memberships (committees served on, awards): _____

_____

_____

_____

Foreign Languages (read, write, speak fluently): _____

_____

Foreign Travel: _____

_____

Awards: _____

_____

Publications: _____

_____

Community Service/Involvement (organizations, offices held, etc.): _____

_____

Interests/Hobbies (avocations, non-business pursuits): _____

_____

Availability (immediate or extent of "notice" required): _____

Present Employer Contact: _____
(Is present employer aware of your prospective job change? May the employer be contacted?)

Salary Desired: _____
(NOT included in resume, but know what you would expect.)

BUSINESS/PROFESSIONAL/ACADEMIC REFERENCES:

Full Name: _____

      Position: _____

      Address: _____

      Phone/E-mail: _____

Full Name: _____

      Position: _____

      Address: _____

      Phone/E-mail: _____

Full Name: _____

      Position: _____

      Address: _____

      Phone/E-mail: _____

PERSONAL REFERENCE:

Full Name: _____

      Relationship (neighbor, teammate, etc.): _____

      Address: _____

      Phone/E-mail: _____

RESUME EVALUATION CHECKLIST

CATEGORY	Excellent	Average	Poor	How to Improve
APPEARANCE:				
Is the format clean?				
Is it easy to follow?				
Are headings effective?				
Does it make the reader want to read it?				
CONTENT:				
Do my qualifications stand out?				
Is the language clear and understandable?				
Have I used short phrases?				
Have I used verbs (action words)?				
Is it brief and to the point?				
Are all important skills and qualifications included?				
Does it create a true picture of me?				
Is irrelevant personal information left out?				
PROOFREADING:				
Is it error free?				
Spelling?				
Punctuation?				

APPENDIX D

SAMPLE RESUMES

Historical/Chronological Resume

WILLIAM A. SMITH
10 South First Street
Minneapolis, MN 55404

Home Phone: (612) 555-5650
Work Phone: (612) 555-9123

PERSONAL   Date of Birth: 6/3/79, 6′ 0″, 175 lbs. Married, one child. Will relocate.

EDUCATION

1997 - 2001   NORMANDALE COMMUNITY COLLEGE
                Bloomington, Minnesota
                Associate Arts Degree and Law Enforcement Certificate.
                    Member of football team.
                    Photographer for school paper.

1997   BLOOMINGTON HIGH SCHOOL
                Bloomington, Minnesota
                High school diploma. Honor student.
                    Member of football team.

**WORK
EXPERIENCE**

1998 - present SECURITY OFFICER
                Dayton's Department Store
                Minneapolis, Minnesota
                Hired as store detective. Duties include plainclothes observation of retail sales
                    area to observe and arrest shoplifters. Assist in loss prevention seminars
                    for store employees.

1995 - 1998   WAITER
                Fancy Joe's Burger Joint
                Bloomington, Minnesota
                Hired as dishwasher. Promoted to busboy and then waiter. Duties as waiter
                    included taking customers' orders, delivering food and beverage items to
                    the table, and assisting other wait staff.

References available on request.

254

Functional Resume

WILLIAM L. SMITH
10 South First Street
Minneapolis, MN 55404
Home Phone: (612) 555-5650

Personal Data: Date of Birth 6-3-75, 6'0", 175 lbs., Single.

Objective:
Position as a law enforcement officer.

Work History

1997 - present

Security Officer:

Southdale Shopping Center
Edina, Minnesota

- Hired as uniformed security officer. Duties include patron assistance, emergency first-aid response, enforcement of property rules and statutes. Assist in training new employees by providing presentations on company rules and state criminal statutes. Frequently appear as witness in court cases resulting from my position. Work with the area law enforcement officers hired to assist during holiday seasons. Act as company representative to Minnesota Loss Control Society.

1995-1997

Office Worker:

Kenny's Market, Inc.
Bloomington, Minnesota

- Hired as assistant to the vice-president. Duties included typing, filing, and telephone reception. In charge of confidential employee records. Assisted in organizing the company's first loss prevention program.

Education

1995-1997

BA, University of Minnesota, Minneapolis, Minnesota.

1993-1995

AA, Law Enforcement Certification, Normandale Community College, Bloomington, Minnesota.

1996

Emergency Medical Technical Technician Registration, Hennepin County Vo-Tech, Eden Prairie, Minnesota.

References available on request.

Analytical Resume

WILLIAM L. SMITH
10 South First Street
Minneapolis, MN 55404
Home Phone: (612) 555-5650
Work Phone: (612) 555-9123

Job Objective: Apply my proven ability in loss prevention.

Qualifications:

- Retail Security: Have developed knowledge and skills in the profession while employed as loss prevention officer for several retail stores. In addition to providing undercover and plainclothes loss prevention services as a store detective, have provided extensive training on the subject to store employees. Excellent performance reviews at each position. Continued increases in apprehension statistics. Received "Employee of the Month" award six times for excellent work as a security officer.

- Supervisory Skills: Promoted to supervisor of 17 loss prevention officers at most recent position. Duties included training, delegating duties, and scheduling. Performance statistics for the crew increased significantly.

- Organizational Skills: All jobs have required detailed activity reports. Hands-on-experience using computers to organize data. Often provided oral reports to supervisors.

Employers

1993 – present   Donaldson's Department Store, Edina, Minnesota.

1992 – 1993   Tom Thumb Stores, Inc., St. Paul, Minnesota.

1990 – 1992   Automobile Club of America, St. Louis Park, Minnesota.

Education

1993   Associate of Arts and Private Security Certificate, Normandale Community College, Bloomington, Minnesota.

Other

1994   Participated in organization of 1994 American Industrial Security Association National Convention.

References available on request.

APPENDIX E

SAMPLE COVER LETTER AND FOLLOW-UP LETTER

Sample Cover Letter

Ms. Jane Smith
1234 Second Street
Los Angeles, CA 90017

July 15, 2001

Lt. Pat Jones
Mytown Police Department
1234 First Avenue
Denver, CO 80203

Dear Lt. Jones:

I am responding to your ad in the *Los Angeles Times* for the position of police officer. With an AA degree in law enforcement and three years' experience as a reserve officer with the Los Angeles Police Department, I am ready to enter the law enforcement profession and hope it will be with your department. A resume highlighting my background, qualifications and experience is enclosed.

I will call you the week of July 29th to make sure my resume was, indeed, received and to arrange for a personal interview. I will look forward to talking with you then.

Sincerely,

Jane Smith

Encl. Resume

Sample Follow-Up Letter

Mr. Scott Anderson
1234 Second Street
Boulder, CO 23456

July 21, 2001

Protection Plus Security
1234 First Avenue
Denver, CO 12345

Attn: Mr. Ronald Smith,
         President

Dear Mr. Smith:

Thank you for the opportunity to participate in the hiring process for the position of security officer. I delivered my resume to your office yesterday and am sorry to have missed you.

I remain extremely interested in the position and look forward to the possibility of being considered for the job. Please call if you need any further information.

Very sincerely,

Scott Anderson

AUTHOR INDEX

259

SUBJECT INDEX